COMMANDO
DESPATCH RIDER

By the same author

Marine Commando, Sicily and Salerno 1943
with 41 Royal Marines Commando, Robert Hale Ltd 1988,
re-issued in paperback 1994.

They Did What Was Asked of Them,
41 (Royal Marines) Commando 1942–1946
Firebird Books, reprinted 1996.

COMMANDO DESPATCH RIDER

WITH 41 ROYAL MARINES COMMANDO IN NORTH-WEST EUROPE 1944–1945

by

RAYMOND MITCHELL

WITH A FOREWORD BY
MAJOR GENERAL JULIAN THOMPSON
CB, OBE

LEO COOPER

First published in Great Britain 2001 by
LEO COOPER
an imprint of Pen & Sword Books
47 Church Street
Barnsley
South Yorkshire S70 2AS

Copyright © 2001 by Raymond Mitchell
ISBN 0 85052 797 X

A CIP catalogue record for this book is
available from the British Library.

Typeset in 11/13pt Sabon by
Phoenix Typesetting, Ilkley, West Yorkshire.
Printed and bound by
CPI UK

Dedicated to the memory of

Ply/X 111113 Marine H.T.W.B. (Bill) SWINDALE
No. 41 (Royal Marines) Commando

Killed in Action, 6 June 1944
Lion-sur-Mer, Normandy

a fellow 'Geordie' and good friend

CONTENTS

FOREWORD

by
MAJOR GENERAL JULIAN THOMPSON
CB OBE

Before Ray Mitchell reached the age of 24 he had taken part in four of the major Allied amphibious assaults of the Second World War: Sicily, Salerno, Normandy and Walcheren, all with 41 (Royal Marines) Commando. This book is about the latter two; his experiences in the first two operations are the subject of an earlier book, *Marine Commando: Sicily and Salerno 1943 with 41 Royal Marines Commando*. His latest book is more than just an account of the great events of June and November 1944, it is also a marine's eye view of the campaign in North-West Europe.

Ray Mitchell kept a diary, which, for security reasons, was forbidden. This, now lodged in the Imperial War Museum, is the basis for his new book. As an author who has spent much time researching in the archives of the Imperial War Museum, I can vouch for the value of books based on diaries written at the time. Time can play tricks with even the sharpest of memories and Ray Mitchell's book is all the more valuable as a testimony to one Royal Marine's experiences because he can refer to his diaries as a back-up to his recall of events.

Anyone not familiar with commando soldiering might regard being a despatch rider (DR – or Dog Roger in the phonetic alphabet of the time) as a 'cushy number'. Starting with landing on Sword Beach on D-Day carrying a 75 lb Welbike (folding motorcycle) in his arms, down the see-sawing wooden landing plank of one of the infamous Landing Craft Infantry (Small), Ray Mitchell's experiences as a DR varied from 'hairy' to 'hilarious', mostly the former.

ix

A DR's life was both lonely and dangerous. Carrying despatches necessitates knowing exactly where you are going and how to get there, including avoiding any route that will lead you straight into enemy hands, all of which requires good map-reading. Road and tracks were usually pinpointed on the enemy's map and treated to frequent doses of artillery and mortar fire. If that was not enough, 'friendly' traffic was an added hazard. DRs were, of course, also required to take their place as riflemen from time to time.

Churchill wrote about the Westkapelle operations at Walcheren, 'The extreme gallantry of the Royal Marines stands forth'. Ray Mitchell was one of the Commando DRs selected to land with his comrades of the 4th Special Service Brigade to capture the five great batteries of coastal guns guarding the entrance to the River Scheldt. He recalls that, in contrast to Normandy five months earlier, 'The task force had been put ashore, and all craft still seaworthy had been withdrawn. There would be no streams of supplies, no back-up, no reinforcements: the Brigade was on its own'. The only way off the saucer-shaped island, whose centre had been deliberately flooded, was by silencing the batteries sited on its sand-dune rim, a costly and hazardous operation.

In 'normal' circumstances 'man proposes, God disposes'. In battle it is the other way around, 'God', in the form of the higher command, may propose the strategy, but the outcome will ultimately depend upon what someone called the most exclusive club in the world: the relatively small number of those who do the actual fighting. The Royal Marines Commandos occupy a special corner of that club. This is a fascinating account of the second part of one marine's very busy war in that company.

GLOSSARY

Ack-ack	*Anti-aircraft*, from early signaller's spelling code for radio or telephone – e.g. 'A' for *Ack*, 'B' for *Beer*, 'C' for *Charlie*, etc., and was applied to both the guns and to the bursting shells.
ADS	Advanced Dressing Station – the next stop for a casualty after he had been 'patched up' at his Unit's RAP (qv).
AMGOT	Allied Military Government of Occupied Territories
AVRE	Armoured Vehicle, Royal Engineers, basically a Churchill heavy tank but specifically adapted for attacking reinforced concrete fortifications. Its primary armament was a 290mm spigot mortar which hurled a 40-pound missile, known as a 'flying dustbin', a distance of some 80 yards.
AWOL	Absent Without Official Leave.
Bangalore Torpedo	A six-foot length of 2½ inch diameter steel tubing packed with explosive, used for blowing a gap in barbed wire and detonating mines. Two or more could be fixed together and pushed forward to deal with broad defences.
Benghazi Cooker	Metal container, such as a biscuit tin, partially filled with sand which would be doused with petrol and set alight to heat water for a 'brew up' (qv).
Blighty one	A wound that was severe enough to get a serviceman sent back to the UK – or *Blighty*,

	a corruption of the Hindi word *bilayati*, meaning *foreign*.
Bren (Gun)	A Light Machine Gun (LMG) named from the first two letters of the Czechoslovakian town *Brno* where it originated and *Enfield* where it was later manufactured – 0.303 inch/7.65mm calibre.
Brew-up	1. Make a brew of tea. 2. A tank bursting into flames after being hit by a shell.
Buffalo	Common name for a *Landing Vehicle Tracked*, (*LVT*) qv.
Burton *(Gone for a . . .)*	Been killed. Originating in the RAF, as the medical centre for new intakes in Blackpool was set up in the former premises of *Burton the Tailor*.
Buzz	Naval term for 'rumour', hence *buzzmonger*, one who spreads them.
CCS	Casualty Clearing Station – the primary function of which was to ensure that all casualties were fully documented.
Compo	'Composite'. The standard Field Rations of WWII. All the creature needs for fourteen Service Personnel for one day – tinned food, cigarettes (seven per person per day), confectionery and toilet paper – were packed in stout hardboard boxes and labelled 'A' to 'E', according to the food content.
CS	Continuous Service. The usual name for a 'regular' Royal Marine as opposed to an HO (qv).
D-Day	The day on which any planned military operation was to be initiated, now synonymous with 6 June 1944 – the biggest one of WWII.
Dead ground	Any area which lay below the line of enemy small arms fire (qv) and was therefore safe from that form of attack.
Dhobying	Washing clothes – in the Indian Army a *dhobi* was a washerwoman.

Dog Tags	Identity discs, two in number and of different shapes, stamped with the bearer's Name, Regimental Number and Religion. All Service personnel were required to wear them around their necks and, if killed, one was snipped off for the records, while the other would identify the dead man.
Dripping	Naval term for grumbling, hence *Dripper*.
DUKW (Duck)	Amphibious wheeled vehicle, being the factory coding of the manufacturer, General Motors, D=1942, U=Amphibious, K=all-wheel drive, W=dual rear axles; naturally, they were known as 'ducks'.
Eighty-eight	German gun of 88mm calibre, originally designed as an anti-aircraft weapon but quickly to become their most effective general artillery piece – most especially as an SP (qv).
Erk	Slang term for an aircraftman, possibly derived from 'erg' the unit of work or energy in physics (i.e. a force of one dyne acting through a distance of one centimetre).
False Beach	A submerged sandbank on which a landing craft could ground, forcing the attacking troops to wade or swim ashore.
FDL	Forward Defended Locality – the 'Front Line', when there isn't a continuous line of trenches, as there was in WWI, denoting the boundary of territory held by a military formation.
Flak	Anti-aircraft fire, arising from the initial letters of 'anti-aircraft gun' in German – *Flieger Abwehr Kanone*.
FOB	Forward Officer Bombardment. A Royal Navy Officer who landed with a Military Unit to call for, and direct, naval gunfire when required.
FOO	Forward Observation Officer. A Royal Artillery Officer who was the Army equivalent of an FOB. The arrival of FOB and FOO

	personnel was a clear indication that a Unit would soon be going into action.
Gunga Din	The name of Rudyard Kipling's fictitious water carrier, which was applied to the Unit water truck, and also to its driver.
Head or Heads	The naval term for toilet, going back to the days of sail when the only facilities were lavatory seats fitted outboard near the bows or *head* of the vessel.
H-Hour	The precise time when any military operation was to be initiated.
HO	Hostilities Only. Term applied to a Royal Marine who had enlisted, 'For the duration of the present emergency' as opposed to a CS (qv).
Jeep	American General Purpose (i.e. 'Gee P') vehicle.
Jerrican	German-designed petrol can holding 20 litres (4½ gallons), the design was unashamedly filched from the Jerries.
LCA	Landing Craft Assault, 41ft 6 long, 10ft beam, draft 2ft 3in, carried 35 fully armed and equipped troops.
LCF	Landing Craft Flak, an LCT MkIII (qv) with crew of twelve and fifty Royal Marines to man the twelve 2-pdr pom-poms or 20mm Oerlikons.
LCG (L)	Landing Craft Gun (Large). Basic particulars as LCT with crew of forty-eight, including Royal Marine gunners, main armament two 4.7 inch naval guns.
LCG (M)	Landing Craft Gun (Medium) vessel with a displacement of 380 tons, crew of thirty-one (including RM gunners), main armament two 17- or 25-pounders.
LCI (L)	Landing Craft Infantry (Large), 387 tons displacement, crew of twenty-eight, load nine Officers and 196 Other Ranks.
LCI (S)	Landing Craft Infantry (Small), 110 tons

	displacement, crew of seventeen, load six Officers and ninety-six Other Ranks.
LCS (L)	Landing Craft Support (Large), of 116 tons displacement with a crew of twenty-five including RM gunners, armament one 6-pdr in Valentine tank turret, twin 20 mm Oerlikons and twin 0.5-inch machine-guns.
LCT	Landing Craft Tank, the Mark III had a displacement of 640 tons and the Mark IV 586 tons; carrying capacities of 300 and 350 tons respectively.
LCT (R)	Landing Craft Tank (Rocket), basically an LCT Mark III but fitted with 1080 (Mark 1) or 936 (Mark 2) rocket launchers; all these missiles being electrically fired in a succession of 24-bomb salvoes.
Lee Enfield	The standard service rifle of WWII, 0.303 inch calibre, weight 9 pounds.
LMG	Light machine-gun, see *Bren*.
LVT	Landing Vehicle Tracked, the Mark II, the *Buffalo*, was 26 feet long overall, stood eight feet high on its tracks and could carry twenty-four fully equipped men or three tons of cargo at 25 mph on land, 5.4 knots in water.
Mae West	Inflatable rubber life jacket, worn around the chest, named after a female film star of the time who was well-endowed in that area.
Matelot (Matlo)	The French word for 'sailor' but 'Royals' (qv) apply it to all naval personnel.
MMG	Medium machine-gun, usually the 0.303 calibre, belt-fed water-cooled Vickers gun.
MOA	Marine Officer's Attendant or batman.
Monitor	A shallow-draught naval vessel designed to get close inshore in order to bombard enemy positions with its two large-calibre guns.
Mortar	An infantry weapon which is, basically, a steel tube to direct bombs on to the enemy. Unlike an artillery piece, the bore is not rifled and there is, generally, a fixed firing-pin at its

	base, so the only 'firing' that is required is to slide a bomb down the barrel.
Nutty	The matelot's (qv) name for chocolate, with or without nuts.
Oerlikon	20mm magazine-fed gun developed in Switzerland. It fired explosive shells at 450 rounds a minute and was used primarily as an anti-aircraft weapon, in either a single or twin mounting.
O-Group	Order Group, when the commander calls appropriate personnel together to issue his orders for a coming operation.
Oppo	Close friend, the 'opposite number' of a two-man team.
Out pipes	Stop smoking, even cigarettes.
PIAT	Projector, Infantry, Anti-tank. A very effective infantryman's answer to tanks. Weighing 34 pounds, it fired a 2¾lb bomb capable of penetrating 4" of armour at a range of 120 yards.
Pom-pom	A 40mm calibre quick-firing anti-aircraft weapon, which could project an explosive shell weighing 1.684 lb (but generally referred to as a '2 pounder') to a height of 13,000 feet. Used in a single barrel mounting but more often in a quadruple mounting, making it a *multiple pop-pom*.
Pusser/Pusser's	Anything which is of indisputable official origin (*pusser issue*) or anyone who acts strictly 'in accordance with the book', (*a pusser officer*) but used in many lighthearted ways such as *pusser's dust* for instant coffee, while *a drop of pusser's* means real naval rum. The word is a corruption of Purser, the RN name for the Paymaster and Supplies Officer in days gone by.
RAP	Regimental Aid Post, the first stop for anyone wounded in action, manned by RAMC Medical Orderlies or RN SBAs (qv).

Rear Echelon	That part of a Military Unit which remains in the rear areas when the fighting element goes 'Up Front'.
Royal	In addition to its use as an adjective – e.g. when referring to the House of Windsor – it is also used as a noun by naval personnel, who generally refer to a Royal Marine as a 'Royal'.
SBA	Sick Berth Attendant – the naval equivalent of a Medical Orderly.
Sin Bo'sun	A naval Padre, also known as a Sky Pilot.
Small Arms	Small calibre weapons, automatic or otherwise, which fire bullets, as opposed to bombs or shells.
SP	Self-propelled, referring to guns, and particularly to the German 88 (qv).
TCV	Troop-carrying Vehicle. Standard American 2½ ton six-wheeler truck fitted with fore-and-aft slatted seats.
10 (I-A)	No. 10 (Inter-Allied) Commando – formed from foreign nationals, including Germans, who had volunteered to fight as Commandos for the Allies. The Troops (of 60–70 men) were organized by country of origin, e.g. there were Belgian, Dutch, French and Norwegian Troops.
Tiddley	Smart, of neat appearance, not to be confused with *tiddly*, which is tipsy.
2 i/c	Second-in-Command.
TSMG	Thompson, sub-machine-gun – the 'Tommy Gun' of Chicago gangsters in the 1920s. During WWII the military version had a 'straight down' 20-round magazine instead of the gangsters' circular 50-round version.
Weasel	Small 'jeep-sized' amphibious tracked vehicle capable of carrying half a ton of crew and equipment at 25 mph on land, or 5 knots in water.
Winger	Same as 'oppo'.

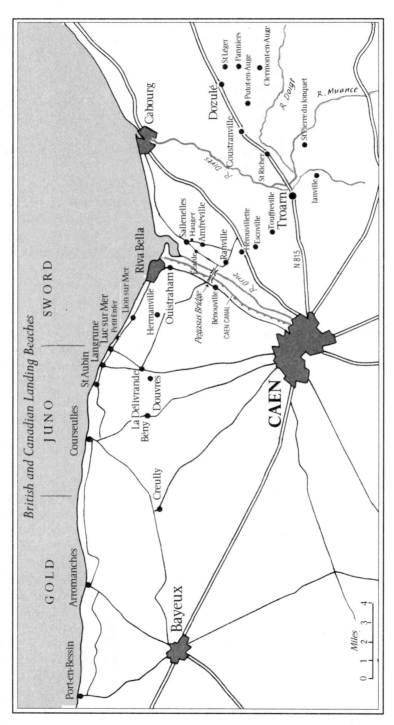

The Normandy Beachhead and the 'Breakout'

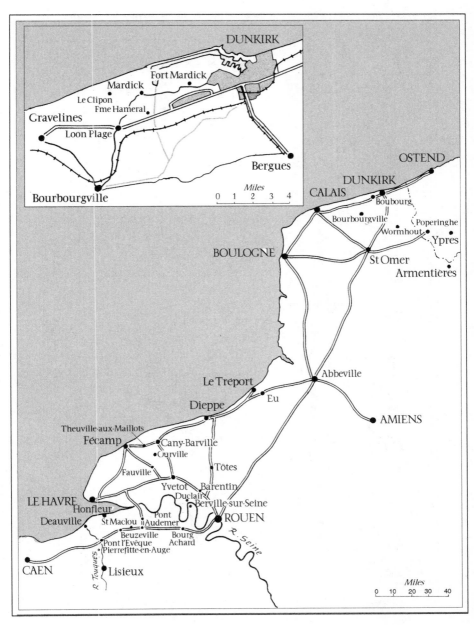

From the River Seine to Dunkirk

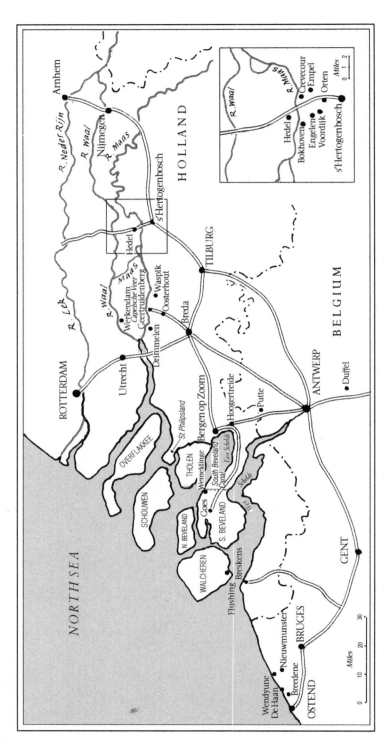

The Scheldt Estuary and the River Maas

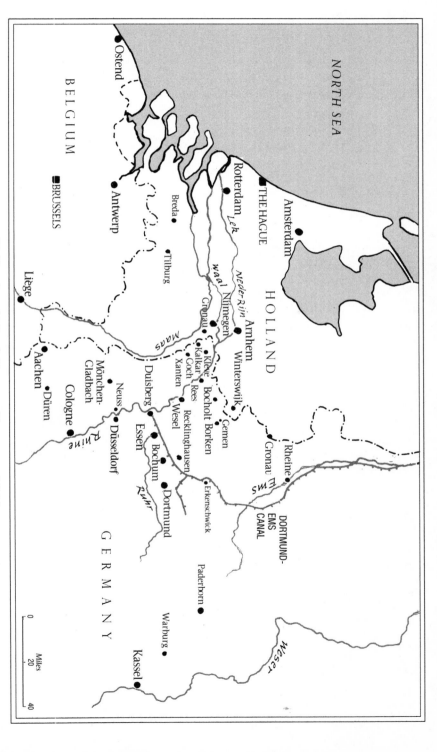

Holland and North Eastern Germany, 1945

AUTHOR'S PREFACE

On 3 September 1939, when Britain declared war on Germany, I was just two months short of my nineteenth birthday and keen to 'get into it'. My eldest brother Rex, six years my senior, was a Sergeant-Pilot in No. 220 (General Reconnaissance) Squadron of the RAF and, wishing to follow in his footsteps, I applied to an RAF Recruiting Office. Very quickly, however, an eyesight test confirmed that my colour vision made me unfit for full flying duties. Suspecting that this defect would also go against me if I tried for the Royal Navy, I opted for the Army and, deciding to go for an élite regiment, wrote to the Coldstream Guards. The reply stated that their age limits for recruitment were 20 to 38 years, so there was no possibility of enlisting there.

Two weeks later my brother was killed. He had been second pilot of a Lockheed Hudson aircraft which, on returning to Thornaby-on-Tees RAF Station from a patrol over the North Sea, crashed on to a house in Darlington. All on board died, but no civilians were harmed. As my other elder brother, Lawrence, was a deck officer in the Merchant Navy, I felt it would be too much for my parents if I were to volunteer for the Services at that time, so I made no more attempts to join up until late February 1940. I then wrote to the Royal Engineers, but the reply was, 'It is regretted that your age, which is considerably under the required standard, prevents your enlistment into the Army at present.'

This seemed to be the end of the line for me, until I learned that the Royal Marines were accepting younger men. On 26 June I

1

applied to the same Recruiting Centre which had written the above letter and was issued with an Identity Card certifying that I had applied to serve in the Royal Marines and would receive instructions later. A week or so afterwards I was called to present myself for medical examination and, barely three weeks after my original application, received a communication stating – 'If you are still willing . . .'! to report for instructions on 3 August and that I would be required to join my Depot four days after that.

In consequence, on 7 August 1940 I was one of a batch of recruits 'collected' at Woodbury Road halt, on the railway line from Exeter to Exmouth, and a Sergeant 'marched' us to the nearby Royal Marines Reserve Depot, Exton. Since the war this depot has been completely redeveloped and renamed as The Commando Training Centre Royal Marines, Lympstone.

After six weeks' initial training, followed by three weeks in the Records Office at Chatham Barracks, I was back at Exton, where the 103rd Royal Marines Brigade was being formed and I was posted to the 8th Battalion as Orderly Room Clerk. More and more recruit squads were allocated to create the Battalion, but, within a matter of weeks, the reverse process was being put in train, as drafts left the embryo Battalion, posted to other Royal Marines formations more urgently in need of men.

By the end of January 1941 the Battalion had been reduced to a nucleus of the Commanding Officer, Second-in-Command, Adjutant, other chosen Officers, most of the Senior NCOs, plus a few score selected Junior NCOs and men. On 8 February this 'hard core' of a Battalion took over the empty Thurlestone Hotel in South Devon to create and operate the Royal Marines Officer Cadet Training Unit. After six months of being engaged in this task, by which time NCOs were also being trained at Thurlestone and the establishment had been renamed the Royal Marines Military School, the original staff was released to re-form the 8th Battalion as a fighting unit. On 24 August the unit moved to Dalditch Camp, on Woodbury Common, only a few miles from the Exton Depot. On completion of their initial training at the Depot, squad after squad of men were marched up to Dalditch Camp and allocated to either the 7th or the 8th Battalion, both of which were being brought up to operational strength at the camp. In addition to military training, the men would also spend a few periods each

2

week on 'Camp Construction', helping civilian contractors to replace the Bell tents and marquees with Nissen huts.

At Dalditch my long-standing request to 'escape' from the Orderly Room and return to General Duties was finally granted and I was posted to the Mortar Platoon. A few weeks later, however, the Battalion received its allocation of Bren Gun Carriers and there was a call for volunteers to form the Motorcycle Section of the Carrier Platoon, so I put my name down. My experience as a motorcyclist extended to no more than 'once around the block on my brother's Rudge', but I was accepted. My job in the Section was anti-tank rifleman and I remained as such throughout the following twelve months or so of Battalion and Brigade training in Devon, and in South Wales, until October 1942. The 8th Battalion, then stationed in Llanion Barracks, Pembroke Dock, was chosen to form the second Royal Marines Commando. The first, known as 'A' Commando, had been formed early in the year and had taken part in the ill-conceived Dieppe Raid; our Battalion was to create 'B' Commando.

As the strength of a battalion was something over 800 men, and a Commando comprised only about 450, there would have to be a major slimming down in numbers. Most tradesmen would be automatically excluded – there would be no place for cooks, for example, as the Commando would be living in civilian homes, nor for transport drivers, as the new unit would 'carry it all on their backs'. Older men, and those less fit, could be expected to be passed over and the reshuffle no doubt presented an ideal opportunity to shed 'undesirables'. Nevertheless, for two days everyone was on tenterhooks as to whether they would be 'in' or 'out'. At a parade of the entire Battalion on the Saturday morning the composition of the new Troops was announced and it was a great relief to learn that the Carrier Platoon was being transformed into 'Q' Troop of the new Commando and that I had become a rifleman in No. 7 Section of that Troop.

Two days later 'Q' was one of the Troops which moved to Weymouth to begin living in civilian homes and to becoming accustomed to getting themselves to the specified place of parade at the required time of day, which could equally well be ten o'clock at night as eight o'clock in the morning. During the next few weeks, all seven Troops – six Rifle Troops, 'A', 'B', 'P', 'Q', 'X' and 'Y', and Headquarters Troops – were located on the Isle of Wight and the unit was restyled 'No. 41 (Royal Marines) Commando'.

Commando training proceeded on the Isle of Wight and in Scotland until mid-June 1943, when the Commando, along with the original Royal Marine Commando, now styled No. 40, boarded two Infantry Landing ships, already well-packed with untold hundreds of Canadian troops, which were part of a large convoy lying in the Clyde Estuary, off Greenock. That convoy was to carry the entire Canadian First Division, together with all of its arms, munitions, transport, stores and supporting units, to join General Montgomery's Eighth Army for the invasion of Sicily. The two Commandos spearheaded the Canadians' landing, near the town of Pachino in the south-east corner of the island. An account of this, and the Commando's part in the US Fifth Army's landings on the Italian mainland two months later, are covered in my book *Marine Commando, Sicily and Salerno 1943 with 41 Royal Marines Commando*, published in hardback by Robert Hale, London 1988, now reissued in paperback.

The present book takes up the story from the time of the unit's return to the UK early in January 1944 and covers the next two years until my release from the Royal Marines in 1946. Soon after arrival in England in 1944 my role changed from Rifleman to that of Despatch Rider and in that capacity I participated in the D-day landing, spent the ensuing weeks in the Normandy beachhead, followed by the pursuit through northern France; the Walcheren landing to open the Port of Antwerp on 1 November; winter months on the Maas River Front in Holland and, finally, occupation duties in Germany until November 1945.

During the war it was, technically, an offence to keep a diary, lest it should fall into enemy hands and divulge military information. However, I began jotting things down as soon as I joined up at Exton before knowing that I was committing an offence. Later, I felt that the ban surely couldn't apply to anyone as lowly as myself so far away from the enemy. My 'diary' entries were, in general, simply a matter of recording something as and when I felt in the mood, so there were gaps in the narrative which had to be filled by other means. Fortuitously, the crucial year of 1944 was recorded by me on a day-to-day basis, thanks to a 'Gentleman's Diary', which gave much information about shooting seasons, etc.! It was inscribed 'From Mother, Christmas 1943'. I passed that Christmas Day in Algeria, so didn't receive the diary until January 1944, on disembarkation leave following the Commando's return to the UK.

When released in 1946 I had a motley collection of six books/diaries, which are now lodged in the Imperial War Museum, and the inner conviction that some day I would string the contents together to give a cohesive account of my five and a half years in uniform, if only for my family's sake. Those years in uniform, however, had persuaded me that I should aspire to something more than the clerking position I had left behind, so I applied to the City Engineer of Newcastle upon Tyne to become an 'Engineering Learner' and, on being accepted, began to study, at nights and weekends, to become qualified as a Civil Engineer.

In consequence of this, then getting married and raising a family, the work of setting down my wartime experiences proceeded slowly, 'by fits and starts', over the years, which eventually lengthened into decades. When I had eventually linked together my own records of the period from August 1940 to March 1946, I obtained a copy of the Unit War Diary, to ensure accurate correlation with official records. Then, considering the possibility of publication, I decided to concentrate in the first instance on the Mediterranean period, which I finalized and this was subsequently accepted for publication by Robert Hale.

In 1992 the Veterans of the WWII 41 RM Commando felt that a History of the wartime unit should be written and I undertook the task. Thanks to the efforts of a small Publication Committee, which invited financial support from former members of the unit, publication of the resulting book, *They Did What Was Asked of Them, 41 (Royal Marines) Commando 1942–46*, was achieved in 1996. This was on the basis that, when all costs of publication had been met, and such advance financial support repaid, all subsequent proceeds would be donated to the Royal Marines Museum Heritage Appeal Fund, and this situation was achieved within twelve months of publication. My deep involvement in the Unit History, which extended to supporting the Committee in advertising, sales and distribution matters, further delayed the completion of the present work, but it did ensure that the overall facts of the campaign in North-West Europe were refreshed and that their presentation is correct.

5

I couldn't end this Preface without acknowledging the immeasurable assistance, in gaining information and sorting out facts, which I have received from a number of official organizations. Firstly, my deep appreciation and thanks go to the Director and Staff of the Royal Marines Museum for their long-standing help in clarifying doubtful episodes. Then, grateful thanks must also go to the staffs of the various departments of the Imperial War Museum which I have consulted over the years for their courteous help. This has ranged from supplying details of WWII weapons and military vehicles, cartographical information and copies of official war photographs. I also appreciate the help given by the Air and Naval Historical Branches of the Ministry of Defence, the Public Record Office, the Army Museum and the Royal Air Force Museum.

In conclusion, I would, once again, like to acknowledge my deep appreciation of the continuing support I have received from my wife, Joan. Over many years she has typed and retyped drafts of this work, giving useful comments upon the 'flow', 'understand-ability' and punctuation in the process, then undertook a final 'proof read' to check that I had complied with her suggestions!

Chapter 1

FROM RIFLEMAN TO DESPATCH RIDER

At 0600 hrs on Tuesday 4 January 1944 the docks at Gourock, on the Firth of Clyde, were wet with drizzle, cold and misty. For the hundreds of men lining the rails of the recently-berthed troopship, SS *Otranto*, their first sight of Britain after months of absence was bleak and unattractive. There were no fluttering flags, no military bands, no cheering crowds – none of the 'Welcome Home!' trappings which the cinema screen generally accords to troops returning from a successful campaign. Just a glistening quayside bustling with khaki-clad figures humping loads of military equipment and being bawled at by their NCOs to 'Come on! Get fell in!' More long files of men in full marching order, each burdened with his personal weapon and kitbag, many shivering involuntarily in the unaccustomed winter chill, were gingerly picking their way down slippery gangplanks to swell the throng below.

For the British at least, Gourock meant 'Blighty', 'the UK', 'Home', so for them it was sufficient just to be back there all in one piece, with the uninviting weather no more than a minor irritation. Not so fortunate were the hundreds of Commonwealth troops who had travelled on the same ship. They were still thousands of miles from their own countries and couldn't even hazard a guess as to how many more months or years it would be before *they* saw their homes again. Some other passengers must have had even more doubts in their minds, a few score German prisoners of war, unshaven and still dressed in crumpled Afrika Korps desert uniforms with, here and there, an Iron Cross dangling from a

7

ribbon around the neck, who were yet to be put ashore. Nevertheless, for the whole heterogeneous mass of service personnel, women as well as men, that seemingly inhospitable corner of Britain at War did at least mean the end of a cramped ten-day sea voyage from Algiers.

Amongst those going ashore were the four hundred or so officers and men of 41 (Royal Marines) Commando and a rifleman in 'Q', one of the six Rifle or 'Fighting' Troops, was CH/X 100977 Marine Raymond Mitchell, author of these memoirs. The Commando had returned to the same Scottish port from which it had embarked for overseas service six months previously.

On 28 June 1943, a hot and brilliantly sunny summer's day, the Unit had sailed from the Clyde on board the SS *Durban Castle*, a 35,000-ton luxury liner of the Union Castle Line, then doing its war service as an Infantry Landing Ship, with rows of LCAs (Landing Craft Assault) lining her tall sides. She had been one of a large convoy carrying the entire Canadian First Division, some 18,000 men, with all its artillery, tanks, transport and stores, to join General Montgomery's Eighth Army in the invasion of Sicily. 41 Commando, together with her sister Unit, No. 40 Royal Marines Commando, had been given the task of neutralizing Italian coastal strong points which could threaten the Canadian landings. These two units were the first British sea-borne troops to go ashore – at 0246 hours on Thursday 9 July 1943 – and by spearheading the return of Allied Armies, absent from the continent since the débâcle of the fall of France in 1940, they initiated the liberation of Europe.

Two months later, on 10 September 1943, then as part of US General Mark Clark's Fifth Army, 41 Royal Marines and No. 2 Army Commandos, had made a night assault across the beach at Vietri sul Mare, as part of the Allied landings near Salerno aimed at the capture of Naples. Both Commandos suffered heavy casualties during the nine days of touch-and-go fighting before the Fifth Army had established itself securely on the Italian mainland.

When withdrawn back to Sicily, less than two weeks after it had sailed from there, 41 could muster little more than half of its original strength. The Unit had lost most of its commissioned officers and was without a Commanding Officer as Lieutenant Colonel B.J.D. 'Bertie' Lumsden RM had been seriously wounded on the second day ashore. During the last minutes of the Commando's action at Salerno, I myself received a leg wound from a German hand-grenade and was evacuated to a Canadian hospital in North Africa.

After first returning to Aci Castello, its starting point for the Salerno operation, the Commando later moved into 'winter quarters' in Catania. With replacements arriving from the UK and wounded re-joining from hospital, the Unit was being re-formed. In mid-November we sailed for Algiers, to be shipped back to the UK, but were disembarked at Bizerta in Tunisia, supposedly to complete the journey by train. However, after three days in World War One '40 men or 8 horses' wagons, during which only 120 miles were covered, the Unit reached Bône (now Annaba) and marched to a tented camp on desert sand.

There the Commando languished for six weeks, while the 'Top Brass' debated whether it should be sent back to the UK to take part in the Second Front, the invasion of France, or be employed in Jugoslavia. In November Lieutenant Colonel T.W. Gray arrived to take over as Commanding Officer, but the Commando was kept waiting until, like a bolt from the blue, two days before Christmas, he announced that a ship was lying in Algiers harbour, ready to take us home.

Early next morning, Christmas Eve 1943, 41 Commando left No. 4 Transit Camp in a convoy of American TCVs (Troop Carrying Vehicles) and flurries of dust. Forty hours later, after alternate roasting under the African sun and freezing in the near-zero night temperatures, very late on Christmas Day the Unit climbed laboriously up a steep ladder on to the deck of the SS *Otranto*. Ours must have been her last intake of passengers; in the very early hours of Boxing Day the engines throbbed into life at the start of what turned out to be an uneventful voyage to the Clyde.

At Gourock, after assembling on the dockside and being 'mustered', Troop by Troop, the Commando marched off. Minds became occupied with the possibility of a customs or military police examination before clearing the docks area – a number of men had picked up 'souvenirs' such as binoculars, cameras, German Lügers or Italian Beretta automatics, which it would have been very galling to have had to surrender. Another concern was to get home while the oranges, lemons and tangerines bought in Bône were still edible. At that stage of the war citrus fruit was unobtainable in the UK and

9

a supply of vitamin C would be almost as welcome as ourselves. One minor personal concern was whether our Padre, the Rev John Wallis DSC, would go ashore still wearing the 'full set' of moustache and beard he had grown overseas. I had wagered a day's pay that he wouldn't, but he did.

In the event no Customs Officers nor MPs (military policemen) were encountered, but, after a short march to a docks railway platform, it was found that a reception committee was indeed awaiting our arrival. Despite the early hour and the miserable wintry weather, a dozen or more ladies of the WVS (Women's Voluntary Service) stood at the ready beside a line of trestle tables piled high with either packets of sandwiches or morning papers. Every man, as he filed past, was handed one of each. Then, like excited children off on a Sunday school outing, we clambered on board the waiting LMS (London Midland and Scottish Railway) train.

As soon as kitbags and rifles had been stacked in the corridor and weighty webbing equipment heaved up on to the racks, everyone was in holiday mood. As well as the fillip of being newly back from a war zone, that journey would be the first in a 'real' train since travelling to that same station, for embarkation, the previous June. In comparison with the '8 chevaux ou 40 hommes' wagons from Bizerta to Bône, British Third Class railway coaches would be the height of luxury.

When the train chuffed off every openable window was crammed with as many heads as could be poked out and it left to the accompaniment of whoops of delight and rounds of hurrahs. So it continued throughout the day; everyone encountered en route, standing at level crossings, passed at a distance in the fields, or waiting on the platforms of the many stations we speeded through was greeted with gales of spontaneous cheers and wildly waving arms. Every girl in sight, within earshot or not, pretty, plain or downright ugly, was bombarded with salvoes of wolf whistles.

The journey continued in a general mood of high hilarity, although there were a few minor grumbles from time to time. These started early with our Scottish comrades from Clydeside, passing within a few miles of their homes, bemoaning the fact that in a few days' time they would have to travel all the way back to those very stations on disembarkation leave. Then the men from the Borders became vociferous about the nearness of their firesides, followed by the Northern English and by afternoon it was the Midlanders.

As was commonplace during the war, stops were frequent, often long and invariably unexplained. The railway authorities must have considered that the then current admonitory warning, 'Careless Talk Costs Lives' applied to their operations, so the train moved, stopped then started away again, all without explanation. The exuberance continued until the early darkness of a winter's evening required the black-out blinds to be pulled down. The carriages quietened as men turned to reading newspapers or became involved in card schools of pontoon, solo or brag. Eventually these too gave way to an untidy sprawl of sleeping Marines draped over any convenient surface of seat or floor, while the train continued to rumble fiftully on.

With daylight it fell to the Londoners to point out their own particular neighbourhoods of 'The Smoke' as the train kept rolling ever southwards. At about half past nine a final squeal of brakes heralded the Commando's arrival at its destination – Deal. Commands to detrain, get rigged and get fell in rang out along the line of carriages and, to the hiss of escaping steam, stiff men tumbled out to form up on the station platform.

The weather, in marked contrast to the previous morning, was Spring-like and bright with sunshine. Kit bags were stacked for collection by a fatigue party and, when reported 'All present and correct', the Commando marched out of the station. The initial euphoria of returning to the UK had evaporated, the six months' sojourn in the Mediterranean area was over and here was just another march. Minds became occupied with the prospect of food, a wash and shave, and wondering what the billets would be like.

It was pleasant enough to march through quiet residential streets, find ourselves entering the Royal Marines Barrack and then to be led on to the wide expanse of the parade ground. The Commando was halted Troop by Troop, turned into line and given the usual orders of 'Stand at – ease!' and 'Stand easy!' On the far side of the parade ground a few squads of immaculately uniformed recruits were being put through their paces at close-order drill under the critical eye of an officer, resplendent in 'blues' uniform, peaked cap and gleaming brasswork, obviously the Depot Adjutant.

Then our presence on *his* parade ground impinged upon his

11

consciousness and he suffered what could only be described as an instantaneous attack of mobile apoplexy. Pivoting on his heel, he steamed across the vast expanse of concrete towards 41's officer group and it was patently obvious that our grubby, dishevelled and unshaven presence was desecrating his holy of holies. Six months' active service, terminating in a ten-days' troopship voyage, followed immediately by twenty-seven non-stop hours on a troop train, were as nothing compared with the niceties of protocol attaching to the parade ground of a Royal Marines' Barracks! The Commando was called to attention and marched off.

After dispersal to mess halls for a belated breakfast, there came the allocation of barrack-rooms, a wash and shave, and the issue of new battledress uniforms to ensure that, in future, we would conform to the sartorial requirements of the barracks. The remainder of the day was given over to cleaning weapons and equipment in preparation for an inspection, scheduled for the following morning, by General Sturges, Royal Marines, Officer Commanding the Special Service Group. In May 1942 he had been in command of all the land forces involved in taking Diego Suarez, Madagascar, from the Vichy French to ensure that the naval base didn't fall into Japanese hands.

While preparing for his inspection, I went time and again to the depot Post Office hoping to send a telegram home, but it was always swamped with scores of others with the same idea in mind so I never managed it. That night most of the unit luxuriated in real beds for the first time since leaving Troon some six months previously.

On parade next morning it was abruptly announced that the General's inspection had been cancelled and the Commando would go on leave instead. Then followed a mad 'flap' of queueing-up for the issue of leave passes, travel warrants and ration cards, and a pay parade. Transport got us to the railway station just in time to catch the early afternoon train to London.

My travelling companion was Bill 'Geordie' Swindale, the fellow Tynesider to whom I have dedicated this book; he lived in Gateshead. We just managed to squeeze on board the crowded 20.20 out of Kings Cross, but got no further than the corridor, as all compartments were packed to overflowing. That was where we passed the journey, and it was 05.10 next morning before we stumbled from the fuggy train on to the chilly No. 8 platform of Newcastle Central Station. Nine hours to cover two hundred and eighty miles wasn't at all bad for rail travel in wartime Britain.

I arrived home to find that my mother was in Oxford, where sister Evelyn was daily expecting to give birth to her second child. My eldest brother Rex, a Sergeant-Pilot in the RAF, had been killed in November 1939, and the next eldest, Lawrence, was at sea as a Deck Officer in the Merchant Navy. With my father at work all day, and my younger sister and brother, Marjorie and Douglas, both at school, there was no alternative for me but to take over as cook. It was, therefore, something of a relief to be able to escape to Oxford for the last few days of leave, to see my mother and inspect baby nephew Peter Charles. His sister, Pauline Ann, four years old at the time, still retains a vivid memory of that visit, in the form of a pair of 'enormous boots', as she describes them, pushed close to her nose as she crouched shyly under the bed.

The normal time for the expiry of a period of Service leave was '2359 hrs' – one minute before midnight – but on Friday 21 January 1944 train timetables dictated that, to avoid being AWOL (absent without official leave), I had to arrive in Deal at 1700 hours. The town was under a 'shell warning' – like Dover and other nearby coastal towns, Deal was within range of the heavy German cross-Channel guns – but it proved to be a quiet night.

Next morning we received General Sturges' delayed 'Jolly good show, chaps!' address, but his inspection had been cancelled and later in the day came the welcome news of an early move into 'civvy billets' in the Margate/Ramsgate area. Living with civilian families was an integral part of the commando training system, designed to inculcate a degree of independence and self-reliance in the men. Everyone was individually responsible for getting himself to the next place of parade on time, whether it was at 8 o'clock in the morning for a 'pusser' parade and weapons inspection, or 10 o'clock at night with blackened faces and rubber-soled boots for a 'night stunt'.

To the 60-odd men of 'Q', however, the day also brought the bad news that the Troop was to be disbanded. The 'Raiding Party, carry it all on your backs' concept of Commando Units had been abandoned and in future they would be provided with transport. The overall structure of Units had also been changed by reducing the

13

number of Rifle Troops from six to five and upgrading the Heavy Weapons Section of HQ Troop (Vickers medium machine-guns and 3-inch mortars) to full 'Support Troop' status.

The prime factor in choosing 'Q' as the Troop to go was undoubtedly because it had ceased to exist as an entity on 11 September 1943, on Dragonea Hill above Vietri sul Mare, near Salerno. Heavy casualties had been suffered that day, which included all three commissioned officers – Troop Commander Captain R.M. Stott and Lieutenant D.C. Lloyd killed, and Lieutenant P.H. Haydon seriously wounded. Lieutenant Haydon was awarded the Distinguished Service Order for his action that day and, at barely twenty years of age, was the youngest Royal Marines Officer in World War Two to receive that high award. Many months later, promoted to Captain, he re-joined the Commando as a Troop Commander, but was killed in action on the island of Walcheren, Holland, in November 1944.

Another consideration in the choice of Troop for disbandment was likely to have been that, when 41 Commando was created from the fully-trained 8th Battalion Royal Marines, 'Q' had been formed largely from the Carrier Platoon. Bren Gun Carrier drivers and men of the Motorcycle Section possessed skills which would be useful in the motorization of the Unit. Corporal George 'Jan' Maley, for example, was appointed Transport Sergeant and Bill Smith, Bren gunner in the Motorcycle Section, became a Despatch Rider. The rest of the Troop was 'shared out' amongst the other Rifle Troops and I went to 'P'.

On Monday morning, 24 January, 'Q' Troop paraded for a final period of drill and a valedictory address by Captain Grant. He had been with us in the Carrier Platoon, then was a Lieutenant Section Commander in 'Q', before transferring to 'Heavy Weapons', and was at that time Troop Commander of 'S', the newly formed Support Troop.

On Tuesday 25 January the Commando assembled for a 'pep talk' by its new Commanding Officer, Tim Gray, and next day marched out of Deal barracks – 'B' 'S' 'X' and 'Y' Troops heading for Margate, 'A' 'P' and HQ going to Ramsgate. Much of the route lay along the coast road with the seawards view obstructed by broad barbed wire entanglements, anti-tank obstacles and gun emplacements. In Ramsgate itself there were more evidences of being in a 'front line' position on the south coast – numerous plots of grass-covered empty space where once there had been buildings.

I was billeted with Harry Weiss in Moss Rose Cottage, fronting the main street, where our host family was very welcoming, as we found everyone in Ramsgate. Nevertheless we weren't too happy about having to remove a dog or a cat from any comfortable chair in the house before sitting down, so we decided upon a move and began looking for new digs. We soon found another billet, with the Sayer family in Hardres Road and, not wishing to hurt anyone's feelings, said that we were to move closer to our Troop Office, which was true, if only by about two minutes' walk. 'P' Troop Commander, Captain Bill Sloley, nothing if not unconventional, had located his HQ in a back room of the North Pole public house on the Margate Road. Commando Daily Orders were pinned up behind the bar of 'the public', so there was always a good reason for being outside the Troop Office with a drink in your hand. Also behind the bar was a small blackboard on which the landlord kept a tally of air raid and shell warnings and, at 2230 hrs on Friday 28 January 1944, as I was reading Daily Orders, he amended the total to '2409'.

Earlier that day our previous CO, Lieutenant Colonel Lumsden, badly wounded at Salerno some four months earlier, came to welcome his old Unit back to the UK. The Colonel was accompanied by Sergeant 'Nigger' Branchett, who had been a Marine clerk with me in the Orderly Room of the 8th Battalion in 1940/41, who offered me a 'square number' (cushy) job. He needed a clerk at Brigade Rear Echelon, which would remain in Canterbury no matter where the rest of the Brigade went, but I wasn't tempted.

Nevertheless, despite refusing that offer, I was soon to get a change of occupation and, as had been the case when first getting into clerking with Nigger, without really wanting it. I had, fleetingly, encountered Jan Maley in his new role of Transport Sergeant and he, being fully aware of my motorcycling background, had called out, 'Hey, Mitch! – I'm getting nine motorbikes tomorrow'. My automatic, and unthinking, response had been to reply, 'You'll be wanting some DRs then,' but thought no more of it.

On the Sunday afternoon Harry and I were occupied in moving to our new billet and, in consequence, missed the first showing at the local cinema (Sunday cinemas were a wartime innovation) and were queueing-up for the second house when the first one came streaming out. Amongst the flood of people emerging was Jan Maley and, on catching sight of me, his invariably cheerful face widened into a broad grin. Too far away to talk, he extended both arms in line with his shoulders and, while nodding his head vigorously, went through the motions of operating a motor cycle twist grip with his right hand.

The meaning of Jan's pantomime was unmistakable to me and next morning it was conveyed to the rest of the Commando. Part II of Daily Orders, which dealt with pay, promotions and appointments, carried the item: Transferred from 'P' Troop to HQ Troop as Despatch Rider – CH/X 100977 Mne Mitchell, R.

Chapter 2

UK TRIPS AND CONCENTRATION CAMPS

That my transfer from 'P' Troop to HQ had appeared in Daily
Orders made it a *fait accompli*. The only way to alter the situation
would have been to put in a formal request to return to General
Duties, which would have put Jan in an awkward position as he
had clearly thought that I was seeking the transfer. At the same
time, with the break-up of 'Q' Troop, I was back with friends of
long standing because, in addition to Bill Smith, two other former
motorcyclists of the Carrier Platoon, Jackie Horsfield and 'Killer'
Barker, had become DRs, while the two former Despatch Riders of
the 8th Battalion, who had not previously been in the Commando,
now came back. Despatch Riding carried no extra 'tradesman's'
pay but there was no doubt that it would be a much less strenuous
occupation than being a rifleman in a Fighting Troop, so I decided
to bide my time.

My Lee-Enfield rifle and bayonet were returned to store in
exchange for a Colt 45 automatic pistol and I was issued with
riding gear – breeches, riding boots, crash helmet, jerkin, mackin-
tosh coat, gloves and goggles. The motorcycles were 350cc
overhead valve Ariels, nippier machines than the heavier side-valve
Norton 500s we had used in the Carrier Platoon, but all were well
past their first flush of youth.

The Unit's complement of six despatch riders, with a Corporal-
in-charge, came under the command of the Signals Officer who was
responsible for maintaining round-the-clock communication links
within the Commando, with Brigade Headquarters and with such

17

other units as was necessary. The nerve centre was the Signals Despatch Office (SDO), where telephone exchange, radio links and Despatch Riders were based. In Ramsgate the SDO was set up in an empty semi-detached house in a steeply-sloping street leading down to the wired-in seafront near the western edge of town.

In the UK Despatch Riders delivered everything that couldn't be transmitted by telephone, including officers on occasions, while in the field they carried all written messages and were the 'last resort' when neither field telephone nor radio contact could be made. Two were 'Duty' at any time, for a 24-hour tour starting at 0800 hours, and slept fully clothed on the SDO floor, ready to depart at a moment's notice. Two more acted as 'Stand-by' during the day to carry out any trips needed when both Duty men were out. They returned to their billets at night and, next day, took over from the Duty DRs, who went 'Off Duty' to carry out maintenance and repairs, and undertake any special trips which might be required.

Most trips were in the Ramsgate/Margate area, but others could be of fifty miles or more, and every day there would be at least two runs to Brigade Headquarters in Canterbury, which involved a round trip of some 40 miles. As it was mid-winter not all journeys by motorbike were pleasant affairs, but the life-style of a DR was remarkably unfettered compared with that of men in the Fighting Troops. Nevertheless, my mind continued to be niggled with thoughts of transferring back to 'P' Troop, although, as more Carrier Platoon personnel gravitated to transport roles, the urge tended to become less strong.

On the whole, life as a DR proceeded smoothly, but some days were packed with incident. One such included three round trips to Brigade, two mechanical breakdowns, running out of petrol and being booked for speeding. To crown everything, that evening I was ordered to Canterbury again, with instructions to take the Brigade Duty Officer, with an important message, to Brigadier 'Jumbo' Leicester, out on a training exercise 'somewhere in Kent'. Surprisingly, my instructions were to report to the officer at a hotel in town, where he gave me a shilling for a drink and instructions to report back nearer closing time!

On my return he climbed on to the luggage rack – our bikes had no pillion seats – and off we went into the obscurity of a blacked-out wartime winter's night. The masked headlamp illuminated little more than the front wheel, so intense concentration plus a measure of good luck were needed simply to keep us out of the roadside ditches. The officer was supposed to know where we were going, but it seemed to be entirely a matter of trial and error, and it was midnight before the Brigadier's HQ had been tracked down to an isolated farmhouse. By the time the officer had conducted his business, had been returned to Canterbury and I had found my way back to Ramsgate the early hours were well advanced before I was able to curl up on the SDO floor.

Some daylight journeys could be equally demanding. One such was a fifty-mile round trip to Folkestone in near-Arctic conditions, riding over ice-covered roads through driving hail, with the left forearm shielding my face and only the right hand to control the bike. As some small recompense, on the return journey I made a five-mile detour to RAF Hawkinge, where I knew a hometown friend, Doug Blair, was stationed with a Servicing Commando which always had a cup of tea handy.

Living with the Sayer family in Hardres Road was pleasant and comfortable. He was a civilian employee at the nearby Manston RAF station and Harry and I would occasionally join him and Mrs S at their local, Hennekens. Their daughter, Betty, serving in the Women's Land Army, came home from time to time and I suspected that Mrs Sayer thought of me as a likely lad in that direction.

Duty evenings in the SDO were generally quiet and, having an urge to learn how to drive, the presence of some of the Commando's vehicles parked overnight on the roadway outside the office proved an irresistible temptation. The smallest, and so the most appropriate for my purpose, was the water truck, invariably known as the Gunga Din after Rudyard Kipling's fictitious Indian water carrier. Therefore, after spending some time familiarizing myself with the controls, I took a deep breath, switched on and pressed the starter. The engine blurrrped into life and, after a few starts and stops, getting accustomed to the response of the accelerator, I decided that that was enough for a beginning.

On a subsequent evening the water truck was parked last in line offering an easy return to base, so I decided to have a go. The engine started easily and, without putting it in gear, releasing the hand-brake allowed the gradient of the road to get us moving. After steering away from the kerb, then making sure that the footbrake was working, I engaged bottom gear and we were off! The streets were completely empty and, without changing gear, I managed to negotiate four right-hand turns to bring us back to the starting position, feeling rather weak and sticky. On future occasions I ventured into higher gears, but it was always a touch-and-go business, and too risky – both the actual driving and the possibility of being caught at it – to do more than crawl around the nearby streets.

The Gunga Din was fitted with slatted walkways along the top of the tank, to give access to the filling manhole, and these were often used as repositories for tools, etc, when carrying out vehicle maintenance. On the morning after one of my driving jaunts, everyone within earshot was subjected to a tirade of accusations from the Signals Sergeant, demanding to know who had 'swiped' an oil can he had left on the water truck the previous evening. I slunk away, wondering vaguely at which street corner it had fallen off.

As it turned out, that was my last driving session in Ramsgate as, on returning from seven days' leave on Good Friday 7 April 1944, I learned that I was to leave next day with an Advance Party going to Hastings to arrange billets for the Commando. When the Main Body arrived a week later, I was put with Harry Weiss and Bill Marshall, both jeep drivers by that time, in St Anne's Hotel, a private guest-house in Grosvenor Gardens, where some elderly ladies were still in residence. Brigade Headquarters had remained in Canterbury, so every Brigade trip – and there were still at least two every day – now meant a hundred miles in the saddle.

Since sailing from Algiers the previous December it had been common knowledge that the Commando was earmarked for the Second Front invasion of Europe and now, as the first months of 1944 were passing, it was clear that it couldn't long be delayed. An indication that things were beginning to move came towards the end of April with rumours of an imminent large-scale exercise, codenamed Fabius. By all accounts it was to be more logistic than military, designed to gather together some tens of thousands of the

20

men who would be involved on 'the Day' and rehearse the arrangements for their transportation, accommodation, feeding and embarkation.

Fabius remained no more than a rumour until Friday 28 April, when Killer Barker and I were abruptly detailed-off to join the Commando contingent leaving next day, our dress to be 'fighting order' and without motorbikes. I welcomed it as a chance to test the few residual feelings I had about returning to General Duties, but just the minor chores of cleaning and assembling the webbing equipment, then parading for inspection, foreign to us for more than three months, gave a slight jolt to the nervous system. The march to the railway station raised more question marks about the wisdom of any such change.

The Unit detrained at Botley, near Southampton, where a string of TCVs was waiting to take us on a circuitous journey through rural Hampshire which ended up at an immense tented town labelled simply 'C8'. It was a 'concentration camp', in the original Boer War sense of 'bringing together', and was as security-conscious as those notorious ones in German-occupied Europe. Its eight-feet-high perimeter fence, topped-off with barbed wire, was patrolled by armed guards rehearsing the role they would carry out when it would be necessary to ensure that no one who might let slip military information could leave. C8 was already bursting at the seams with many hundreds of troops and the fact that they were mainly Canadians probably accounted for the good food and the wide choice of film shows which we enjoyed in the evenings.

The first stage of Fabius was simply to exercise the camp staff in housing and feeding immense numbers of men; all we had to do was collect and eat our meals at specified times. Food was issued on a slick production line basis with long files of men continuously moving in front of lines of trestle tables laden with steaming dixies of food and drink. Behind the tables stood cooks with ladles at the ready and, as each man reached a dixie, the two parts of his mess tin in one hand and enamel mug in the other, he received a splodge of 'meat' in one and a splodge of 'sweet' in the other, while his mug caught a splosh of liquid – tea for us, coffee for the Canadians.

The processes of eating and the washing of mess tins and mugs afterwards were equally expeditious. A brief sojourn on a wooden bench alongside one of the scores of long tables in huge marquee mess-tents sufficed to dispose of the food, then out again. First to scrape any uneaten remnants into a bin as pig swill, then to a row of three forty-gallon petrol drums of water, kept on the boil over wood fires, for a quick swish of utensils in each one in turn, then everything was ready to be packed away again.

Sunday was a repeat performance, but on Monday, May Day, TCVs transferred us to another camp which looked precisely the same but was labelled 'C3' this time. The staff there must have needed practice in dealing with officers, because each man was issued with a camp bed before joining the food queue.

Next morning a more active phase of Fabius began when TCVs transported the Commando to a backwater of the Solent, in readiness to board LCI(S)s Landing Craft Infantry (Small), the type of craft we would soon be using 'for real'. These vessels could carry ninety fully armed men in three small 'holds', but, having wooden hulls covered with steel 'scales', they were poor 'sea boats'. The sea was judged too rough for them, so, after hanging around all day vainly hoping that conditions would improve, we were returned to camp.

Wednesday started off similarly when, like a few hundred pawns in a mammoth game of chess, we were transported to a different Southampton backwater and again settled down to wait throughout the morning. A sister unit, No. 45 (Royal Marines) Commando, was nearby doing just the same until a football was produced and an inter-Commando match was quickly organized. The powers that be must have waited prudently until the game had gone to full time because the final whistle was also the signal for NCOs to start shouting, 'All right lads! Get rigged and get fell in!' and almost a thousand men trooped on board the waiting craft.

When the ten LCIs carrying the two Commandos had been eased out of the small creek into the wide expanse of Southampton Water they became only one small part of a vast assemblage of shipping. In every direction lay untold numbers of ships and landing craft of all types, shapes and sizes. We steamed out into the fairway, moored to buoys until dusk when, together with a large part of the armada, the LCIs cast off and sailed off into the night.

Early next morning 41 Commando's LCIs were moving in line

22

abreast towards the shore to carry out mock attacks on objectives in and around Littlehampton. The craft were rammed on to the beach, the ramps splashed down into about three feet of water and everyone sprinted, rather wetly, ashore. With no specific role in the attacks, we DRs simply tagged along behind, to be told in due course that the Commando had 'achieved its primary objectives' by 0830 hours. The unit's part in the exercise was over by noon, but it was evening before a train arrived to return us to Hastings.

On the following Monday four DRs were detailed off to accompany the Commando for more landing exercises, again without motorcycles. In the early evening civilian coaches took the Commando to Newhaven where, after putting weapons and equipment aboard the allocated landing craft, we were given the 'freedom of the dockyard' until 2200hrs, when the flotilla sailed out. By next morning the craft were once again moving in line abreast towards the beach at Littlehampton. Crewmen launched the ramps and everyone doubled ashore, only to be called back to get on board again. The ramps were retracted, the LCIs pulled off, circled out into deeper water, re-formed into line and came in again. This procedure was repeated time and again, seeming to indicate it was for the Navy's benefit rather than ours. After a few hours of this occupation the LCIs returned the Commando to Newhaven and trucks delivered us back to Hastings.

The increasing frequency of exercises made it clear that the day for the invasion of Europe, D-Day, was drawing near. All military operations were planned to begin at 'H-Hour' on 'D-Day' and these two reference points enabled the entire sequence of events, before and after the initial assault, to be planned in advance of any starting date having been fixed. All phases of preparation – moving troops, tanks, supplies, aircraft, ships, etc – would be 'D minus 30, 20, 10 etc', while reinforcements, supplies, etc, would be fixed for 'D plus 1, 2, 3, etc.' There were a multitude of 'D-Days' during the war and no one could have foreseen that the term was to become synonymous with 6 June 1944.

Shortly after the Newhaven exercise it was revealed that the four DRs who had been chosen to take part were the ones who would go ashore with the Fighting Troops on D-Day. By that time I had come to accept that I would remain as a Despatch Rider and was pleased to know that I was 'in' for the invasion of France.

During the second week of May we received the motorcycles to be used during the first days in France – 125cc, two-stroke Famous James. They were primitive and slow in comparison with our 350cc Ariels and their small, squeaky, bulb horns would have better suited a child's kiddicar. As the bikes had no speedometers the actual speed of travel wasn't known but, for the fifty-mile journey to Canterbury, it was simply a matter of twisting the throttle wide open then sitting patiently until you arrived there about one and a half hours later. We soon convinced the Signals Officer that they weren't fast enough to cope with the greatly increased flow of signals traffic in the lead-up to D-Day, so we reverted to the Ariels.

By this time all the unit's transport, apart from motorcycles, had been waterproofed by encasing the electrics in a waterproof, plasticine-like material and extending exhaust pipes and air intakes up to the top of the cab. In addition, every vehicle had been allo-cated the precise load of men, guns, ammunition, tools, spares, rations, Famous James etc, it was to carry ashore, with a detailed loading plan specifying precisely where each item was to be placed. The exact order of loading and unloading was practised by drivers and others involved until they could do both blindfold.

41 Commando's move towards D-Day was initiated on 17 May when a batch of fully-loaded jeeps, accompanied by the DRs who would not be going ashore on D-Day, left for an unknown desti-nation. Later that same day the four 'D-Day DRs' were each issued with a third machine, a 98cc Excelsior Welbike or 'parascooter' to be carried ashore.

The Welbike had been designed to fit into a standard parachute container and, with handlebars, seat and footrests folded, the overall dimensions were no more than 4'3" × 1'3" × 12". It had a wheelbase of little more than 3 feet, with wheels fitted with 12" × 2" tyres and weighed 75 lbs. It was good fun to tootle around the streets of Hastings on such miniature motorbikes, occasioning turned heads, raised eyebrows and questioning stares, but we were very quickly and curtly told to 'KEEP THEM FOR THE DAY!'

During the following days more and more vehicles rolled away to unknown destinations. On May 23 the last of our operational transport left and with them went Bill and Harry. Our landlady, 'Ma' Sheldrake, shed a few tears as she kissed them goodbye, but had to quickly dry her eyes as the door had barely closed behind them before she was opening it again to admit three Army Commandos, arriving to take over the billet. I was moved down to the basement for what turned out to be my last night in St Anne's Hotel.

Next day, 24 May, Empire Day in 1944, I was suddenly relieved as Duty DR, with orders to pack all kit and equipment and report to HQ by 1730 hours. At the appointed time the 'D-Day element' of the Commando paraded outside their various Troop offices all ready to go, but were told that departure wouldn't be until early the following morning. Arms and equipment were stacked in the offices and shore leave was granted until 1030, when all returned to bed down on the floor beside their gear. By that time a goodly proportion of our number, officers as well as men, were exhibiting the effects of a real humdinger of a 'last night ashore', to the obvious disgust of our Commanding Officer.

By six o'clock next morning the Unit, sore heads and all, was on its way by train, and TCVs completed the journey to another of those huge canvas concentration camps, where once again we found ourselves incarcerated with many hundreds of troops, mostly Canadians. For a change, this one was near 'civilization', on West Common, Southampton; it was soon dubbed 'Stalag C19'.

That evening, although all others were allowed to spend the evening in town, 41 was confined to camp by our CO as a punishment for the previous evening's over-indulgence by a minority. That had in fact been the last opportunity for a night ashore; the camp was 'sealed' next day and thereafter no one was allowed out except in a supervised party. It was galling to see civilians going about their normal business on the other side of the fence, close enough to touch, but it was forbidden even to speak to them. We were as effectively cut off as if already overseas.

For my part, after months of living almost like a civilian with the comparatively light duties of a Despatch Rider, it wasn't a pleasant change to have to sleep on the bare ground, to spend an hour fire-watching most nights and be unceremoniously roused by 0630 reveille. As this was followed by morning parade and weapons inspection, perhaps followed by a route march, I was glad to be able to console myself that my real job was still that of a Despatch Rider.

On our second day in camp we were allocated to the specific craft that would carry us ashore on D-Day. Each craft had been given a serial number and thereafter all instructions given over the Tannoy public address system were by those serial numbers, rather than Units or Troops. To ensure that the loss of a single landing craft would not result in losing the entire command structure, Headquarters Troop had been distributed between the five landing craft allocated to the Unit and I had to respond to 'Serial Number two-five-six . . .'. Also distributed between the serials were the dozen or so German-speaking men from No. 10 Inter-Allied Commando who would accompany patrols and act as interpreters when the Commando was in contact with the enemy.

In Stalag C19 a previously-made suggestion by Captain Peter Howes-Dufton, CO of 'Y' Troop, that the Unit should be allowed to grow beards for the invasion was given the go-ahead by Colonel Gray and a 'Best Beard by D-Day' competition was instigated. As naval personnel, Royal Marines were required to 'put in a chit' (i.e. submit a written request) for 'permission to grow', and removal too was subject to 'permission to shave off'. A period of grace was allowed before having to make a beard 'official' and in my case the results after a few days – tufts of hair sprouting out here and there, with wide expanses of nothing in between – decided me to shave off. All except the moustache, that is, which has been retained as a *'souvenir de la guerre'*.

The weather, which had been hot and sunny on our arrival in C 19, grew hotter over the next few days and by Sunday 29th, Whit Sunday, the country was under heatwave conditions. In the afternoon the Commando paraded in 'shirt sleeve order without arms or equipment' to be led out of camp on a training-cum-keep-the-mind-occupied march. With three days' growth of beard, we undoubtedly looked a pretty scruffy lot and, dressed in khaki shirts without collars, sleeves rolled up and trouser braces exposed, no one could possibly have guessed that those nondescript marchers were normally spick and span Royal Marines. On that hot holiday Sunday afternoon, there were few civilians in the city streets, hardly any girls for the wolf whistle treatment and little of interest.

Beyond the city limits, however, things were more interesting, as the shady country roads, completely devoid of people and of traffic, were virtually a never-ending Quartermaster's Store. Along the grass verges edging every carriageway, hidden from the air beneath the canopies of hedgerow trees, were continuous lines of military vehicles of all descriptions, parked nose to tail with hardly any room for a playing card between them. Where there weren't vehicles there were incredibly long stacks of munitions and other military stores. Some stretches were protected from the weather by low arches of corrugated iron, while others were completely shrouded in tarpaulin sheets, stoutly roped to prevent ingress. On each batch, painted white and large, were reference letters and numbers which told the RASC personnel precisely what lay concealed there. Untold quantities of military supplies were waiting in readiness alongside good roads and needing only to be loaded into trucks for transportation to the nearby docks for shipment to France.

The Mediterranean weather continued into Whit Monday when we spent much of the day in a closely guarded, swelteringly hot 'Operations Marquee', as briefing for the forthcoming invasion started. We were given the overall picture of the operation, code-named, as is now well known, OVERLORD, and learned the major specific units that would be taking part. As details of the airborne, infantry and armoured divisions, and other units to be involved, the air and naval support to be provided, radar diversions to mislead the enemy etc, etc, etc, were unfolded, we were overawed by the unbelievable immensity of the scheme.

By reference to large-scale topographical maps of the area to be attacked, with all actual place names replaced by code-words such as 'Ganges', 'Vienna' and 'Poland', a detailed exposition of the invasion plans was given. It was learned at first hand all those things which are now common knowledge – the five main landing beaches, two code-named UTAH and OMAHA for the American First Army under General Bradley at the western end of the invasion coast, and three, GOLD, JUNO and SWORD for General Dempsey's British Second Army, with its substantial proportion of Canadian troops, to the east.

On each flank of the fifty-mile invasion front airborne troops – American west of UTAH and British east of SWORD – were to secure river crossings ready for the breakout from the beachhead. On the British eastern flank troops of the Sixth Airborne Division would land, by parachute and glider, some hours before the seaborne assault began. They had three tasks: to seize the bridges

27

spanning the river and canal linking a town code-named 'Poland' with the Channel coast, to neutralize a German coast defence battery which commanded the landing beaches and to hold a bridgehead on the enemy side of the river 'Ganges', for the eventual breakout from the beachhead of the British Army.

It was crucial for the reinforcement and supply of the Airborne troops that the bridges, lying some four miles from the sea, should be taken intact. The plan therefore was to set down gliders on the narrow strip of land between river bridge and canal bridge, and close enough to the abutments, to enable the troops to get out, reach the bridges and overcome the German guards before they had time to detonate explosive charges thought to be already in place.

The D-Day objectives of the various units were divulged and we were particularly interested in the tasks of the two British Special Service Brigades which were to be involved. These Brigades were No. 1, comprising 3, 4 and 6 Army and 45 Royal Marines Commandos, and No. 4 made up of 41, 46, 47 and 48 Royal Marines Commandos, the strength of each Commando being of the order of 450 men. No. 1 Brigade, which would form the extreme left flank of the entire Allied seaborne landing force, had the task of pushing rapidly inland in order to link up with the Airborne troops at the bridges. Of No. 4 Brigade, 41 and 48 Commandos would land straddling the junction of SWORD and JUNO beaches, to clear the coastal towns in the area, while 46 was to be held in reserve to go ashore next day, D+1, as reinforcement. 47 was given an independent D-Day role on the western flank of the British forces, the capture of Port-en-Bessin, and would land on GOLD beach.

On this occasion the employment of the Commando forces was to be different from usual. Instead of spearheading the attack, they were to land through 'holes' punched in the strong German beach defences by the tanks and guns of more heavily equipped infantry divisions. The Commandos' job would be to widen the point of attack by neutralizing enemy positions remaining along the coast.

The infantry brigades were to concentrate all their efforts upon pushing inland, without concerning themselves about what they might be leaving behind, which meant that none of their tanks, artillery or mortars would be available to support the Commandos in their tasks. 41 Commando was to land behind the leading elements of the 3rd British Infantry Division (3 Div) on SWORD beach, while 48 would follow the 3rd Canadian Infantry Division (3 Can Div) on to JUNO. The two Commandos would then move east and west respectively to clear the coastline between the two points of attack.

Once ashore, 41 Commando was to strike westwards to attack Lion-sur-Mer, a small coastal resort defended by two German positions, a strongpoint at a crossroads near the town and a nearby fortified château. To deal with these, the unit was organized into 'Force I', led by the Commanding Officer, and 'Force II', under the Second-in-Command, Major Barclay. After that the Commando was to attack another town further along the coast and there link-up with 48. The primary D-Day task of the entire British and Canadian attacking force was to be the capture of the town, some eight miles inland, codenamed 'Poland' on the briefing maps.

At the conclusion of that first briefing session each man was handed a small booklet entitled *France*, similar in format to the one called *Italy* we had received before the Sicily landing almost twelve months earlier. It gave sketchy information about the country, its people and language, plus the usual instructions on how troops were expected to behave towards the civilian population, but, more than that, it negated the entire rigmarole of false names on the maps! Its frontispiece is a small map of France, with all the real place names, so it required no more than a glance to recognize the shape of the invasion coastline. This, as is now well-known, extended from the Cherbourg peninsula to the River Orne; it was the Orne bridges that were to be secured by the Sixth Airborne Division, and 'Poland', the 2nd Army's D-Day objective, was the city of Caen.

That evening the DRs, riding their parascooters, were escorted to a nearby petrol filling station where RASC men topped up the tanks. We enjoyed a pleasant if brief outing, but it did occur to us that, as the Welbike's fuel tank held little more than 6 pints, the whole operation could have been accomplished by one man with a jerrican of petrol and a quart of oil!

Over the next few days more details were given of the part the Commando was to play in the landing, without us having to admit that we already knew the general location of the area of disembarkation. We also studied aerial photographs of the SWORD

29

beach area, to visualize the Commando's route to its objectives and to learn more details of the German defences in the area.

H-hour on SWORD beach was set for 0720 hours, but, in the hours of darkness before that, detachments of Royal Engineer and Royal Marine divers would be at work in the shallow inshore waters, rendering harmless German defences planted there to impede landing craft. The action proper would be initiated by a massive naval bombardment of the coast defences; then, prior to the infantry going in to assault, 'swimming tanks', launched from landing craft a few miles offshore, would touch down on the selected beaches. From a hull-down position in the sea, with only their gun turrets exposed above water, the tanks would engage any remaining German defences at close range.

These tanks had flotation girdles – six feet high canvas 'walls' – fitted to the hull which, when erected by compressed air, completely surrounded that part of the tank above the tracks, enabling it to float. On beaching, the walls would be collapsed at the touch of a lever to lie like a skirt about the hull and the tank could go into action immediately. They were fitted with twin propellers turned by the main driving shaft, which gave them a speed of five knots in water and also their technical name of 'Duplex Drive', or simply 'DD', tanks.

After the DDs, it would then be the turn of the Crabs or flail tanks, to explode mines buried in the sand. These were modified Shermans fitted with two massive arms supporting a steel drum, to which lengths of heavy chain were attached. As the Crabs trundled up the beach, with drum rotating, the chains flailed the beach ahead, exploding any mines in their path, leaving a safe route for the infantry to follow. 41 Commando was scheduled to go ashore at 0840, by which time things could be expected to be hotting up, both weather- and other-wise.

At a pay parade later that day we received the equivalent of ten shillings (four days' pay) in 'invasion money' – 200 francs of the French currency issued by AMGOT (Allied Military Government of Occupied Territories) which enabled those who had run out of English money to get back into the card schools; it took the bankers very little time to adjust to handling pounds, shillings – and francs.

The heatwave continued until Wednesday 31 May when part of HQ Troop unexpectedly departed for an unrevealed destination.

June began with appreciably cooler weather and a day of talks. First the Padre, then the Medical Officer, gave us counsel in their respective fields, after which it was the turn of the Commanding Officer. The CO's basic job was to convey General Montgomery's Message to the Troops: 'If things go as planned, and every man does his job to the best of his ability, Germany will be out of the war by October or November – and Japan six months later.' In the event, things didn't turn out that way, so perhaps there was someone who didn't do his job quite to the best of his ability. Such dates, however, didn't impinge upon us very greatly because at the time we firmly believed that, once the invasion forces had been securely established ashore, all Commandos would return to the UK, to be held in readiness for any further landings that might be required.

Every evening in C19 the mess tents doubled up as cinemas and the camp was well provided with films. By wandering around the vast canvas town you could find a different show every night. Many were recent releases, including *Yankee Doodle Dandy* and *And the Angels Sing*. We also felt chuffed at seeing Bing Crosby playing the Roman Catholic father in *Going My Way* some time before the film's general release in the UK.

Cinema shows were the only form of organized entertainment available to the rank and file, as the camp was completely 'dry'. To partially redress this last fact, immediately after the trio of talks on hopes, health and the hereafter, there was a second pay parade when each man received another ten shillings of due pay, in English money this time, to enable us to visit a public house.

This sounded great and engendered gleeful anticipation of another 'Glorious First of June' – it just happened to be the 150th anniversary of Admiral Howe's victory over the French off Ushant in 1794 in which Royal Marines had played such a useful part. In the event it turned out to be rather a low-key affair, far removed from any normal 'few pints at the local'.

After the evening meal all volunteers for 'Operation Pub' were fallen in and marched out of camp. The rendezvous had obviously been reconnoitred in advance and any thoughts of resting an elbow on the bar whilst chatting-up a barmaid, or even passing the time of day with mine host, were quickly dispelled. We found ourselves crammed, shoulder to shoulder, into a small garden area behind

31

the hotel and told to stay there. Orders were taken by officers and senior NCOs, who brought out the drinks, to be consumed where standing. Two pints per man was the ration, after which it was: 'All right lads, that's your lot – Get fell in outside', followed by a brisk march back to camp. The British tend to take their pleasures rather seriously.

The weather continued cool, as more briefings and final preparations went ahead. On Friday 2 June we were issued with a few items of 'Commando' equipment, designed to help us escape in the event of being taken prisoner, to be secreted about our persons. These included maps printed on very fine silk which could be folded into amazingly small dimensions, small files and a variety of compasses, for sewing into pocket flaps or uniform linings. To a casual observer my compass was no more than a pair of standard brass trouser buttons, but one was fitted with a needle-point fulcrum and the other had tiny steel inserts which caused it to behave as a magnetic needle. I also opened up one of the seams of the trousers to conceal a three-inch-long file.

On the morning of Saturday 3 June it was announced that we would be leaving C19 next day; D-Day was scheduled for Monday morning, 5 June. Personal ammunition and enough food to feed ourselves for the first two days ashore was issued, then came an unexpected packing problem. Each man received a free issue of a hundred cigarettes which had somehow been wangled by our Padre, the Rev Caradoc Hughes, but whether or not by divine intervention wasn't revealed.

During the last few days in C19 the stream of military traffic passing the camp had increased to flood proportions. By day and night guns, tanks, trucks and jeeps had clanked and rumbled past, no doubt some of the build-up forces moving into marshalling areas vacated by the D-Day vehicles already loaded on board their craft.

At 0820 hrs on Sunday morning a Communion Service was held for those who wanted it and this was followed at 1000 hrs by a regular Church of England Parade. We had kitted-up ready to move off when given the bombshell news that the invasion had been postponed! Maybe for only twenty-four hours, but. . . . We returned to waiting and playing cards, and, to my great astonishment, I won 250 francs at pontoon – maybe a good omen.

Rain began to fall during the evening and by lights-out the

weather was cool, wet and definitely dicey. We turned in, with our minds full of conjecture. Would we move off next morning or would the whole complicated business have to be gone through again in time for the next 'propitious' day for tides which wouldn't be for another month?

Chapter 3

D-DAY, SIXTH OF JUNE 1944

Monday dawned bright and clear and, even as we awoke, the message was in the air – OVERLORD was ON! D-Day would be one day later than originally planned but the long-awaited Allied invasion of France was all set to go ahead next day, Tuesday, Sixth of June.

Blankets were returned to store at 0900 hours and, after a meal at noon, we boarded TCVs for the short, dusty ride to the embarkation point which we had used previously, at Warsash on the River Hamble. After the inevitable, unexplained wait, the Commando filed on board the five LCI(S)s which were to carry it to France. Late in the afternoon the craft eased away from their berths, steamed a short distance and moored to buoys anchored in the fairway. These indicated our allotted position in the vast armada being gathered together in Southampton Water and spilling out into the Solent.

Those who had been involved in the Commando's two previous landings in the Mediterranean had already experienced similar vast build-ups of the almost unbelievable numbers of ships and invasion craft needed for an assault upon an enemy-held coast and this one re-awakened our amazement and wonder. Everywhere we looked there were more and yet more vessels of all sizes, shapes and types, and this, we knew, was only one of goodness knows how many other such marshalling areas along the south coast of England. Other convoys from more distant locations were already at sea. We had been slotted into our own little niche in the overall scheme of things and could at least draw comfort from the fact that, whatever the morrow might bring, there would certainly be a lot of our own people over there with us.

1:50,000 maps of our stretch of the Normandy coast were produced and we began to learn the names of the towns and villages soon to be seen at first hand. The Commando would go ashore on the beach of Hermanville-sur-Mer, a small town lying a mile or so inland, and would move on to clear Lion-sur-Mer, then press on to Luc-sur-Mer and link up with 48.

Familiarizing myself with our area of operations, I noticed the name of a small place lying between Lion and Luc – Petit Enfer, and thought that, next morning, 'Little Hell' could very well live up to its name. I also learned that the gun battery on the far side of the River Orne, said to threaten the landing beaches, was at Merville.

The armada assembling off Southampton continued to grow ever larger throughout the afternoon and evening until, at around 2130 hours, our craft were unhitched from the buoys. We took our place in the seemingly unending stream of vessels moving down the Solent, passing the Isle of Wight and into the English Channel. There was nothing for us to do but await the passage of time, putting our trust in God and the Royal Navy to get us unscathed to the right place at the right time next morning.

Most remained on deck, marvelling at the unbelievable sight of the innumerable black shapes sailing with us, until they became lost in the overall darkness. Then we moved down to the messdecks, three small 'boxes' each accommodating about thirty men with only an army blanket to wrap around oneself before settling down on the deck. We were accustomed to bedding down just where and when directed, so slept reasonably well throughout what turned out to be an uneventful night.

We awoke next morning to feel the landing craft being tossed about by a very disturbed sea and the sound of heavy guns engaging enemy shore installations coming down to us. Called out on deck, we stretched legs and cleared lungs of the fuggy fumes of the cramped messdeck, finding the early morning sea air, even in 'Glorious June', to be breathtakingly cold. The coastline of France was no more than a dark smudge on our port bow and all around were the silhouettes of the multitude of other vessels moving with us relentlessly towards the shore; some of our number were being sick over the side.

It would be more than an hour before we could expect to touch down and it was breakfast time. As we carried our own rations, we had the choice of menu, so I opted for the self-heating soup. The can was fitted with a chemical element running down the centre which, activated by a ring pull, had the contents piping hot within a few seconds. Mine appeared to be tomato and it tasted marvellous on the way down, but the rolling and pitching of the LCI suddenly persuaded my insides that they would feel very much better without anything like tomato soup to contend with. I joined the others at the ship's rail.

Ahead, along the coast to the west, we could see the rippling flashes of gunfire from sea and shore. The rumble of the Naval bombardment, pouring salvo after salvo on to the German defences, and the enemy's reply, grew louder by the minute. We were enjoying a ringside seat for such a momentous occasion, but weren't allowed to watch for long. 'All right! (it was always "all right", even when we knew that things were anything but right) Back to your messdecks and wait to be called up'. No reason was given for cooping us up, certainly no one had any thoughts of jumping overboard and swimming home.

The messdeck, although still slightly fuggy, was warm and cosy after our chilly sojourn on deck. We kitted up, checked weapons and equipment yet again, then sat around smoking and wondering. I was still somewhat apprehensive about humping the parascooter ashore. I had extended the seat, handlebars and footrests ready to wheel it along the deck when the time came, but realized that the tricky part would be heaving that 75 lbs of metal on to my shoulder and getting down the ramp, with goodness knows what kind of 'muck' flying around.

For the next half-hour or more it was frightening and frustrating to be confined below decks. Moving into calmer water closer inshore, the rolling and pitching became much less pronounced, but, as we came within range of the German guns, the landing craft's movements became violent and spasmodic. The shriek of incoming shells came to us quite clearly, but all we could do was to hunch our shoulders and exchange wry looks at each uncontrolled bounce and sway resulting from nearby explosions.

The cacophony of noise coming down to us increased in intensity; there was no way of sorting out the causes and meanings of all the whines explosions and thumps, but they told us that we were getting very close to the beach. By then we were not so much concerned about what was going on ashore as just getting our feet on dry land before the craft caught a packet.

The urgent notice of our release came at last, bawled down from the deck, 'All right, lads! We're touching down – on deck quick!' We crowded out into the daylight to be immediately assailed by an incredible medley of sights, sounds and smells. There were momentary glimpses of an untidy, straggling line of craft nosed up onto a crowded beach littered with tanks and other vehicles, many of them burning, scurrying figures and bodies in the water. Then there were the smells of cordite and of smoke drifting from burning ships and tanks. Everything taking place, the swaying of our landing craft, the crackling small arms fire, the whines of shells and their crashing detonations, were absorbed by impressions; there was no conscious looking about, the overriding concern was to get ashore in the shortest space of time.

I was on the port side, crouching low against the midships deckhouse, grasping the handles of my parascooter, ready to start pushing, when the urgent shriek of an incoming shell terminated in a shattering explosion on the starboard side of our craft. There was no time to assess whether it had been an actual hit or a near miss, nor even to wonder who, if anyone, had been hit; the voice of authority was urging us to, 'Keep moving! Get the hell out of it!! Get ashore!!!' I began to push the bike along the deck, closely following the man in front and being chivvied to move faster by the one behind.

At the bows there was a bottle-neck. Our LCI was wallowing skew-on to the beach; the bottom of the port ramp had floated away and was leading down into deep water in the general direction of England. Only the starboard ramp was usable and that was on the skew, both with the LCI and with the shore; men were queueing to get on to it. With only its bows in contact with terra firma, the craft was rolling helplessly in the sloshing motions of the sea. The only dry way down to France was via a narrow strip of timber gangway which was bucking and swaying like a cakewalk at a fair.

From my eye-level view, some fifteen feet above the beach, it was obvious that shouldering the Welbike and attempting to run down the ramp would probably have resulted in one very wet Marine and a waterlogged and useless piece of machinery. When my turn came to descend, therefore, I cradled the machine in my arms, stepped on to the ramp and sat down! Then, like a small child making its way downstairs nursing a teddy bear, I executed a rapid boots-and-bottom descent until I could swing my legs into shallow water and hop off. I splashed through a few yards of sea and kept on running over the deep soft sand, following a string of men disappearing into a large crater some twenty yards from the water's edge. I dropped the bike on the edge and rolled in beside them.

That temporary refuge, blasted out of the sand by an aerial bomb or large-calibre shell, was perhaps twenty-five feet across and five deep, and already occupied by a score of men. Some were lining the inland edge, firing rifles and a Bren in the direction of a wire fence, looking more like chain link than barbed wire, only a few dozen yards away. A fleeting impression of field-grey uniforms on the other side of the wire was cut off a split second later when a Churchill tank trundled to a halt between shell-hole and fence. The hatch was flung open, two crew members rapidly emerged and, standing exposed on the turret, reached down to drag out one of their comrades, who dangled limp and bloody from their hands. They were lowering him gently to the sand when our officer gave the order to follow him and doubled off along the beach to our right.

Even as I was humping the bike on to my shoulder the others were moving away and I was soon falling further and further behind. After only a dozen yards of stumbling through the soft sand, the weight became too much, so I dropped the machine and began to push it. The small wheels sank down to their axles and, instead of turning, simply gouged a furrow in the sand. For several minutes I alternated between trying to push the bike and heaving it up for another carry, until I was sweating like a stuck pig and my muscles could take no more. The others were out of sight, having disappeared through a gap in the tall hedge bounding the beach a few hundred yards ahead of me; it was obvious that my only hope of catching up would be to abandon the machine. I was then alongside a knocked-out Churchill tank, three of her crew crouching on the sand alongside. I dropped the Welbike in front of the first one and gasped, 'Here, Jack! Want a motorbike?' Without waiting for any response, I flexed aching muscles and ran on.

Relieved of the strain of concentrating everything upon coping with the parascooter, even as I ran my eyes and mind absorbed a little more of the turmoil about me. The landing had been timed for high tide, to enable craft to pass over obstacles in the water, so the action was concentrated on a narrow strip of dry sand. Tanks and other vehicles were burning on the beach, shattered craft were on fire at the water's edge and shells were falling here, there and anywhere. Amongst the floating debris being lapped against the shore, dead men, still supported by their Mae West life jackets, were bobbing about like corks. Other bodies lay scattered haphazardly over the sand.

Running past one of those dead men, I heard the urgent swishing of an incoming salvo which was obviously going to land very close and he seemed to offer an improved chance of survival. Without hesitation, I flung myself down alongside the body hoping, as proved to be the case, that the shells would land on the other side of him. I'm sure he would have understood. Fortunately, in soft ground, missiles go deep before exploding and their effect is directed upwards rather than outwards, so that their killing range is more confined.

No sooner had the shells burst than I was up and running, quickly reaching the gap through which the others had disappeared, where I was amazed to find two infantrymen digging a slit trench right there in the sand. They must have been new to the invasion game as the first rule of any landing was GET OFF THE BEACH! – to some place for which the enemy didn't have the map coordinates displayed in front of every artillery piece within range.

I ran through the gap to find myself on the narrow, unmetalled coastal road made familiar by maps and aerial photographs. The simple act of stepping on to it effected an instantaneous transition from the chaos and death of a crowded invasion beach to the deserted, if still noisy, seclusion of a residential area. There were some evidences of destruction, the road was strewn with rubble and draped with a tangle of wires from shattered telegraph poles, but the far side was lined with towering, three- or four-storeyed, half-timbered houses with steeply sloping roofs and pointed gables over their upper windows.

I had turned right and was running westwards in the direction of Lion-sur-Mer. From our briefings I knew that, a hundred yards or so ahead, this coastal track formed a junction with a road leading inland towards Caen. A short distance further on would be a Y-junction, both arms of which led to Lion, but the actual one to be used by the Commando had been left to be decided by 'prevailing circumstances' after the landing.

Just before reaching the junction I came upon a wounded infantryman, slumped against a wall bounding the right-hand side of the track. He had suffered a pretty bad leg wound, which I knew I couldn't do much about. 'Anything I can do for you, mate?' I asked. 'I'm OK,' he answered, 'but I wouldn't mind a fag.' I lit a cigarette and placed it between his lips. 'I'm OK,' he repeated, 'better push off and catch up with your pals.'

I left him with a 'Best of luck, chum!' and, on reaching the junction, came upon two stragglers of the Commando, crouching low in a ditch as an assortment of missiles passed over. They were debating which of the two roads to Lion to take and we all moved forward to have a closer look at the alternatives. At that moment an angry multiple whine heralded the imminent approach of another salvo of shells which weren't going to pass over. Instinctively we dived to the nearest cover, the shop premises forming the apex of the angle between the two roads to Lion, which was already devoid of a door and had no glass in its windows.

After the shells had exploded unpleasantly close we raised our heads to find that our refuge had been in the local Post Office-cum-Stationers. Amongst the debris littering the floor were scores of picture postcards, two of which caught my eye, one of Hermanville Plage where we had just landed, deserted apart from a solitary rowing boat, while the other was of the shop we were in. I pushed them inside my battledress blouse.

Of the two routes to Lion the left fork skirted open country, being built up along the right-hand side only, while the other, lying nearer the sea, was narrow, overhung with trees and high walls ran along both sides. That one looked safer, so we started off at the double, but, almost instantaneously, another batch of shells shrieked in to impact on the carriageway only a few score yards ahead. We hesitated momentarily, but guessed that shells, like lightning, probably wouldn't strike in the same place twice. We ran on, over the shell craters, very shallow ones as the shells had fallen on a hard, paved surface, passing through the last vestiges of smoke and the lingering smell of burnt explosive. A few minutes later, reaching the edge of a more built-up part of Lion we came upon the tail end of HQ Troop, crouching on the pavement against the walls of buildings on the left hand side of the road.

They were awaiting orders to move forward into the centre of town and weren't slow in giving us a ribbing for having fallen behind. Hardly had our trio flopped to the ground for a breather, however, than everyone was ordered to their feet and we were running at full pelt along the narrow pavement, making very little noise in our rubber-soled 'brothel creeper' boots.

We were passing within a few feet of the abutting houses and, framed in a number of the ground-floor windows could be seen the faces of curious, apprehensive, inhabitants of Lion-sur-Mer. The presence of British troops in their small French town would have made it abundantly clear to them that the Second Front in Europe had indeed started and that they were right in the middle of it. For a fleeting moment I gained the impression of an open view to our right in the direction of the English Channel, then once again there were buildings lining both sides of the street. We were halted and told to 'Wait Here!'

Sweating profusely from the combination of the now hot June sunshine and our exertions, we dropped to the pavement and sat with backs against the wall of the buildings sucking in lungsful of air. Given permission to 'Carry on smoking', green berets were removed to wipe streaming brows and also to get at the cigarettes and matches stashed there, to better their chances of a dry landing. Our group of HQ Marines had landed on the forecourt of a small shop and, surprisingly, its door was standing open for business. One of our number, who had left his matches in a trousers pocket and found them damp and useless, called across, 'Hey, Mitch! This is a paper shop. They probably sell matches. Go and buy us some will yer?' My few words of schoolboy French had put me on the spot, but it was a case of *noblesse oblige*, so I searched the depths of memory for the right words, took his five franc AMGOT note and went inside.

There was a young girl and an elderly lady behind the counter and when I said, '*Avez-vous des allumettes, s'il vous plait?*' Matches were produced, the note I proffered was accepted and they gave me change. Looking back, I have puzzled over how they had treated my request so phlegmatically, as though it was an everyday occurrence to sell matches in the middle of an invasion and to accept a previously unseen currency in payment. Nevertheless that, undoubtedly, must have been the very first 'invasion money' spent in the OVERLORD operation.

There is no doubt that the situation of our group of HQ personnel at that time was rather incongruous. Barely a mile away the beach of death and destruction on which we had landed was still receiving a pounding of artillery fire, yet here we were, sitting on the pavement in the sunshine. The morning air all about was filled with the sounds of whining projectiles and crumping explosions, but nothing was coming our way so we had time to reflect upon our great good fortune at having survived the greatest seaborne landing of all time. Similar but more distant sounds of gun-fire were coming to us from the direction of other landing beaches further along the coast beyond Lion-sur-Mer.

Then we began to hear the sounds of lighter explosions, probably mortar fire, coming from only a few hundred yards away, which indicated that forward elements of the Commando hadn't progressed very far. Whether the fire was 'ours' or 'theirs' was a matter of conjecture, but it was quite close and slightly disconcerting. However, there was obviously nothing that our particular little batch of HQ Troop was required to do for the time being, so we just sat in the sunshine, smoked and chatted.

We hadn't been there for long when an agitated French lady approached from the direction of the town centre. She clearly had something of import to impart so, as the only Britisher around with even a smattering of French, I went across to help. After asking her to speak more slowly, I gathered that there was a wounded soldier in her house and, with one of our Sick Berth Attendants, accompanied her through narrow alleyways then upstairs into her front bedroom. Sure enough, lying fully clothed on the bed was an Army private who had oozed a sticky mess of blood onto her snowy sheets and pillow from a jagged gash in his shoulder.

The SBA removed the soldier's battledress blouse, tore open his

42

shirt, cleaned the wound and applied a field dressing. We talked about moving him, but the lady intimated that she didn't mind him staying for the time being. With his wound neatly dressed, the pongo's main concern became the fact that he had lost the fighting order pack containing his food, so we left him some of our own to be going on with.

Hardly had we returned to the paper shop than someone called out, 'Hey, Mitch, what does, "*blessay*" mean?' Another lady had come to report that she too had a wounded soldier. I persuaded a different Sick Bay Tiffie to go with her by himself. I couldn't afford to give away too much of my food ration.

We had been waiting for orders for perhaps an hour when a pro-nounced build-up of mortar/artillery fire in the immediate vicinity confirmed the fact that the forward Troops of the Commando were having problems. It was clearly unsafe to be hanging around in the open streets, so we were quickly moved into the grounds of a church and set to work digging slit trenches.

I was assigned to a position alongside a tarmacadam path near where a trench for the Headquarters Signaller was being excavated. As we were digging, driblets of information filtered through and we learned the names of some of the numerous men of the Unit who had become casualties. The dead included my oppo, 'Geordie' Swindale from Gateshead, killed by a shell burst; the RSM 'Horace' Belcher, who had trodden on a mine, and our Second-in-Command, Major Barclay who, not many weeks earlier, had docked me three days' pay for speeding.

In view of the loss of his 2 i/c and some Troop Commanders, Colonel Gray had taken over command of Force II as well as Force I and attempted to proceed with the Unit's tasks as planned. Heavy casualties on the beach, however, had delayed assembly and greatly reduced the number of men available to him for the attacks on the Commando's two objectives. On top of this, all the Navy's bom-bardment signallers, assigned to the Commando for the first wave, had been wounded on the beach and their radio sets rendered useless, so it was impossible to call for any supporting gunfire. In addition, the attached Centaur tanks had been knocked out early in the day and, in consequence, the Fighting Troops had no close-up artillery support when moving in towards their objectives.

In view of heavy losses on the beach, tanks of any description had been at a premium, but, after the Centaurs had been knocked out, three AVREs (Armoured Vehicles, Royal Engineers) had been made available to support 'P' and 'Y' Troops as they moved forward with the South Lancs to attack the Lion-sur-Mer strongpoint. Those vehicles were based on Churchill tank chassis, but their function was to attack reinforced concrete fortifications at close range, not to provide infantry support. Their single artillery piece was a huge 290mm spigot mortar, designed to hurl 40lb 'flying dustbin' missiles at concrete blockhouses. Their range, however, was no more than 80 yards and they had a maximum rate of fire of only three rounds per minute.

The AVREs, nevertheless, led the Commando's advance upon the strongpoint, firing their Besa machine guns, primarily providing an armoured shield for our men. Unfortunately, at a range of about 100 yards, a well-sited German anti-tank gun (later identified as a 50mm PAK 38) opened up on them and, one after another, all three were knocked out. 'Y' Troop Commander, Captain Peter Howes-Dufton was killed and the Troop suffered other casualties before they could take up positions in houses on both sides of the road from which to engage the enemy.

The arrangements for these operations, and putting them into effect, occupied most of the morning. Then 'B' Troop, pushing forward towards the château, had come under heavy fire from German mortars and a field gun. By that time 41 Commando's own mortar section had expended all of its immediately available ammunition, so couldn't retaliate. Being without any artillery or mortar support, 'B' Troop was unable to move forward and was ordered to hold fast where they were.

As this was going on, Headquarters Troop, as well as excavating some protection for itself, had been operating the overall command functions. All Signals, Intelligence, Medical and general co-ordinating requirements had been carried out from holes in the churchyard. At an early stage a push bike was produced and I had been given signals to deliver in the vicinity. As the morning advanced the mortar fire became heavier and closer. Men were having to distinguish between the urgent, short, sharp 'SWISH! SWISSH!, SWISSSH!'es, which meant, 'heads down quick', as a batch of missiles was going to land very close, and the more leisurely, 'SSSWWIIIISSSSHHH'es of those bombs which were on a flatter trajectory, and so would fall at a safe distance, so far as they were concerned.

It was probably around noon when an officer called me across to the Signals trench to say that some of the Commando's jeeps, together with a Famous James motorbike, would soon be coming ashore at Hermanville Plage, and sent me off to bring them up. Once clear of the churchyard, cycling back to the beach, conditions were appreciably quieter until nearing the Post Office again, as that area was still receiving attention from German artillery. During the few short hours since diving for cover in the shop, the deserted coastal road had been transformed. A continuous flow of military vehicles of all descriptions was now streaming from the beach area, while an impeccably turned-out military police sergeant was on point duty at the road junction. Wearing white belt, anklets and gauntlet gloves, his arms were in continuous motion, chivvying drivers to keep moving and directing them to make the left turn towards Caen. As I neared the junction a flurry of incoming shells prompted another dive for cover, but the MP on point duty carried on imperturbably.

Beyond him the secluded residential road I had to myself that morning had also changed beyond all recognition. The hedge had been bulldozed out of existence, the road lay open to the beach and was choc-a-bloc with a one-way, nose-to-tail stream of military vehicles with many many more seeking an opportunity to join in.

The beach too, still littered with burnt-out tanks and other debris, had also changed remarkably. The tide had ebbed, so there was now very much more of it and, except for those sunk and disabled still lying in the shallows, the LCIs had gone. In their place were dozens of LCTs (Landing Craft, Tank) disgorging guns, trucks, jeeps, ambulances, staff cars, mobile workshops and every other item of military mechanization. Strip after strip of steel Somerfield tracking funnelled them across the soft sand, to continually feed the flood of vehicles heading towards the MP on point duty.

I had been given the serial number of the LCT to find, but guessed that it would be simpler just to look for the Commando's own identification number, '93', painted on the front and rear of every vehicle. I had to ride the push-bike along a much greater length of road than I ran along earlier in the day, but, suddenly, 'Bingo!'

– there was an LCT which had obviously just dropped its ramp and a bunch of 93s was clearly visible. They had a short, splashy trip ashore, but the waterproofing of the engines proved effective and there were no problems. On the back of one of the jeeps reclined a Famous James motorbike. When it was lifted off I swung my leg over the saddle, depressed the kick-start and the engine burst into life. A triumphant squeeze of its pathetic little bulb horn, however, produced no more than a gurgling squirt of seawater.

Leading the string of jeeps back along the track, I had to convince the MP that my little convoy was indeed the exception and that our route lay not inland towards Caen but along the coast to Lion. After moving past him, the road was deserted once more and in a matter of minutes we were back with Commando HQ at the church. The shell/mortar fire was much worse than when I had left and everyone was preparing to move out.

It appeared that 'A' and 'B' Troops had been heavily attacked as they neared the château and Colonel Gray, anticipating a general enemy counter-attack and still being without any artillery support, had decided to pull back a short distance to hold a more defensible line. The jeeps I had led forward were immediately put to good use in moving Commando HQ and evacuating casualties.

HQ travelled about half a mile down the road, through a gateway in the hedge on the left-hand side and up a track on the other side of the hedge leading to the apple orchard chosen by Colonel Gray for his HQ area. To the right of this track open fields stretched away towards the coast and about three hundred yards away, half-left from the gateway on a slight rise in the land, stood a large modern bungalow. It was reasonably intact, but had obviously been badly damaged by a shell or bomb and was deserted.

With Commando Headquarters being in the orchard, some two hundred yards from the gate, the jeeps, on their return from ambulance service, were parked alongside the hedge, hidden from the air by the overhanging trees and camouflage netting. We all set-to digging slit trenches in the narrow verge between track and hedge, a slow and laborious business with the one-piece entrenching tool comprising no more than a 6" long 'pick' at one end, and a 6" × 5" 'shovel' at the other. Work was halted from time to time by the arrival of shells or mortar bombs, so the afternoon had advanced into evening before sufficient earth had been removed to create holes large enough to enable us to curl up below ground level and sleep with a reasonable degree of safety.

Whilst engaged with this digging, although the rank and file didn't know it at the time, the Commando had come under the command of the 9th British Infantry Brigade (9 Bde), which hadn't come ashore until H + 6, i.e. around 1330 hours. Two of their battalions, the 5th Lincolnshires and the Royal Ulster Rifles, had been sent to assist 41 in the coastal sector, where the Brigade Commander had deployed them to extend the perimeter begun by Colonel Gray earlier in the day. Fortunately, one of the jeeps brought forward had been that of the RN Forward Officer Bombardment (FOB) who finally made radio contact with destroyers lying off-shore and called for a prolonged shoot onto both the château and strongpoint. It lasted from 1700 hours to 1800 hours and, whilst in progress, Lieutenant Stevens reported back with half of 'A' Troop which had been cut off when the unit had pulled back earlier in the day.

As the shadows lengthened there seemed little doubt that HQ would spend the night in that position and, as no other transport had reached us, there wouldn't be any blankets for bedding down. The only coverings in our equipment were waterproof sheets and anti-gas capes, so Bill Smith and I decided to reconnoitre the bombed bungalow. The interior was a shambles of demolished walls, wrecked furniture and shattered household goods, but amongst the rubble we came across a dusty red quilt, which we decided to 'liberate' and returned to our hole with it in some glee. The quilt performed yeoman service that night and for many more nights thereafter, but we never did get the opportunity of returning it to its owner.

By dusk all was quiet in our vicinity. The sky to the north-west, beyond the open fields abutting our narrow track, glowed bright orange in the setting sun and was streaked with long, grey clouds. The Isle of Wight lay barely a hundred miles away in that general direction, but we might have been at the other side of the world.

Then the calm of late evening was disturbed by the drone of many aircraft engines and men tensed themselves ready to dive for cover. However, when long strings of aircraft could be distinguished, as silhouettes against the colourful sky, it was obvious that they were coming from England. As they came nearer it could be

47

seen that each one was towing a glider; it was the Sixth Air Landing Brigade, going in to reinforce the Sixth Airborne Division and No. 1 Special Service Brigade, holding a bridgehead on the far side of the River Orne.

As the aerial armada drew near a few shells burst amongst the aircraft, showing that there were still a few enemy anti-aircraft guns within range, but the planes didn't falter. They had appeared from about half-left, looking towards the coast and, as they flew across our front, spontaneous bursts of cheering came from the men on the ground. When the leading planes disappeared from sight below the trees a few miles away to the right, however, a build-up of crackling anti-aircraft fire subdued all jollity. Barely five miles away, beyond the Orne bridges, the gliders were swooping down to a hot reception. All we could do was to wish the troops in them a silent 'Good luck, chaps'.

Within a matter of minutes the leading planes, having released their gliders, were heading back the way they had come. Altogether our unexpected session of evening entertainment lasted little more than twenty minutes from the first rumble of approaching engines to the last planes disappearing northwards. As they were leaving there was the inevitable wag within earshot whose thoughts had perhaps been in other minds. 'Just think,' he said, 'those bloody RAF pilots'll be back swilling beer in their canteens in about an hour's time,' but most of us would much rather not have been reminded of that sort of thing.

With darkness came the enemy bombers, but they weren't after us. Their target was the mass of shipping lying off the invasion beaches and it was clear that they were directing their attention not towards nearby SWORD beach, but further west in the direction of GOLD and JUNO. Anyhow, that gave us something else to watch – tracers arching skyward, exploding ack-ack shells and the flashing explosions of bombs silhouetting the skyline of the inter-vening landscape. It was all happening some miles away, so we were no more than interested spectators. Bill and I eventually settled down for our first night in French soil and, thanks to the borrowed red quilt, it was warm enough. Apart from taking our normal turns on guard duty, the hours of darkness and the inevitable dawn stand-to passed without incident.

Not until long after the war did I learn more about the action our Commando had been involved in that day. At the time it was happening there was no opportunity to ask questions, it was largely a case of just being thankful that 'Number One' was still in one piece and concentrating your other thoughts upon such things as food and rest. It seems, however, that the German defenders in the Lion- and Luc-sur-Mer area, which lay between the 41 and 48 Commando beaches, had managed to maintain their positions after the first assaults and that a battalion of Panzer Grenadiers, supported by tanks, had, later in the day, attacked from the direction of Caen to link up with them.

By evening six tanks and a Company of infantry had in fact reached the coast where they managed to contact Germans still in position there. This had created the possibility of developing a wedge between the British and Canadian forces. The arrival of the 6th Air Landing Brigade, which we witnessed without knowing just who they were, had, perhaps, persuaded them to pull back.

The Official War Diary of 41 Royal Marines Commando for D-Day records that the unit suffered 140 casualties, including four Officers and twenty-two Other Ranks killed, out of a total landing strength of 437 officers and men.

Chapter 4

IN THE NORMANDY BEACHHEAD

Like every day in the forward areas, Wednesday 7 June, D + 1, on the outskirts of Lion-sur-Mer, began with a dawn stand-to. Attacks were sometimes initiated when there was just sufficient daylight to enable attacking troops to maintain contact in the hope of catching the enemy before he was fully organized. All ranks were, therefore, wide-awake and in defensive positions well before sunrise just in case. Not until full daylight had been well established, there having been no attack, were we stood down to flex cramped muscles and think of breakfast.

With stand down, however, the unit was alerted for an 'immediate' move off, so it was a case of getting something into one's inside as quickly as possible. The tin of hot soup which had ended up in the English Channel twenty-four hours previously would have been ideal, but I had to make do with dehydrated porridge. The individual block of porridge oats, dried milk and sugar was intended to be crumbled into a mess tin of boiling water, but I ate mine like a bar of chocolate and achieved the porridge effect by drinking hot tea.

Then, kitted up ready to go, we awaited the order to start engines, and waited, and waited. Intermittent salvoes of shells and mortar bombs were being exchanged in our general neighbourhood and sporadic outbursts of small-arms fire could be heard from the direction of the strongpoint and château. Although some elements of the German army were still active in our area, the main forces of both sides were now some eight or nine miles inland, in the vicinity of Caen, the D-Day objective which had not been achieved.

The waiting had continued for about two hours when sounds of approaching air activity drew all eyes skyward, to see Spitfires in hot pursuit of three German Heinkel bombers flying low in our direction. Attention concentrated on one of the latter with some puzzlement when a large cylindrical object was seen to fall from its belly, but when it opened to disgorge a tumbling cascade of small silvery objects, the truth clicked home. Urgent yells of 'Anti-personnel . . . !! sent us scattering for cover and there was barely time to dive into the narrow gap between jeep and hedge before scores of small bombs were bursting like vicious fire crackers all around.

Hundreds of the bombs had been scattered over a wide area and, although the men who had been by the jeeps were unscathed, in the Headquarters orchard a few score yards away four had been killed and nine wounded. Two of those killed were attached personnel, the Royal Artillery Forward Observation Officer and the Corporal-in-charge of the Brigade Headquarters Signals Link. The wounded included our Commanding Officer, Colonel Gray, and the Chaplain, the Rev Caradoc Hughes RNVR. One HQ Signaller who had dived into his foxhole was unhurt but found his steel helmet, left on the soil outside, had been lacerated by bomb splinters.

With the Colonel evacuated and Major Barclay having been killed the previous day, (ten out of twenty-two officers of the Commando had become casualties in 24 hours), command of the unit devolved upon the Adjutant, Major John Taplin. He was then aged only 23, having joined us as a Second Lieutenant fresh from Cadet School almost three years earlier.

Shortly after the casualties had been evacuated the Commando received its orders. The bulk of the unit was to support 5 Lincs in an attack on the château, while HQ and one Fighting Troop would move around the German positions to make a sweep further inland towards Luc-sur-Mer. Bill Smith was the Despatch Rider chosen to accompany the Lincolnshires, so I was obliged to hand over the Famous James and proceed on foot.

The out-flanking party moved off inland – long, snaking files of men spaced out along each side of the road, weapons at the ready, eyes scouring the countryside. It was empty apart from a few groups of tank men removing flotation girdles and transport drivers 'de-waterproofing' their engines. After about a mile the straggling column turned on to a minor road lined with 'bocage'-type dykes, which ran roughly parallel to the coast in the direction of Luc. Two château-like estates were encountered en route and we made searches of the buildings and grounds; the occupants, interrogated by officers, appeared reluctant to seem too friendly, perhaps thinking that the Germans might return and consider them collaborators.

There was no hint of any urgency in the progress, the column just meandered along through a hot summer's afternoon. News came that the attack on the château had been successful, with very few casualties but not much effect upon the Germans, as most had managed to escape. 5 Lincs and 41 Commando had then moved on towards the other German position, the strongpoint.

By late afternoon the marching column was passing small farms and groups of cottages where the people were obviously delighted to see us. Women and young girls stood by the roadside clutching bunches of roses and, as we trudged past, blooms were pushed into battledress pockets, behind ammunition pouches or under the shoulder straps of webbing equipment. Old men sitting in the sunshine were not so demonstrative, but most held up two fingers in the V sign; there were shouts of '*Vive les Anglais!*' All in all it engendered the feeling of being a hot and sticky conquering hero!

In the early evening the column was halted where it would spend the night and Commando HQ set about organizing itself in a farm at a crossroads on high ground giving a view of the sea about a mile away. With the Signallers, the DRs were assigned to a straw-covered, smelly but cosy corner of the farmyard, where it was a great relief to shed arms and equipment. Soon we were able to enjoy the civilizing luxury of the first wash and shave since leaving Stalag C19 at Southampton. Was that only two days ago? It seemed like half a lifetime!

News filtered through that the attack on the Lion strongpoint had been successful, although no details were forthcoming. 41 had not been involved as 9 Brigade had detached the unit from 5 Lincs and sent it forward independently to Luc-sur-Mer, which they had occupied without opposition earlier that evening. 46 (RM) Commando, after landing that morning, had cleared Petit Enfer against some determined opposition, but all was now quiet there too.

Spruced-up but hungry, we finished off the last of the individual 48-hour rations we had carried ashore and, as darkness fell, our 'evening entertainment' began. From our high vantage point we watched a succession of German bombing attacks on the ships lying off the beaches and the impressive ack-ack barrage blasted into the sky to counter them. In the farmyard, much removed from all that, we passed a pleasantly quiet night, interrupted only by a two-hour stint of sentry duty.

By next morning, 8 June (D + 2), it was abundantly clear that the tide of battle had left us far behind. There was no dawn stand-to; we were allowed to sleep in the straw until 0600 hrs. The initial Allied push towards Caen had been contained by the Germans throwing reinforcements into the line piecemeal, just as and when they arrived in the battle area, ignoring losses. The British and Canadians had only been able to counter this by rushing more and more men and materials from the beaches until conditions were stabilized. It would be many weeks before Caen was eventually taken, but, so far as we were concerned, the main German forces were at least eight miles away, it was a pleasant summer's morning and there was time for a leisurely breakfast.

Our individual supplies of food were finished, but the '14 men for one day' boxes of composite ('Compo') rations had reached us. This meant breakfasting on tinned bacon or tinned sausage (depending upon the box received by the group), bulked out with hard tack biscuits. Someone, hoping to better this, called out, 'Hey, Mitch! Go 'n see if you can buy us some eggs.' My French was successful and the asking price of 5 francs each (about 2½ pence then, 1p in decimal currency) was reasonable. At first the farmer's wife was sceptical about accepting the 'invasion money' proferred, but was finally persuaded and our little group enjoyed two fried eggs each to supplement our basic issue.

After breakfast we quitted the farm for the short march down to Luc-sur-Mer, where a vacant house near the centre of town had been taken over for Commando Headquarters. By the time we arrived signallers were stringing out field telephone lines to link HQ with the other troops. With the radio jeeps parked in a small garden at the rear of the premises, and the drivers busy with their daily maintenance, it was very much like being on a 'stunt' in the UK.

46 RM Commando had moved out of Luc that morning, heading for La Délivrande, a small town some two and a half miles away, near which some Germans were holding out in two fortified radar stations. 41 RM Commando had become responsible for the area around Luc-sur-Mer and Petit Enfer, so most of the men were positioned for local defence, although some, aided by French Resistance men, were engaged in rounding up collaborators and searching the countryside for German snipers.

In Luc-sur-Mer a cheerful, bubbling holiday atmosphere prevailed and the streets, bright with sunshine were thronged with people. Café doors stood open and, when a passing Frenchman invited me to join him for an apéritif, I was happy to accept. Unfortunately his choice was Pernod, a liquor for which I never acquired a taste, so I politely declined a second. Later in the day, Claudie, a boy of about four, spent some time with *les Anglais*, providing French conversational practice nearer my own level of expertise.

On that day, too, I first encountered Abdul, a swarthy hook-nosed individual of undoubted Arab origin, who was standing stiffly and proudly to attention facing the HQ doorway. He wore a crumpled lightweight blue uniform with brass buttons, right hand grasping the sling of an antiquated but well-cleaned rifle slung over the shoulder, left hand resting on a battered bugle dangling from a tasselled golden cord across his chest and on his head he sported a French steel helmet. As I looked in his direction, the cheeky, self-laudatory smile on his face widened into a jubilant ear-to-ear grin of large white teeth.

I passed him with a nod, to ask the Orderly Room clerk, 'What the heck . . . ?' The Arab, apparently, had been discovered on D-Day in one of the houses in which 'Y' Troop had sought cover when it came under fire, moving forward with the AVREs, firing his rifle at the German position. A slave-worker with the German Todt Organization working on the coast defences, he had decamped when the invasion started and now wanted to stay with the Commando! The idea of anyone, particularly a non-European, seeking to join up with Royal Marines in the middle of a war seemed too absurd for words.

The Unit's sojourn in Luc-sur-Mer was short-lived. The very next day, 9 June, 41 followed 46 to La Délivrande, where 4 Special Service Brigade was to form a perimeter around the radar stations. These were understood to be occupied by some 200 men housed in deep reinforced concrete bunkers, proof against all but the very heaviest artillery shell, and with substantial artillery and mortar capability. The original garrison had been augmented by Panzer Grenadiers who had escaped from the château and strongpoint.

Next day 41 Commando moved forward to take over positions occupied by a battalion of the Black Watch of the 51st Highland Division (51 Div), but were kept waiting for almost two hours before being able to occupy the prepared positions. As usual, the Germans were aware that a change-over was in progress and peppered the area with artillery and mortar fire in the hope of catching men in the open. The weather was unfriendly too, having changed to cool and overcast.

When the Germans appreciated that their fresh adversaries were in position they ceased firing and the unit passed a relatively quiet night. For much of it the advanced elements were sending out patrols, probing forward towards the German blockhouses to get acquainted with the lie of the land. On the other side of the perimeter 48 Commando were making similar sorties from their positions near Douvres.

That situation lasted a bare twenty-four hours because, on the evening of 11 June, 4 SS Brigade was temporarily split up. 47 and 48 Commandos, together with Brigade HQ, were placed under the command of 6th Airborne Division and moved off to join them in the bridgehead on the other side of the River Orne; 46 Commando was transferred to Canadian Command, so moved into their sector. This left 41 to look after the radar stations on its own, but without 'S' Troop, temporarily placed under command of 48 Commando.

The depleted Commando, with no more close-up support than two Centaur tanks, was spread out to form a loosely-held perimeter around the entire German position. HQ moved out of holes in the ground to a hutted complex in a wooded area nearer Bény-sur-Mer, which had been the radar stations' control base. Two of the Fighting Troops were positioned along the forward edge of the woods facing the German barbed wire and other Troops of the Commando took over the positions on the far side of the German pocket vacated by 48.

The military situation at the radar stations was complicated by the fact that the flat farmland between them and Bény was being rapidly transformed into an advanced airstrip for the RAF. Less than half a mile from Commando HQ part of the Bény wood was being bulldozed out of existence to provide the required length of runway. By this time a batch of the Commando's transport, including the Ariel motorcycles, had caught up with the unit and the DRs were trying to settle down to a 'normal' routine. However, with the Troops of the Commando strung out around an indeterminate enemy position a mile or more in diameter and an airfield being constructed on the doorstep, it proved to be a rather hairy business, far removed from carefree riding along quiet roads in rural England.

The initial, crucial problem was to pinpoint where the Headquarters of the five Fighting Troops had been set up, because, during the first hours in every new location, even Commando HQ didn't know precisely where they were. On my very first trip at the radar stations, an Officer handed me a signal for 'P' Troop on the other side of the German position. Then, describing a circle on the map with his index finger, said, 'You'll find their HQ somewhere in that area, make a note of where it is and let me know when you get back.'

From my map I determined the appropriate roads to get me around to the other side of the German position and the one leading towards the roughly-indicated HQ position, and off I went. I knew that the most I could hope to find, by way of identification, would be a cryptic 'P HQ' chalked on a gatepost, on a chunk of stone in the verge, or on a plank of wood propped against the hedge. So, when heading down the last leg of the trip, I was travelling very slowly, eyes searching both sides of the road. Nevertheless, I was suddenly assailed by an urgent shout coming from behind me, 'Come back, you silly bastard!!' I stopped in a hurry and turned my head to look down the muzzle of the Bren gun of one of the Troop's forward positions, well-camouflaged in a ditch.

The gun's crew weren't at all happy about the possibility of my having given away their position to a German OP, which might direct mortar fire upon them. My suggestion that they should put up some bloody signs to let people know where the hell they were wasn't received with any gratitude. I was rapidly given directions to Troop HQ and shoo-ed away, but at least I was able to ensure that the next DR going to 'P' knew when to stop.

That was a foretaste of life as an operational DR. Invariably the job involved periods of scary loneliness, riding between the SDO and the forward Troop, wondering if you really were on the right road and with no great confidence of actually finding their HQ even if you were. Then, after you had done the almost impossible and found what you were looking for, it was an odds-on bet that they would be in no way pleased to see you. The first confirmation of having achieved your goal could very well be a shadowy figure lunging out of the darkness of the night to grab you by the shoulders and hiss in your ear, 'For Christ's sake, shut that bloody thing off! The whole fricking German army can hear you.'

The day after 41's take-over of the radar stations I was handed a despatch for 6th Airborne Division on the other side of the River Orne. With it came the usual imprecise directions, 'You'll easily find their HQ – it's in Ranville'. I traced out the route on the map – three miles to Luc, then six more along the coast road to Ouistreham, to turn right and follow the river inland. It was another three miles to Bénouville, where a sharp left-hand bend would take me towards the canal and river bridges; Ranville lay about one and a half miles away on the other side. Almost as an afterthought I was advised, 'Don't dawdle on the bridges. They are under enemy observation.'

I left Commando HQ with mixed feelings of curiosity and trepidation. The journey would be a fourteen-mile sortie into unknown territory and was undoubtedly 'up front'. I knew that the 6th Airborne's bridgehead on the other side of the River Orne and Caen canal was still very much as it had been immediately after the initial assault. It had been reinforced by No. 1 Special Service Brigade linking-up with them on D-Day and, two days ago, by 47 and 48 Commandos, but this meant only that the original slim perimeter on the far side of the Orne bridges had been strengthened, not extended, and every part of it was well within the range of German artillery.

After three quiet country miles I reached the coast road which took me past the bustling beach areas of Riva Bella and Ouistreham. There un-ending streams of trucks carrying arms, ammunition and stores were pouring ashore, to augment huge stockpiles being built up along the front, and all to the intense interest of crowds of French civilians in holiday mood. Turning inland at the mouth of the Orne, however, those scenes of comforting activity were immediately replaced by the belt of 'nothingness' which invariably lay between the 'rear' and 'forward' areas. An empty, meandering road took me through a completely deserted countryside. There was no traffic, no sign of human beings, no animals in the fields, and even the birds seemed absent. I was the only moving thing in that dead landscape and the unmistakable crumps of exploding shells in the middle distance ahead grew louder by the minute.

At Bénouville a sharp left turn revealed an empty ribbon of road leading down to the two bridges, only five hundred yards apart, which span the Caen canal and the River Orne. Beyond the bridges the road climbed towards high ground where spurts of billowing smoke around a belt of trees on the skyline indicated a multiplicty of bursting shells. I paused briefly for reflection and decided that the best chance of getting across before any guns could be brought to bear would be to twist the throttle wide open and – 'GO!'

The Ariel swept down the hill just as fast as it would go, skimmed over the bridges, then, roaring up the hill on the far side, I eased back on the throttle. Shells were falling uncomfortably close and, not being entirely sure of the route, I was contemplating ditching the bike and taking cover to consult the map. At that point, however, a head followed by an arm making urgent 'Stop!' signals materialized from the grass verge on the left-hand side of the road. Rapidly braking to a halt revealed a Military Policeman who, amazingly, wasn't crouching low in his slit trench, but standing upright in one so deep that his chin was at ground level!

'Airborne HQ?' I queried, mentally wondering just how he would get out of that hole in a hurry should the occasion arise. The arm waved up the hill, while the head said, 'The right fork and straight on to the village', then both disappeared again. I opened the throttle and pulled away. His directions were adequate; 6th Airborne HQ was located in the basement of a shell-shattered house and ten minutes later I was back on the road with a reply. Speeding down towards the bridges again, there was no sign of the MP, so either he was way down in his hole or I was travelling too fast to see him.

The bridge over the Caen canal has gone into the history books and on to the maps of Normandy as 'Pegasus Bridge', named after the winged-horse symbol of the 6th Airborne Division. Ranville too has its place in history, being the first village in France to be liberated, and a plaque on the wall of Place du 6 Juin 1944 records that it 'was wrested from the Germans at 2.30 a.m. on June 6th, 1944, by the 13th (Lancashire) Battalion, Parachute Regiment'.

At the radar stations life for the Fighting Troops had settled down to a cat-and-mouse situation of exchanging shells. Should either side consider it necessary to fire off a few rounds, the other felt obliged to send some back in return. The Corps Commander, Lieutenant-General Crocker, had directed that no unnecessary casualties were to be suffered in trying to take the radar stations: the operational requirement was simply to ensure that the Germans stayed where they were and created no problems for the Allied forces.

From time to time the Royal Artillery would have a go with their '7-point-2s' (7.2" howitzers), but even their hefty 200-pound shells weren't heavy enough to do more than chip the massive concrete bunkers emblazoned, as I saw later, with the names of earlier German military leaders such as HINDENBURG and LUDENDORFF. Nevertheless such loads of explosive would probably have disturbed the inmates and perhaps prompted them to wonder just what they were achieving by remaining there. To augment the close-up artillery support provided by the two Centaur tanks, 'P' Troop had found a German anti-tank gun with a supply of ammunition and were delighted to blast it off at the slightest pretext.

In the early hours of 13 June the senior of our German-speaking 10 I-A Commando men, CSM O' Neill (Czechoslovakian by birth but with a wartime British name), led a party with bangalore torpedoes to blow a gap in the outer German wire and minefield defence to enable AVRES to get in close enough to hurl 'Flying Dustbins' carrying 26-pound demolition charges against the German bunkers. The AVREs completed their shoot without attracting any return fire and two men of 'A' Troop, led by Lieutenant Stevens, passed through and blew a gap in the inner wire. This provoked the Germans into opening up rapid fire with machine guns and machine carbines from four separate positions. But they were shooting wildly in the darkness, not knowing where the Marines were and, after a fifteen-minute fire fight, the 'A' Troop men withdrew without casualties. For a protracted period thereafter the Germans vented their spleen with mortar and shellfire.

Later that same day I had a second trip across the River Orne to our own Brigade Headquarters, which I would find 'Somewhere along the road to Sallenelles'. It was another lonely ride beyond Ouistreham, a similar brief pause at Bénouville to survey the bridges and another 'belt' down into the valley and up the other side. There was no sign of the MP this time as I swept up the hill to take the left fork leading down river towards the sea and Sallenelles, instead of going right to Ranville.

Once around the bend I was in 'glider country', where the Sixth Air Landing Brigade, seen flying in on D-Day, had come to earth. The fields abutting the road were littered with gliders, lying so close together that it seemed as though they had been lowered in by crane. Some had wings torn off by colliding with trees or other gliders, many had split open on landing and a pitiable few were no more than heaps of shattered timber and perspex. How so many had managed to get down, at night, without engines and without killing everyone on board, was little short of miraculous. There are worse ways of going to war than landing from the sea.

Brigade HQ was found without trouble. After a couple of miles along the road a good '4 SS HQ' sign in the verge directed me up a narrow track to a farm. On the return trip I had passed the glider fields and was rounding the bend towards the Orne bridges when a shell exploded in the field directly ahead, barely fifty yards away, quickly followed by another and another and another. Instinctively I 'rode to ground' – a technique learned for precisely any such self-preservation situation – and landed in a shallow depression against the hedge, with my bike lying alongside.

Lying there, hugging Mother Earth, I realized that here was another 'minus' of a Despatch Rider's life – the noise of a motorcycle engine drowns the whine of approaching shells. With the engine silenced, I could follow it all – German shells coming in towards Ranville and the bridges area, and our guns opening up in retaliation. After a while there was a lull, as if both sides were pausing for breath, so I hauled the bike upright and raced off down the hill, kicking the engine into life on the move. Bike and I shot back over the bridges to the relative peace of the beachhead as if the bats of hell were close behind.

In marked contrast, there were trips 'back' to British landing beaches, which stretched from the mouth of the Orne in the east to St Aubin and Courseulles in the west. On such trips, once clear of any 'hate session' which might be in progress around the Douvres/La Délivrande position, it was no more than taking a spin in glorious weather along empty roads winding through pleasant countryside. Then it wasn't unknown for me to attract the curious stares and shrugs of locals as a mad Englishman rode past carolling his own version of Maurice Chevalier's song, '*Auprès de ma blonde, il fait bon, fait bon, fait bon . . .*'!

Many buildings in that coastal strip of Normandy had been damaged by bombs or shell-fire and one unusual example lay on the route to Courseulles. Nearing Langrune the top of a slender church steeple could be seen poking above the trees and roofs, but not until rounding a bend in the road could it be seen that there was a neatly-drilled hole about half-way up. Clearly, a shell had passed through without exploding, leaving the main supporting timbers and most of the tiling still intact.

At Courseulles the quiet countryside of rural Normandy had been transformed into an unbelievably vast military stores complex, a noisy world of trucks, bustle and dust. Behind the beaches of Sicily there had been huge stockpiles of war *matériel*, growing larger by the minute, as DUKWS ferried load after load ashore from supply ships anchored close inshore. Then, more recently, prior to D-Day, we had marched past mile after camouflaged mile of vehicles, stores and munitions lining the country roads around Southampton, but at Courseulles it looked as though the entire countryside was being submerged beneath never-ending supply dumps. Whole fields had become open air warehouses, containing row after row after row of towering stacks of boxes, crates, cans and drums of food, petrol, oil, arms and ammunition – everything, it would appear, from chinagraph pencils to Churchill tanks. Between the interminable lines there was just sufficient width for trucks to enter and be loaded for the Front.

The extent of the supply dumps was so great that it had apparently been considered futile to make any attempt at camouflage and to rely solely upon the RAF keeping the Luftwaffe away. In any case, much of the area must have been partially hidden by the continuous clouds of dust raised by never-ending lines of trucks trundling from beach to stockpiles and from stockpiles to the forward areas.

My first trip to Courseulles was at the instigation of the Adjutant, on the off-chance that there was an Army Post Office there which might be sitting on some mail for the Unit, because none had reached us. After much riding around and many enquiries, I eventually located the APO and, sure enough, there was a bag of mail for 41 RM Commando awaiting delivery or collection. It was a relief to be able to escape from the turmoil around Courseulles and head back to the relative quiet of Bény woods, and with a sense of great achievement – a bag of mail draped over the luggage rack! That was probably the only occasion on which my arrival anywhere was greeted with general jubilation, but there was nothing in the bag for me.

Most days included at least one plastering of the radar stations by the RA's 7.2s and most nights Commando patrols would go out, perhaps to blow additional gaps in the enemy barbed wire or just to clear away a few more mines. On some nights, however, they would quietly worm their way right up to the gun slits of the block-houses, so that our 10 I-A men could eavesdrop on German small talk and learn something about enemy intentions and morale. On one such occasion Sergeant Hazelhurst of 'A', before leading the patrol back, felt incensed enough to bang on the steel door of one of the blockhouses with his Tommy-gun butt, bawling at the occupants to stop being such bloody fools and come out! There were undoubtedly some inmates who understood what he said but there was no response.

From time to time a German would sneak out to surrender and one of them volunteered the information that they were getting short of food and water. The next night the Luftwaffe did make a parachute drop but 'P' Troop got to the container first. Instead of food and water, however, the drop comprised small arms ammunition, replacement breech blocks for anti-tank guns and booby traps.

One evening an Allied aircraft was seen to be in trouble, almost directly overhead, and we guessed that the pilot had been making for the almost completed airstrip nearby when he found that he couldn't make it. Seven crew members baled out and all parachutes opened. As they floated safely earthwards the parachutes drifted out of our sight below the treetops and bursts of machine-gun fire were heard coming from the radar stations, although nothing was learned of the outcome.

The Bény airstrip became operational on 14 June when a squadron of 'Tiffies', rocket-firing Typhoon aircraft, started flying from there. Their flight paths for take-off and landing took them close to the radar stations and it must have been disconcerting for the pilots to have German machine gunners greet them with streams of bullets. On one occasion the Commando HQ area too was disconcerted when a Tiffy was being 'bombed up' and a rocket launched itself from the aircraft's wing and tore its fiery way through our wood.

It was undoubtedly the complications of having a pocket of active enemy and their 'containing' troops living cheek by jowl with an operational RAF airstrip that persuaded the Corps Commander that enough was enough. On 16 June, therefore, Lieutenant Colonel E.C.E. Palmer RM, who had arrived to take over command of the unit only two days previously, received orders to terminate the German occupation of the Douvres/La Délivrande radar stations. He was allocated the support of the tanks of the 22nd Dragoons and the AVREs of 5 Assault Squadron RE – forty-four armoured fighting vehicles in all – to help the Commando do it.

The plan was that, after a 30-minute barrage by 7.2s, three teams of Crabs (flail tanks) would make gaps in the German wire and minefields, then would provide covering fire for the AVREs to go forward to loose off their flying dustbins. Some Royal Engineers would dismount from their vehicles under smoke cover to place charges against those blockouses the AVREs could not reach. The finale would be tanks acting as an armoured shield for the Royal Marines of 41 Commando: 'B' 'P' and 'X' Troops, with 'Y' in reserve, would advance through the gaps to 'winkle out' the Germans in the larger southern radar station, while 'A' would take care of the small northern one.

At 1630 hours on Saturday, 17 June (D+11), an intense barrage of 7.2s opened up and half an hour later, right on schedule, the Crabs started on the minefield. At 1720 the AVREs moved in to bombard the blockhouses for twenty minutes. Then, at 1740, the Commando moved in and, as the Unit War Diary records: 'the enemy had been dazed, shocked or frightened into surrender and came out in large numbers with their hands up.' By 1830 it was all over, the 'bag' of prisoners being five officers and 222 other ranks. The Commando suffered only one man wounded; there were two RE casualties and one Crab was knocked out. 41's total casualties around the radar stations had been three killed and three wounded.

In a BBC radio broadcast on 18 June 1944 Frank Gillard reported that some of the Douvres bunkers extended to four stories below ground, although I didn't get to see inside any of them until fifty years later when some were reopened as a tourist attraction.

My role in the assault had been no more than being one of those 'who only stand and wait', at the Signals Despatch Office, ready to deliver any messages that might be required. There weren't any, so it was merely a case of listening to the 'noises off'. In consequence, I saw none of the wrist watches, bayonets, Leica cameras, Zeiss binoculars, Lüger pistols and Nazi officers' ceremonial swords which invariably changed sides on such occasions. The only 'souvenir' that fell into my hands I found in one of the small peripheral pillboxes when poking about afterwards. It was a German/French phrase book entitled, *Wie heisst auf Französisch . . . ?* and clearly its previous owner, a German soldier destined for a British prisoner of war camp, had realized that he would have no further need to know what things were called in French. The book wasn't much use to me either.

On the evening of that same day, riding back to HQ, I took an unaccustomed 'exploratory' route and came upon a small, roughly-painted sign set in the roadside verge which read, simply, '3210 SC'. Cryptic as it was, it told me a lot – I had stumbled across Doug Blair, the fellow Novocastrian and boyhood friend whom I had visited at snowbound RAF Hawkinge some months previously. I turned into the gateway and was soon being accorded the welcome of an honoured guest – a cup of tea and a place in their pontoon school.

Doug's unit was one of the RAF's Servicing Commandos whose job was to closely follow-up invasion forces to get captured enemy airfields (or, as at Bény, newly constructed advanced airstrips) operational as quickly as possible and keep the squadrons flying until their own ground crews arrived. 3210 SC had come ashore on D + 1 and, without either of us knowing it, Doug and I had been next-door neighbours for more than a week.

Return to Commando HQ that evening was to a 'hot buzz' that, with the radar station episode finalized, 41 was on the top line for return to the UK. We were lulled to sleep by the ever-held belief that, once the beachhead had been secured, we would be sent home. A more immediate result of the removal of the Germans from our neighbourhood, however, was the absence of any stand-to procedure next morning. Dawn passed unnoticed and, as it just happened to be a Sunday, we were permitted a 'lie-in' until 0600.

The day continued to be unusually quiet. The Commando had been absorbed into the peaceful conditions of a well-behind-the-lines coastal area and, being off-duty, it was possible for me to pay another visit to 3210 SC. I found that, with the arrival of the Tiffy squadron's own ground crew, their duties at Bény were at an end and they were under orders to move on the morrow, to an airfield near Bayeux. In the meantime, pontoon continued to be the order of the day and the Erks were only too pleased to make room once more for a Bootneck with a few francs in his pocket. That was our last game at Bény and arrival back at HQ was to learn that 41 too would be moving out next day.

Not entirely unexpected, the Commando's move would *not* be the rumoured return to the UK, nor even a comfortable transfer 'back' like 3210 SC. The Unit was destined to join the other two Commandos of 4 SS Brigade on the other side of the River Orne, to add our 300-plus men to the forces holding the bridgehead.

Chapter 5

FIRST WEEKS EAST OF THE ORNE

If you are destined to live in a hole in the ground few things make life more unpleasant than bad weather and Monday 19 June 1944, when 41 Commando moved from the radar stations into the Orne Bridgehead, was wet and very windy.

The Unit followed the same general route I had taken on my previous trips there, but the journey was much more protracted as the men had to march because the bulk of the Unit's transport was still in the UK awaiting slots in the shipping programme. The few vehicles that had arrived kept to the slow progress by leap-frogging ahead, then waiting by the roadside while the long column of well-spaced-out men marched past. Naturally, drivers and DRs alike became the butts of much verbal banter from the passing foot-sloggers, but it did help to divert their minds from the drudgery.

The Germans were aware that reinforcements were on the way and, when the column was approaching Bénouville, their artillery opened up, sending much less light-hearted diversions in our direction. However, with well-tuned ears picking out those shells which demanded a rapid dive into the nearest ditch and the ground having been softened by rain, it is remarkable how men can pass through intermittent shellfire without injury. Conditions became particularly unpleasant as we neared the bridges, but, by making rapid progress during periods of lull, all got across unscathed.

After crossing the river and canal, the Commando came under command of the 51st (Highland) Division and the Fighting Troops relieved a battalion of the Argyll and Sutherland Highlanders positioned around the bridges. Headquarters Troop carried on to take the left-hand curve towards the glider fields, Brigade Headquarters and Sallenelles. With rain dripping from the trees, it was ironic for wet, marching men to pass warning signs designed to curb speeding transport drivers, which carried words such as, 'Slow Down – Dust Brings Shells!'

HQ marched on for about a mile beyond the road junction, then halted in a shallow gravel pit, some 6–7 feet deep extending for many hundreds of yards in all directions. This was to be our resting place for the night and, by then, the wet and rather miserable day was well-advanced so it was time to dig slit trenches. The usual artillery exchange 'hate session' sparked off by our arrival in the bridgehead provided an accompaniment to the work, which was made frustrating by the gravel walls continually falling in. The weather stayed reasonably dry until time to bed down, then the rain started again. It continued for much of the night and most of us found it preferable to remain 'on watch', huddled together for warmth, rather than trying to sleep in wet, gravelly holes.

The bridgehead extended along the east bank of the Orne for little more than six miles, from the Channel coast to the outskirts of Caen, with the bridges over the river and canal lying roughly at the half-way point. It enclosed a narrow envelope of territory which, at maximum, where a salient bulged out towards Troarn, was no more than six miles deep, so the whole area was within the range of enemy artillery and mortars.

Tuesday brought an improvement in the weather. Although still very windy, the rain had stopped and a warming sun began to dry wet uniforms. After breakfast HQ moved a mile or so further up the road, then turned off into an area of flat open fields stretching towards the Orne near Écarde, a handful of farm buildings and cottages. During the afternoon the rest of the unit joined us, having been relieved by the Derbyshire Yeomanry, and the Commando was now under the command of 6 Airborne Div. It would be some days before the fighting troops moved into the forward positions, which were little more than a mile away near Sallenelles; the fields around Écarde would be the 'Rear Echelon' and rest area. The immediate task, in order to get any rest at night, was to start digging; the DRs were directed to one end of a large field and instinctively all selected spots close to a hedge, where it seemed safer.

Frank Barker and I agreed to share a hole and, as it was to be semi-permanent, decided that it should be about double-bed size, say five feet wide by 6–7 feet long, and set to work with our puny entrenching tools. Despite the recent rain, the ground was hard and stony, and hour followed hour as we hacked our way down, only to hit solid bedrock at a depth of less than two feet. Others, digging near different hedgerows, were finding a greater depth of topsoil, but we decided to make do with the hole we had rather than start digging all over again.

Some form of top protection would be essential against air-bursting shrapnel shells, falling splinters from our own ack-ack fire and small calibre missiles, so we set about roofing it over. Branches torn from trees served as roof timbers which were covered with brushwood to support the excavated earth heaped on top. The work extended into the following day, but even on completion we had no illusions about the protection probably being more psychological than real.

In use, the dug-out was claustrophobic as there was barely sufficient headroom to squirm inside with a blanket for covering and a fighting order pack to serve as a pillow. Nevertheless it wasn't long before we had the luxury of being able to read in bed. Lamps were fashioned from the cylindrical '50s' cigarette tins in the Compo rations by punching a hole in the lid for a strip of 'four by two' (the 4" × 2" strips of flannel pulled through a rifle barrel to clean the bore) as a wick and paraffin from the QM's store as fuel. There were drawbacks; the lamp had to be within inches of the reading material to be of any use at all, while oily black products of combustion settled on both page and person, and the confined air space became a pocket of unsavoury fug.

By Thursday 22 June the wind had eased considerably and the day grew very hot. The rough weather during the previous few days, however, had put the entire OVERLORD operation in jeopardy. Gale force winds, the strongest for forty years, and blowing onshore, the worst possible direction, had caused a calamitous amount of damage to the two prefabricated 'Mulberry' harbours being assembled to supply the invasion forces. The one intended for American use at Port-en-Bessin had been damaged beyond repair and had to be abandoned. Parts of it were salvaged to help repair the British/Canadian harbour at Arromanches, but completion was delayed for some weeks.

One immediate consequence of the improved weather was that the RAF bounced back into business and ground troops were treated to the sight of a huge force of heavy bombers passing overhead en route for another attack on Caen. The massed aircraft attracted much German anti-aircraft fire, the sky becoming peppered with puffs of smoke from exploding shells, but all planes passed safely over. Later that day it was learned that 41 would leave Écarde next morning to relieve 48 Commando in the forward positions near Sallenelles, and three despatch riders were to go with Advance Headquarters – 'Dripper', 'Heg' and me. Dripper Thompson was a small, hair-receding, angular sort of chap never without something to grumble or 'drip' about, hence his nickname, whereas Frank Heggarty, a Scouser, was too full of *joie de vivre* to think about grumbling.

The short move forward wasn't accomplished without incident. Naval vessels lying offshore were carrying out a shoot on the German positions, to keep their heads down while the change-over was taking place, but a few of their 'wides' fell near our column, wounding two Marines.

48 had set up their Commando and Troop Headquarters in houses and farm buildings close behind the forward positions held by their Fighting Troops. With no continuous 'Front Line', as had been the case in WWI, small groups of men, armed with Vickers machine guns, Brens or rifles, occupied a string of small, separate slit trenches to form a 'Forward Defended Locality' (FDL).

The 'Headquarters Building', which housed the Signallers and DRs, was a detached two-storey house near the brow of a hill, beyond which the road continued down into Sallenelles. The village was only a few hundred yards away, but completely screened from view by intervening trees. An offshoot of garage and outhouse abutting the carriageway was used as cook-house and George Fradley, a massively-built placid young West Countryman, one of the attached 'Brigade Link' Signallers, acted as cook. To the rear of the house a large orchard fell away to the river, giving a wide panoramic view towards Riva Bella, Ouistreham and the landing beaches beyond. To the right could be seen the estuary of the Orne linking up with the English Channel and, further right, a mile or so of enemy occupied coastline beyond Sallenelles was visible.

The sector taken over from 48 had the distinction of being the extreme left flank of the entire invasion front, which stretched fifty miles to the west, as far as the Cherbourg Peninsula. Sallenelles lay in a no-man's-land between the opposing armies, being untenable by either side because of its low-lying situation. Some of the villagers had steadfastly refused to leave their homes, so it stood like a ghost town with inhabitants.

Also taken over from 48 Commando was Les Aigles, a long, rambling two-storeyed building which they had dubbed 'The Patrol House'. A standing patrol of about thirty men was stationed there, to keep the village under constant surveillance, and it served as a base for reconnaissance (recce) patrols. It also provided a useful vantage point for snipers, watching the German positions some 400 yards away. In 41's first two days there they reported one certain and two probable hits.

On occasions the patrol house came to be patronized by authorized 'sightseers'. A history of 48 Commando, by their Heavy Weapons Officer Captain T.G. Linnell, records a *Daily Telegraph* war correspondent describing his trip there as 'A visit to General Eisenhower's Left-hand Man'. The reporter also made great play of having been able to take a glass of cider in a café in no-man's-land!

That first evening at Sallenelles personnel at Advanced HQ had a grandstand view of a massive parachute supply drop over the landing beaches. Scores of transport planes streamed in to drop stick after stick of containers until the entire sky over the coast was polka-dotted with brightly coloured parachutes. This additional support to the invasion forces had obviously been witnessed by the Germans and, probably frustrated at being unable to do anything about it, vented their spleen upon us, with a prolonged plastering of the Commando positions. This included the Rear Echelon at Écarde and it was widely rumoured that farmers in the area had removed cattle from the fields and taken cover shortly before it started!

The house we were occupying hadn't been strengthened or protected in any way, so, whenever conditions became too hot for comfort, all non-essential personnel would adjourn to their off-duty sleeping quarters, dug-outs in the orchard. The hole allocated to Heg and myself was a first-class effort, with a good three feet of headroom, was about the same in width and had a thick covering of earth on top. It even had a blast wall of two sheets of corrugated iron sheeting packed with earth across the entrance and neatly cut steps for easy access. We always felt reasonably safe down there, even during the heaviest of the many bombardments which came our way, but we rarely had a decent night's sleep as the accommodation was invariably shared with mosquitoes. The French variety were ten times worse than anything experienced in Sicily and there were no mosquito nets. No matter how many of the little horrors we incinerated on the dug-out ceiling with our paraffin lamps, there were always scores more to carry on the attack. It was no consolation to know that there was no danger of contracting malaria.

The role of the troops in the Orne Bridgehead, cut off as they were by river and canal, was entirely different from that of the rest of the British and Canadian forces. In the main beachhead all efforts were being directed towards pushing forward to capture Caen, whereas in the bridgehead the prime requirement was merely to stay put and keep the Germans fully occupied. It was therefore a static war of mortaring, machine-gunning and patrol activity, with the Royal Artillery and Royal Navy indulging in frequent artillery shoots.

By day and night there would be 'standing' patrols in or near Sallenelles, when men would lie up in concealed positions to monitor the movements of the enemy. Most days, too, reconnaissance patrols would probe forward to test out the strength and alertness of the German positions and from time to time fighting patrols would go forward to create alarm and confusion in the enemy lines, inflict casualties and, if possible, bring back a prisoner for interrogation.

Most of these patrols would include one or more German speakers of 10 I-A Commando to interpret any conversations that might be overheard, and it soon became apparent that a large proportion of the enemy facing 41 were not native Germans but less-than-enthusiastic soldiers of the Third Reich, conscripted from Poland, Czechoslovakia and other Central European countries. From time to time some would come across to our lines, extremely happy to have finished with fighting for Hitler. One such deserter volunteered the information that, in two weeks, his ninety-strong company had suffered forty-three casualties.

On the second night after our arrival a fighting patrol from 46 Commando, which was holding the sector to our immediate right, caused considerable havoc in the German lines and Jerry demonstrated his annoyance by directing a prolonged session of machine-gun and mortar fire onto all positions in the sector. A number of bombs fell within the Headquarters orchard, some landing as close as twenty yards from our hole. 'P' Troop's galley received a direct hit, but it was unoccupied at that time of night and the only casualties were a few tins of Compo biscuits.

A sealed tin of these 'hard tack' biscuits provided the bulk and roughage of the '14 men for one day' boxes of Compo rations. Boxes were lettered 'A' to 'G' to indicate the contents, with main meals ranging from steak and kidney pudding followed by mixed fruit pudding, down to corned beef and rice pudding. There was no choice in the matter and, by the time supplies had travelled down from the DID (Divisional Issuing Depot) to a small group in the forward positions, most of the preferred boxes had been filtered out.

With Compo rations the job of cook involved little more than boiling water, some to heat the cans of food and some to make 'Compo tea'. The latter simply meant sprinkling a pre-mix of tea, dried milk and sugar into a dixie of boiling water and stirring, which could result in a reasonable drink but might equally well end up as a dust-covered, curdled, undrinkable concoction. However, the job of cook in the forward areas was not without its own particular hazards.

Close proximity to the enemy ruled out the use of standard field cooking equipment, the hydro burner (a large primus cylinder which shot a roaring tongue of flame between two steel firebars), as the noise would have pin-pointed every HQ in the area. Some quieter means of boiling water had to be adopted and recourse was made to a legacy of the Eighth Army's campaign in North Africa, the Benghazi Cooker or Benghazi Burner. This was simply a metal container (empty biscuit tins were fine) partially filled with sand and dowsed with petrol, two commodities widely available to Desert Rats. When set alight the cookers were very effective in providing heat, but there were two drawbacks – they deposited greasy black soot upon everything within range and the burning time was unpredictable. It was frustrating for a cook to see the flames of his cooker starting to plop out just as the water for making tea was coming to the boil and this sometimes goaded him into acting rashly.

The prudent thing was to wait patiently until the sand had cooled down or at least drag the hot stove outside before refuelling, but some cooks poured petrol on the hot sand. The inevitable result was a grey mist of petrol vapour flowing over the galley floor (we were surprised to learn that it was heavier than air) and, with other stoves burning nearby, there would be a panic evacuation until a massive WHOOOOMP signalled that the freshly-fuelled stove had been rekindled by a neighbour. Few cooks in the forward areas had any eyebrows.

Days at Advanced HQ began very early in the morning with dawn stand-to, were rarely dull and invariably included sessions of mortar and artillery activity. Two days after our arrival a morning barrage from the Royal Artillery lasted for about three hours, then, in the afternoon, the Royal Navy had a shoot of their own; the German response was widespread and prolonged. This was still in progress when Bill Marshall was instructed to put his jeep at the disposal of CSM Morgan, (acting-RSM since Horace Belcher had been killed) and CSM O'Neill of 10 I-A Commando, who, with Corporal Dick Harman of HQ Troop, had a mission 'back to the beaches'. CSM O'Neill elected to drive, so, with CSM Morgan in the front passenger seat and Bill and Dick in the back, off they went. When the jeep returned some hours later, with Bill driving, there were jagged gashes in its side and the only passenger was Dick Harman, in some pain from a badly bruised back. It appeared that, as they were nearing the beach area, a shell had landed close by, wounding both Sergeant Majors, and Dick was struck by a chunk of brick. Bill was unscathed and completed the journey with two casualties for evacuation. One of the CSMs and Dick Harman have given conflicting versions of the purpose of that trip. One was to obtain German anti-tank gun breech blocks from the radar stations and the other to use Royal Marines connections on naval vessels lying offshore to obtain some bread. Take your pick!

Next morning the DRs at Advanced HQ were relieved and

moved back to the holes previously excavated at Écarde. Despite the short distance involved, it was like moving into a different world, conditions were so very much quieter. Also, after carrying out maintenance on our machines, and if no extra duty had been allocated, there was time for other pursuits. Having learned that another of our jeep drivers, Dickie Deeks, had been authorized to make a trip that afternoon to contact an uncle in the RAF somewhere near Bayeux, I was granted permission to accompany him.

Off we went in holiday mood, passing 'our' beach area, smothered with war material and military transport, then via Bény, which was still as quiet as ever. Only a few miles further on, and well short of Bayeux, we located his uncle at an RAF station near Creully. As I had hoped, there was also a sign reading '3210 SC' so, while Dickie was with his uncle, I was with Doug Blair's crowd in another game of pontoon. That night at Écarde a German patrol managed to work its way through the FDLs and we were kept awake much of the time, wondering about the implications of the long bursts of small arms fire we heard from time to time.

At Rear Echelon I learned that 'Abdul', the Arab Todt worker who wanted to fight the Germans, had actually been allowed to stay with the Commando. Dressed in British battledress, only his obvious North African features distinguished him from the rest of us. He had been given some non-combatant occupation in HQ Troop and, despite an almost total lack of English, was popular and happy to be there. I doubt if Abdul recognized me from that first meeting in Luc-sur-Mer, but we got into conversation and it was obvious that he understood my French much better than anybody else's English. Even to my ears, his pronunciation was atrocious, but we struck up a friendly rapport and thereafter looked out for each other on my returns from Advanced HQ. Each time he saw me again his face would light up into a broad grin as he hurried forward calling out, 'Meesh! Meesh!' He never did manage to get his tongue around 'Mitch'.

Rumours of an imminent return to the UK had flared up again – this time to take part in a parade through London on Sunday, 2 July, no less! – but the actuality, was rather different. We moved back up to Sallenelles on Saturday, 1 July, and our arrival there coincided with a heavy plastering of the Commando area. A number of shells fell around the headquarters house, one being close enough to crash a large chunk of casing into a wall near the galley. The evening was relatively peaceful, but when darkness fell things became too noisy for sleep. At 0130 hours everyone was roused to stand-to and a particularly prolonged pasting around 0500 seemed to be the prelude to a concerted attack, but things eventually quietened down again. Maybe the Germans had realized that it was Sunday and a day of rest, so wanted to catch up with the sleep they had lost whilst depriving us of ours.

That Sunday turned out to be a quiet one for Commando HQ and, as a bonus, from our hilltop position overlooking the Orne valley, we became spectators of a neat demonstration of German artillery expertise. Interest was aroused by the 'Crummmmps' of shells exploding at a safe distance. Then the white puffs of their explosions were seen popping up some distance short of a group of farm buildings on the other side of the river about a mile away. After that first salvo there was a short pause and we could visualize the artillery commander giving the order 'Up two hundred' to instruct the gunners to increase the range by two hundred yards, or metres in their case. The next salvo fell at about the same distance beyond the farm as the first had been in front – a perfect straddle. Again we imagined the next order 'Down one hundred' and the third salvo burst neatly amongst the farm buildings. After a few more flurries of shells, with no signs of other activity, it must have been acknowledged that the farm was deserted and the firing ceased.

At Sallenelles the amount of time Despatch Riders spent in riding motorcycles was very small, much of our time being occupied with guard duties and taking cover. In such a compact, static situation, the bulk of the signals traffic was passed by field telephone. With a good earth connection at each end, a single cable, strung out along the hedgerows and between trees, connected the 'subscribers' to the headquarters switchboard. Radio links weren't used as they would be in mobile situations, although the one to Brigade Headquarters was invariably kept open to back up the telephone. On occasions, however, a shell or bomb burst would sever a telephone line and the duty DR, the 'third line of defence', would take the message in writing. A signalman would also have to go out to find the fault by following the line of the wire, tracing it hand by hand in the darkness if need be, until the break was found and could be repaired. One night at Sallenelles a Signalman was doing just that when he trod on a mine and was killed.

Most of the DRs' trips were of short duration – to the headquarters of the other Commandos, 46 was at Hauger and 45 at Amfréville, or back to Rear Echelon at Écarde. The three-mile run to 6 Airborne Div at Ranville was one of the longest. On 6 July I was seconded to 46 Commando for a few days and reported to their HQ at Hauger, a château in extensive grounds, where I was allocated a hole near the entrance gates. Apart from sleeping in a different hole and having different faces about me, conditions there were pretty much the same as at Sallenelles.

Next morning, Friday 7 July, the sky was overcast, with sufficient cloud cover to tempt the Luftwaffe to send over some of their fighter-bomb 'sneakers' on strafing sorties. I had a trip to 6 Airborne at Ranville and, returning along the Amfrévile–Hauger road, came upon four ammunition trucks near le Plein, which had obviously been shot-up a short time before. Three were no more than smoking heaps of hot metal, but the fourth was still burning furiously and making unpleasant explosive noises as I opened the throttle and scooted past.

During the afternoon the clouds cleared and by evening visibility was perfect when the first drone of many approaching aircraft swivelled all eyes skyward. There was no doubt that they were 'ours', a huge straggling air armada of Lancaster and Halifax bombers coming in from the north. Squadron after squadron, widely spaced out like untidy gaggles of geese, were moving unhurriedly towards us. As they passed close by, German ack-ack guns opened fire, sending crackling smoke-puffs of bursting shells spattering the sky amongst the aircraft, and soon there was no doubt as to the planes' target.

Hauger stands on high ground overlooking the flat lowlands which stretch towards Caen, some seven miles away. The city itself was hidden from us by intervening trees, but puffs of smoke, ranging in colour from white to black, were seen rising above them. For perhaps half a minute, as the smoke from the multitude of bomb bursts merged into one continuous curtain, only the steady drone of aircraft engines and the crumps and crackling of anti-aircraft fire could be heard. Then the first thumping detonations of heavy bombs arrived, which soon coalesced into a continuous, awesome rumble as plane after plane after plane released its bomb load.

Minutes after the first puffs had appeared over Caen aircraft, with their mission accomplished, were streaming back, still in formation at the same altitude and at the same unhurried pace. As scores of bombers continued to pass us in two streams, one heading towards and the other returning from a pall of rumbling smoke, the spectacle assumed an unreal quality. The bombers had become an incredible aerial conveyor belt, picking up deadly explosives in England and depositing them on the city of Caen. From time to time an aircraft would issue a trail of black smoke, turn slowly out of line and glide to earth. A few suddenly plummeted out of the sky in vertical dives, to be followed down by a handful of billowing parachutes.

The spectacle lasted for over an hour and, as the dusk deepened, the vast pall of smoke changed into a dull red glow. Then darkness fell, the German ground forces in the area unleashed a mortar and artillery barrage upon everything within range. It continued for most of the night, during which a salvo of nebelwerfer bombs removed all the remaining glass from the windows of our HQ building. Although the literal translation of 'nebelwerfer' is 'smoke thrower', the name was applied to a range of large-calibre multiple-barrelled mortars. The packages of explosives flung into the air announced their approach with a fearsome, unstable, multiple swisssshing sound which was quite different from that of any other incoming projectiles.

The air attack on Caen, on 7 July 1944, was one of the heaviest aerial bombardments in support of ground troops ever mounted. 460 bombers were involved and 2300 tons of explosives had been dropped. Next morning the British and Canadians put in a three-pronged attack and by the following day, Sunday the 9th, all of the city on the north bank of the river had been taken. That evening orders were received to be in our holes by 2200 hrs as all units along the bridgehead front were to supplement the Royal Artillery in a 'harassing task' by engaging the enemy with every available machine gun and mortar, to which the Germans would inevitably reply.

Down in our hole Heg and I were lulled to sleep by the continuous rumble of British gun and mortar fire – 41 Commando's

3" mortars alone loosed off over 350 bombs – but it wasn't until shortly after stand-to next morning that we began to be bothered by salvoes of German bombs in return. As this was followed by prolonged periods of heavy and light automatic fire, we waited tensely for the anticipated infantry attack, but were eventually stood-down for a belated breakfast.

Later in the day it was learned that the 2nd Army had put in a further attack that morning in the River Odon sector and the previous night's activity had been laid on to divert the enemy's attention.

Chapter 6

LIFE IN THE ORNE BRIDGEHEAD

During the next few weeks life east of the Orne settled down into the pattern of four- or five-day stints at Advanced HQ, interspersed with shorter periods at Écarde. Neither place was particularly safe and on occasion both could be dangerous, but we seemed to develop a sixth sense about the imminent arrival of missiles. Having stretched out for an afternoon snooze in the warm sunshine at Rear Echelon, you would suddenly find yourself in your hole as a batch of shells burst nearby.

Rumours about an early return to the UK continued unabated and, even after every successive one had proved unfounded, many would still swallow the next. Naturally, everyone would have preferred to be sleeping in real beds in England, drawing six shillings and eight pence per day rather than bedding-down in the soil of France, receiving only three shillings a day, which included six pence per day Field Service Allowance. However, what niggled most was a feeling that, despite specialized Commando training, the unit appeared to have slipped into the role of the PBI – Poor Bloody Infantry.

For a Despatch Rider with a unit 'stuck in the line', however, life had some pluses to help offset the minuses. These pluses included having the men of the fighting troops between you and the enemy and not being required to risk your neck on patrols. Then there was the mobility which occasioned journeys into more normal areas where there were such things as civilians and cafés. The minuses included having to get on your bike and go when all sorts of 'muck' might be flying about and others were safe in their holes; riding at night without lights along roads you could barely see and with no certainty about where you were supposed to be going.

At Advanced HQ there was never much time to spare between eating, sleeping, delivering signals, being on watch and taking cover, but at Rear Echelon, interspersed between duty requirements, there would be time to call one's own. 'Trips ashore' were non-existent, so letter-writing and reading the few books available were the main pursuits, although some tried their hands at sketching, while others engaged in carving perspex. The windscreens and windows of the scores of crashed gliders littering the fields were soon being fashioned by rear area troops into rings, pendants and, most popular of all, paper knives.

On most days these individual pastimes would be supplemented by some form of aerial activity which varied according to the weather. Whenever the sky was overcast the Luftwaffe would send over 'sneakers', which would swoop in low, inflict as much damage as possible with bombs and cannon fire, then zoom up again to lose themselves in the clouds before RAF fighters arrived. Conditions for sneakers were particularly good during the second week of July when there would be two or three sorties over our area every day each one involving up to a dozen aircraft. As they streaked overhead, flying low through a sky peppered with bursting anti-aircraft shells, we would watch expectantly for signs of any being hit and most days one or two would 'make smoke' and turn away, to our whoops of delight. The loudest cheers came when a plane took a sudden vertical dive and ended up as a funeral pyre of black smoke. On only one occasion was a crippled British aeroplane seen in our air space – a Lightning began falling from the sky, but that too raised a cheer when the crew floated down by parachute.

During fine weather the skies above Normandy were the sole preserve of the Allied air forces and our aerial entertainment would be provided by the bomber wings. One such spectacle, we realized later, had been prefaced by two days of military build-up which had begun on Sunday 16 July. Then all non-vital traffic had been ordered off the roads around Écarde, which were then taken over by an unending stream of every type of vehicle – guns and personnel carriers, tanks on transporters, supply and ammunition trucks, Troop Carrying Vehicles, field kitchens, jeeps, staff cars, mobile workshops, field ambulances, etc, etc, etc, and the flow continued by day and night.

On 16 July too, I learned later, General Montgomery held an investiture in the bridgehead at which two of our Commando were decorated – recently promoted Captain Stevens received the Military Cross and Sergeant Wither the Military Medal. It was also given out that our previous CO, Lieutenant Colonel Gray, wounded in the air attack on D+1, had also been awarded the Military Cross.

At dawn on Tuesday 18 July the entire countryside erupted into multitudinous lightning flashes and thundering explosions as the artillery of the British Second Army opened fire. The uproar was escalated a short while later by the multiple drones and throbbing of many aircraft engines, soon to be followed by the dull rumbling thumps of heavy bomb bursts not many miles away. When the sun rose squadron after squadron of loaded bombers were seen passing overhead and minutes later were returning empty. For hour after hour the medley of noises – the droning of aircraft engines, the crackling and thumps of ack-ack and field artillery fire and the explosions of innumerable shells and bombs – continued as a background to our bridgehead duties.

While it was happening we had no idea what it was all about, but that massive artillery and aerial bombardment had been the softening-up process for Operation GOODWOOD, the attack by British and Canadians to gain control of the high ground commanding the road from Caen to Falaise. Targeted on the German Panzer Group West in the area south-east of Caen, the aerial bombardment had involved 2000 planes which delivered 7700 tons of bombs and was, in the words of Air Chief Marshal Leigh Mallory, 'the heaviest and most concentrated air attack in support of ground forces ever attempted'.

That night the Rear Echelon area was subjected to a vicious German backlash, a prolonged series of air raids aimed at halting the forward movement of supplies to sustain the attack. In our shallow, lightly protected hole, Killer and I passed some hairy hours, with all the sound effects coming through only too clearly. Out of a background cacophony of crackling ack-ack shells and the tumult of aircraft engines would come the high-pitched screams of individual dive bombers as, one after another, they plummeted

81

down to attack some nearby target. We lay helpless and bemused as time and again the whistling bombs were followed by the blasting crashes of nearby explosions. All we could do was to curl up as small as possible and hope for the best. Nearby, two supply trucks were hit and burned well into the night, providing a useful beacon for further attacks.

The GOODWOOD push succeeded in breaking the German lines and on Wednesday 19 July the capture of Caen was completed by the occupation of that part of the city lying south of the river. Despite the colossal land and air bombardments, however, the Germans had been able to put up strong resistance and the 11th Armoured Division alone had lost over 100 tanks. Next day the weather broke and heavy rain poured down for two days, changing the dust of Normandy into the equivalent of Flanders mud; GOODWOOD became, literally, bogged down.

The rain played havoc with the rear areas too, where most of the dug-outs were rendered uninhabitable, forcing men to risk sleeping in the backs of trucks. With inches of mud in the fields, wheeled transport which had previously been using numerous tracks of sun-baked earth, couldn't move off the metalled roads. Riding motorcycles was impossible and the DRs were allocated a jeep. I was very pleased that my limited driving experience wasn't put to the test under such conditions. Early on Saturday 22 July the rain stopped; hot sunshine was soon drying out the soggy countryside and the Second Army resumed its attack.

Next morning, Sunday 23rd, I began another spell of duty at Advanced HQ and, by chance, was given the opportunity of seeing at first hand some of the effects of the bombing of Caen. One of our Troop Sergeant Majors – the lean and lanky, much-tattooed extrovert TSM Crookes of 'A' Troop – had been given permission to seek out his brother, a tank commander with the 2nd Battalion Grenadier Guards, who had been involved in GOODWOOD. They were out of the line somewhere to the south of Caen and I was detailed off to take TSM Crookes there on the back of my motorcycle. As the Ariel had no pillion seat he had to sit on the tubular steel luggage rack, using the rear wheel hub nuts as footrests.

The trip started off towards the bridges, but we didn't cross over, as our route lay through Hérouvillette. There the bike was sucked into a continuous stream of military vehicles, all heading for the southern part of Caen. Being struck in a meandering stream of nose-to-tail traffic was no place for a self-respecting DR, so I began to struggle to make headway. We overtook vehicle after vehicle, through clouds of choking dust, hardly seeing, let alone having time to avoid, the innumerable potholes which seemed to continually increase in number. It was a rough ride for me, with a saddle to reduce the effects, but my pillion passenger must have had a much worse time, having to take it all without any padding.

After a while we entered the industrial suburb of Colombelles which only a few days previously had been the German front line. Two months of almost continuous shelling and unprecedented aerial bombardment had turned it into a moonscape of complete devastation. There wasn't a single undamaged building to be seen; the entire area had been reduced to a series of unbelievable hillocks of shattered bricks and masonry from which protruded roof timbers and the twisted steel skeletons of industrial buildings.

The carriageway was only as wide as bulldozers had been able to clear a route through the ruins and every few yards was pock-marked with roughly-filled bomb and shell craters. Where 12-ton Tallboy ('Blockbuster' or 'Factory Remover') bombs had fallen on the road, the Royal Engineers hadn't attempted to fill the monster craters – some thirty feet in diameter and six or more deep – but had simply bulldozed a new route through the ruins of abutting buildings. Despite the recent rain, everything was covered with a thick coating of dust, being continually stirred up by the long caterpillar of lumbering vehicles. In some places it had settled so thickly that backfilled craters were completely camouflaged and revealed themselves only when the motorcycle began to buck and bounce with bone-jarring jolts.

On reaching the Faubourg de Vaucelles, the inner city area, we were relieved to get a smoother ride. Much of the original road surface was still intact, although greatly reduced in width where buildings had collapsed on to the carriageway. Many tall blocks were still standing and at first glance appeared only superficially damaged, but closer inspection showed that they were no more than bomb-scarred masonry facades, cloaking gutted, rubbish-filled interiors. Over everything, everywhere, hung the unmistakable stench of decaying human flesh.

Leaving the dead city, we entered an equally dead countryside with very different evidences of war – the military wreckage of the fighting that had taken place there only a few days earlier. The roadside was lined, and adjacent fields dotted, with shot-up and burned-out vehicles – tanks, trucks and half-tracks. All the knocked-out tanks we passed were British. Many were no more than blackened shells, having burst into flames ('brewed up' was the current term) on being hit. Some had been blasted on to their sides and lay like monstrous dead beetles; others appeared undamaged until a closer look revealed that one of the tracks had been blown off. At one point, on the left-hand side of the road, a group of four Shermans stood near the top of a grassy knoll in almost precise line abreast and perhaps sixty feet apart. There could be no doubt that German gunners, ready and waiting for them, had picked each one off in turn as it crested the brow of the hill. Just what was in TSM Crookes' mind as we passed through that mile or two of dead tanks would be difficult to imagine.

In addition to the knocked-out vehicles, the entire countryside was littered with the pathetic minutiae of a recent battle. There were heaps of spent shell cases, empty ammunition boxes and mortar bomb carriers, abandoned pieces of webbing equipment, steel helmets, water bottles, entrenching tools – and the dead. Low mounds of earth showed where they lay in their shallow graves. Some were alone – perhaps an infantryman killed as he moved forward – while others lay in small groups, probably the crew of a field gun or tank. Each grave was marked with a rough cross or simply by a rifle thrust muzzle first into the ground and topped with a steel helmet to indicate 'ours' or 'theirs'.

We enquired of the very few British troops we came across as to the whereabouts of the Grenadier Guards and were eventually directed down a narrow lane. There, parked nose-to-tail on a wide grass verge, hidden from the air by the overhang of mature trees, was a line of Shermans. A few tank men were standing beside the first one and, when TSM Crookes asked about his brother, there was an immediate nodding of heads and a shout of 'Crooksey!' went down the line. A face, bearing a marked resemblance to the one on the back of my bike, popped out from behind one of the tanks. Mission accomplished! The tanks were moving up that evening, so TSM Crookes decided to go back to Sallenelles and request permission to return later in the day to bid his brother adieu. We completed another round trip in the afternoon.

That wasn't the end of a busy day and the evening episode was rather more scary. Jan Maley, our Transport Sergeant, required some spare parts, a jeep had to take him back to collect them and, as Duty DR, it was my job to drive. I broke into a cold sweat and my brain raced into top gear. Should I admit that the total extent of my driving experience was no more than a few unofficial trips in the water truck at Ramsgate and so brand myself as a delinquent as well as a non-driver, or . . . ?

'Right-o sarge!' I said and, taking it all very gently, thinking out every move well in advance, we set off. Thankfully there was nothing else on the road that Sunday evening and, on our safe return, there was a great feeling of satisfaction at having accomplished another mission that day. Jan will never know into what suspect hands he had entrusted himself that evening – unless he happens to read this!

Two days after that first 'official' drive of mine the whole Commando was cheered by another 'first' – the first issue of bread since leaving England! It is difficult to comprehend why troops so close to their homeland should have been required to eat dog biscuits for seven weeks, but that's how it was. The first ration was no more than half a slice per man and it was almost two weeks before bread became a regular part of our diet.

By then, too, the basic compo rations were being supplemented by issues of rice and those two wartime innovations designed to save shipping space, dried eggs and dehydrated potatoes. In retrospect, it seems strange that eggs were never 'dehydrated', nor were potatoes ever 'dried'. Then, with water added for cooking, dried eggs were invariably said to have been 're-constituted' – but no one ever talked about 're-constituted' potatoes.

At Rear Echelon there wasn't the same concern about preparing meals as George Fradley bestowed upon those he prepared at Advanced HQ. Without the need for silent cooking, and with more mouths to feed, all finesse had disappeared. The cans could have come from different boxes of Compo and, on occasions, they hadn't been punctured. In consequence, the scalding hot can plopped into your mess tin would not only be devoid of any identifying label but both ends could be domed-out under internal steam pressure. Then, with a handkerchief or green beret, the can would be held firmly on the ground, pointing away from fellow diners, and stabbed with a jack-knife. The resulting spray of steam and scalding liquid undoubtedly lost a few proteins, but the bomb had been rendered safe and could be cut open to discover what was on the menu.

Abdul had soon absorbed an impressive string of English swear words, which he enunciated with relish, if little understanding, but when I was at Rear Echelon we had sessions of exchanging languages. We began with counting and, raising fingers, I would say, 'One, Two, Three, Four, Five . . .', which Abdul would imitate and write down phonetically. Then he would do the same in Arabic and I wrote down the sounds – 'Wahed, Zhooge, Claytah, Rhemah, Rhumsah . . .', etc. We then progressed to the days of the week, 'Kuneen, Claytah, Lairvah . . .' and objects around us, like 'rifle' – umkahlah, 'pistol' – verdeen, 'socks' – treshe . . . etc. etc. His spidery squiggles of written Arabic were no more than worm tracks to me, as, no doubt, were my English words to him.

The most productive outcome of these language sessions was to be able to put him in touch with his family. From his identity card as a slave labourer, we had discovered earlier that his full name was Adelasis ben Assouet, so thereafter we called him 'Ben', rather than having outsiders hear some of His Majesty's Royal Marines refer- ring to one of their number as 'Abdul'. I learned from Ben that he came from Fez in Morocco, and that a brother, Semohammed, who worked for the Post Office there, understood English and French. I decided to try to let his folks know that Ben was safe and well.

As a letter written in Arabic would undoubtedly have confused the military censors, I wrote a brief note in English, saying that Ben was in good health and friendly hands, translated it into French and got Ben to sign it with his worm tracks. The unit's BLA (British Liberation Army) address was given for any possible reply and I put the letter in an Active Service envelope, addressed to 'Semohammed ben Assouet, Bureau de Postes, Fez, Morocco', and Ben addressed it in Arabic. It was a long shot, but it came off! Some weeks later Ben, with an even wider grin than usual and an arm around my shoulder, told me that he had had a reply from his brother.

Throughout July a series of actions in other sectors of the beach- head, of which we were largely unaware, was developing the American 'right hook' through northern France. Concurrently the British and Canadians were keeping up a continual pressure to engage as many German troops as possible, to ease the task of the Americans, and also suggest that the main thrust towards Paris would come from that sector. In consequence of the Allied efforts, on a front of only fifty miles, the Germans were compelled to deploy no less than eleven panzer divisions, precisely half the number on the entire Russian front of eight hundred miles.

With all this activity going on in other parts of Normandy, the continuing 'marking time' in the Orne bridgehead wasn't popular with many of the troops being kept in restraint there. So much so that, towards the end of July, General Montgomery felt it necessary to issue an Order of the Day stressing how vital it was for him to be absolutely certain of the security of his left flank whilst carrying out the various preliminary manoeuvres of the battle plan. The Orne bridgehead, it said, 'was the hinge-pin for the eventual break-out of all the Allied forces'.

Towards the end of July I returned to Rear Echelon to find that we had no dug-out. The field had been taken over by the REs for the construction of a new road to link up with the two pontoon bridges built to supplement the existing road crossing of river and canal. The Germans knew what was happening and, on the 27th, took advantage of cloudy weather to make an unsuccessful attempt to bomb the bridges. On the 30th a thousand-bomber raid was carried out as 'softening-up' for another Second Army attack south of Caen, timed to coincide with the American thrust towards Avranches, which started their wide sweep towards Paris.

During the first week of August the DRs, alternating between Rear Echelon and Advanced HQ, seemed to get 'plastered' in both places. At Écarde German artillery was trying to undo the RE's work on the new road and at Sallenelles the artillery and mortar exchanges had been stepped up in line with increased activity all along the front. On Friday 4 August the Commando suffered eleven casualties and next day we began to hear 'buzzes' about an imminent move into the 'Troarn Bulge'.

All we knew about that sector, some six miles to the west of us, was that there was a salient protruding into the German lines towards the town of Troarn and, from all accounts, it was 'hot'. On Sunday the rumour was confirmed; the operational strength of the Commando was to move into the bulge next day, leaving Rear Echelon where it was. That night the Germans appeared to give the

Commando a prolonged farewell barrage and on the Monday morning, just before moving off, a batch of shells scored direct hits on the row of farm cottages which had just been vacated by the Commando Sick Bay.

That day, August 7, was August Bank Holiday Monday in the UK, but it was no holiday for 41 Commando. Jackie Horsfield and I had been detailed off to shepherd the transport column carrying the Commando to its new location and to remain there with Advanced HQ. The convoy had first to go back towards the Orne bridges, then our route lay via Ranville and Hérouvillette, both badly damaged, then through the ruins of Éscoville, which had been shelled and bombed virtually out of existence. Then we passed into the empty 'nothingness' of the countryside between 'rear' and 'forward' areas. A gloomy, overcast sky matched a rather sombre occasion.

Slow progress was mandatory. Every few hundred yards, nailed to trees or set up in the grass verge, were 'up front' injunctions not to attract shells by raising dust. These ranged from the cautionary 'SLOW! – dust means shells', through more precise 'MAXIMUM speed – 5 mph', to blatantly threatening 'Slow Down! – YOU HAVE BEEN WARNED!!' Despite strict adherence to all such admonitions, our progress into the Troarn Bulge was accompanied by outbursts of shellfire. The screaming approach of shells and their blasting explosions seemed ever more personal the further we travelled. Even without the convoy making dust, the Germans were undoubtedly aware that a change-over was taking place, knew which roads were being used and were hoping to catch some of us in the open.

Nearing the forward area, sections of the convoy were detached to proceed to their own specific locations and the vehicles carrying Advanced HQ and two of the Fighting Troops were halted at a level crossing on the edge of a wood with the order 'No mechanized vehicles beyond this point'. The Unit being relieved, a battalion of the Hallamshire Regiment, had learned the hard way that the Germans in that sector reacted to noise as well as dust. Jack and I propped our bikes against the railway embankment and joined the rest to complete the journey on foot.

The Headquarters area being taken over was about half a mile into the wood and every DR trip had to begin and end with that walk. The two Fighting Troops carried on some hundreds of yards further to occupy forward positions at the edge of the wood, which was the limit of the FDLs of the British salient. The unit had inherited some very good Army holes – large, deep and solidly roofed with heavy baulks of timber and a good thickness of earth. An exception was the Signals Despatch Office, which had been constructed at ground level by digging into a steep bank-side, enclosing the front of the excavation with a thick wall of sandbags and roofing over with stout timbers and a few feet of earth. A narrow entrance was protected by a blast wall of sandbags and a rolled-up tarpaulin sheet was anchored in the earth cover, ready to be dropped at night. From the top of the doorway a spider's web of field telephone wires radiated through the trees. The dugout was just large enough to accommodate a rickety wooden table for the Commando telephone exchange, a chair for the duty signaller and an area of beaten earth behind him for the duty DR.

One unexpected asset of the HQ area was a 'recreation room'! – a hole about ten feet square, with almost six feet of headroom, well roofed-over and protected. Throughout our stay there, at almost any hour of the day or night, no matter how much 'muck' was flying around outside, it would be filled with cigarette smoke and off-watch Marines engrossed in one or more serious games of pontoon, nap or brag.

The 'welcoming bombardment', hoping to inflict casualties before men reached the prepared positions, had had some success, including Lieutenant Robinson and Sergeant Murray of 'X' Troop, both killed, and it kept on coming. For three days and nights, with only occasional let-ups, shells or mortar bombs were falling somewhere in the neighbourhood and, during the whole ten days of the Unit's tenure of that position, most periods of 'quiet' could be measured in minutes rather than hours.

This almost continuous enemy activity made the life of a DR, moving around in the open, far from a snug hole, particularly hairy. In daylight the drawback of the approach of shells being masked by the motorbike's engine was disturbing enough, but rides after dark added other problems. Being on duty at night meant remaining fully clothed, ready to go at a moment's notice. Curled up in a blanket behind the duty signaller, ears were always attuned to the cranking of the call-up handle. A few turns meant that all was well, but when it went on and on, it was time to steel yourself for the Signaller's, 'Sorry sir, I can't raise them, the line must be cut'. The inevitable consequence would be, 'Better send the DR then,' and you would squirm into your riding coat. Then, shoulders hunched against the cold, a half-mile stumble through the trees, kick the engine into life and off on a lonely ride.

If the night was 'noisy', and most of them were, the mind would be too fully occupied in trying to sort out what was happening around you to think of much else. If things were quiet, however, it was easy to imagine that every German for miles around was listening to your approach and getting ready to do something unpleasant about it. When it became necessary to stop and switch off the engine to consult the map or search for a gap in the hedge on foot the complete silence was even worse and there was an immediate itching to start up again, just to hear a friendly noise. Either way, day or night, quiet or noisy, without fail, the first comforting words to greet you at your destination would be 'For Christ's sake, shut that bloody thing off!'

Being in a salient added a further complication because, when travelling laterally across it, 'the front' was both ahead and behind you. In the gathering dusk of one evening, riding slowly along an unfamiliar lane, eyes straining to pick out anything that might direct me to my destination, I was brought to a halt by a shadowy figure, rifle at the ready, materializing from the hedgeline. ''Ere myte!', it said, 'I woon't gow no furvver dahn there – unless yer message is fer the Jerries.' I thanked my Cockney saviour and beat a hasty retreat.

'S' Troop was positioned in the ruins of a well-shelled brick-works, about a mile east of Touffreville. It was less than half a mile from Commando HQ as the crow flies, but to get there circum-spectly by road meant a ride of about three miles, and every trip was guaranteed to be eventful, as 'S' undoubtedly attracted more attention than any of the other Troops. This could have been because the Germans knew that our mortars were based there, or maybe the chimneys, now no more than heaps of brick rubble, had once been artillery 'markers', or simply that the approach road was under observation.

My first ride to 'S' was on the morning after our move-in and I adhered strictly to the 'Drive Slowly! – Dust brings shells!!' warnings by the roadside. I located their HQ hole in the shattered ruins of the brickworks, delivered the message and had the engine running ready to leave when a batch of incoming shells announced their imminent arrival. Dust at that juncture would clearly have no effect, so I twisted the throttle wide open and roared off as fast as I could work my way through the gearbox. Behind me, bursting shells were re-arranging the heaps of rubble and I learned later that two Marines had been wounded.

Despite the frequency of bombardments, 'S' Troop's casualties were relatively light as the kilns and flues, with the added protection of a covering of brick rubble, made effective shelters. A drawback for DRs, however, was that the Troop Commander would move around his subterranean domain, so, when your sole concern was to get rid of the message and go, it was necessary to flit around from hole to hole calling down, 'Is this Troop HQ?'

Two days after our arrival in the Bulge there was a strong buzz that the Germans were pulling back and, simultaneously, we had an unexpected visit from the Brigadier, 'Jumbo' Leicester. Some said that the Brigadier had brought the rumour, but the wags averred that it was more likely that the rumour had brought the Brigadier! That, of course, was no more than a 'family' joke, as 'the Brig' was well respected. Anyhow, a strong patrol went forward to investigate and the Germans, taking it to be the start of a major attack, subjected the Commando area to a heavy pasting for the rest of the day, causing some casualties.

On the fourth day in the Bulge Frank Heggarty and Ray Stillwell arrived by truck to relieve Jack and me, taking over our bikes. Half an hour later we were back in the peace and quiet of Rear Echelon, repairing the roof of our hole which had been stove in by a truck. Then, next day, Rear Echelon moved to a new location near Pegasus Bridge, so we had to dig a new one! The move at least confirmed my acceptance as a driver as I was given the job of driving a loaded jeep to the new location.

Later in the day two incidents demonstrated that, even without enemy action, life in the rear areas had its hazards. The first incident came about whilst we were attempting to perfect an oil-and-water stove. When carefully regulated droplets of oil and water are contrived to fall onto a hot metal plate and set alight, combustion is self-perpetuating. It would have had no practical application for us but it was an interesting experiment. The basic problem was to get the hearth plate hot enough to vaporize the oil, so Jack Horsfield was helping things along with a slosh of petrol when he found he had a flaming jerrican in his hands. Luckily he had the presence of mind to close the cap quickly and the flames soon died away.

Nearby, Frank Barker had the cylinder head off his bike and decided to wash out the engine's innards with petrol before putting everything back together again. He depressed the kick start to move the piston, but, unbelievably, had left the sparking plug on its lead and the bike was immediately enveloped in flames. Showers of dry earth prevented major damage, but the incident certainly prolonged Frank's maintenance work.

Next day, back at Advanced HQ in the Troarn woods, I was given a trip to a quieter part of the salient. This took me onto a deserted narrow road running along the top of a dyke, some six feet or so above the surrounding countryside, and my nose was soon wrinkling with the stench of rotting flesh. The source became apparent when I came upon a German tank keeled over on its side at the bottom of the dyke. The decomposing body of one of the crew dangled by one leg trapped in the turret hatch and he had obviously been there for quite some time as the visible flesh had rotted away until it was almost transparent. Judging from the all-pervading stink, it seemed probable that some of his pals were still inside.

The forward positions of the Troarn Bulge were as lively as ever and casualties were mounting; in six days the Commando suffered a total of forty-four, including three killed. Every man went about his duties continually deciding where he would dive for cover when the next batch came in. This meant that 'going to the heads' was a tricky business, as the latrine areas couldn't be sited below ground level. Should there be a lull in the shelling, suggesting that things would be quiet for a while, and you decided to go, only to hear more shells coming in, you had a problem. I am sure that few of us escaped the indignity of being, literally, 'caught with their trousers down'.

41 Commando's move into the Troarn Bulge had coincided with momentous happenings all along the Normandy front. By Sunday 6 August, the day before the Unit had left Sallenelles, the sweeping

92

American 'right hook', by no less than twenty divisions, had reached Alençon and Le Mans. That same night Von Kluge's Seventh Army had attacked in the direction of Mortain and Avranches in an attempt to cut them off from their supply base in the Cherbourg Peninsula. The British and Canadian Armies had resumed their attack to the south of Caen; with the sole exception of the Orne bridgehead, the entire Allied invasion front was in motion.

Von Kluge's counter-attack was pressed forward for five days, with his troops continually at the mercy of the omnipotent Allied air forces and suffering heavy losses. By Friday 11 August, the day on which I had returned to Advance HQ in the Bulge, they had been forced to abandon the attack and were beginning to pull back. Units of General Patton's US Third Army were then swinging northwards towards Argentan, while the British and Canadians, supported by the Polish armoured division, were attacking strongly southwards in the direction of Falaise. The jaws of the 'Falaise Gap' were beginning to close and the only questions were when and how many Germans would then be cut off, to be killed or captured.

By Tuesday 15 August the British and Canadians had reached Falaise (the gap was finally closed on the 20th) and the Americans, striking towards Paris, were rapidly approaching Chartres. It was clear that the German forces around the Orne bridgehead would soon be forced to pull back too if they were to avoid being completely outflanked. Possibly to help them make up their minds to go, the British artillery barrage rose to a crescendo during the day; it began to look as though Montgomery's hinge was at last beginning to turn.

Next morning, 16 August, conditions in the Troarn Bulge were so unusually quiet that it was generally believed that the Germans had indeed moved back. Early in afternoon, however, such thoughts were rudely dispelled when a heavy rain of shells neatly targeting the HQ area sent everyone scurrying for shelter.

Those shells, however, had been the enemy's Parthian shot. The afternoon advanced with unaccustomed peacefulness and by evening the usual sounds of bombs and shells had been replaced by birdsong. A message from Brigade advised of the imminent likelihood of a German withdrawal and shortly afterwards a deserter, who obviously preferred not to go with them, confirmed that the Germans had been alerted to pull back across the River Muance before dark that evening.

Orders were given for a strong patrol to move off early next morning, probe forward to the south-east of Troarn and re-establish contact with the enemy. 'A' and 'B' Troops were to lead and I was to be the DR to accompany them. As the noise of a motor-cycle engine would be too much of a give-away, it was understood that I would be allowed to use the CO's jeep.

Chapter 7

FORWARD FROM TROARN

During the late evening of Wednesday 16 August, and again at first light on the 17th, Commando patrols failed to make contact with the enemy and preparations to move forward were finalized. My hopes of using a jeep to accompany the patrol were dashed when I was told to report to 'A' Troop Commander, Captain Stevens, with my motorbike. I was given an explicit order not to start the engine until he gave me the instruction personally; until then the bike would be pushed. TSM Jack Hazelhurst positioned me in the long single file of men, 'A' Troop following 'B', which was already snaking its way through the trees.

Pushing a motorbike through rough woodland is no easy matter and after only the few hundred yards to the foot of a railway embankment (the line curves towards Troarn in two sinuous loops from the level crossing where we had had to leave our bikes) I was lathered in sweat. Others helped manhandle the machine to the top, bounce it across the tracks, then ease it down the other side. At the foot of the slope we passed through a narrow gap in a tall hedge on to a minor country road and turned left.

It came as a surprise to me to see just how close to Troarn our positions had been – the first buildings were less than a quarter of a mile away. In that short distance three British tanks were slumped at untidy angles in the roadside ditch; after passing those dead tanks we entered a dead town. It was seemingly intact, even to a church with a slim steeple, but many of the buildings lining the rubble-littered streets were no more than gutted shells. Apart from ourselves there was no sign of life.

My motorbike was very probably the first Allied mechanized vehicle to have entered Troarn since 6 June. In the very early hours of D-Day Major Roseveare, with a few men of 6th Airborne Division, had roared into the town in a jeep to blow the bridge over the River Dives, but he was intercepted by a German patrol and was lucky to escape with his life, on foot. My own journey was in the reverse order – I went in on foot and rode out.

After leaving the town the patrol began moving across country again and, even with some assistance from less-encumbered Marines, it was hard going. After half a mile or so, however, we joined the minor road which follows the River Muance to the small hamlet of Janville, some two miles away.

In marked contrast to the dug-outs and shattered trees of Troarn wood, the countryside was unblemished but completely empty, silent, bare. There were no houses, no people, no animals in the fields, and even the birds seemed silent. There was no sound other than the scuffling of booted feet.

The advance was slow and spasmodic. 'B' Troop was scouting ahead, alert for the first sign of the enemy; the rest followed with alternate men moving along each side of the roadway, weapons at the ready, eyes searching constantly for any sign of movement. I just pushed my bike and looked about.

Janville was reached without incident. The road should have crossed over the River Muance, which at that point has two separate courses, but both bridges had been blown. The carriageway made two V-shaped contacts with the river, but the water was only knee-deep, so men had been able to cross and were pushing on. I was given a signal to take back and allowed to start the engine after having pushed the bike back round the first bend in the road. Then I was in the saddle, bowling through the empty countryside, wondering whether any German snipers had been left behind.

I was given a reply to take back and, on regaining Janville, which I now saw comprised little more than a church, a few houses and the blown bridges, found that 'A' and 'B' Troops were still there, in a position of all-round defence. 'Y' Troop had taken over the lead and was on the other side of the river, moving towards St Pierre du Jonquet two miles further on; the Patrol Commander was with them, so I had to follow.

It wasn't too difficult a job to manoeuvre the bike across the two bridge spans resting on the river bed, through the shallow waters and do a little rough riding up the far bank to regain the road. Then once again I was like The Ancient Mariner, 'Alone, alone, all, all alone . . .', with the added knowledge that this time I was heading forward, instead of back. There was a loaded Colt 45 automatic at my belt, but that was little more than a symbolic protection, and those two miles of recently-liberated France seemed very long indeed. It was a great relief to cruise round a bend in the road and find myself looking down the muzzles of the 'Y' Troop rearguard. There was no doubt that I was back among friends when they bawled, 'For Christ's sake, shut that bloody thing off!' The bike had to be left by the roadside while I went forward on foot to find the Troop Commander.

'Y' were ranged in firing positions along both sides of the road, the bocage-type country, with hedges set upon banks of earth, providing good defensive parapets. The Marines slumped against them were delighted to divert a little of their attention towards a DR without a motorbike.

'What's up, Mitch? Lost your bike?'

'Hey, look! DRs can walk!'

'Is that my leave chit you've got there, Ray?'

'What the hell does Monty want of us this time?'

There was also some unprintable language from the less couth.

I found the Troop Commander on the high ground on the outskirts of St Pierre du Jonquet and handed him the signal. It was clearly the 'Press on!' instruction he had been expecting and, even as I turned to walk back to my bike, shouts of 'All right, "Y", on your feet, on the road, we're moving on' were passing down the line.

As I retraced my steps men were reluctantly easing themselves away from their restful positions against the banksides and adjusting their equipment. There were some 'cracks' about me going the wrong way and I may have smirked a little, but we all had our jobs to do. 'Y' Troop 'bumped' the Germans about half a mile further up the road at the River Dives, where again the bridge had been blown, but this time a rearguard had been left to cover it.

Shots were exchanged, but both sides were content to leave it at that. Brigade was awaiting further orders, so it was just a case of sitting tight. I spent the rest of the day with 'A' Troop at Janville and slept with them in a barn alongside the church.

Next morning, after stand-to, the Patrol was put at instant readiness to continue the advance, but later this was relaxed to one hour's notice. Throughout the day I had trips to HQ, still in the old position, but not until 2030 hours was the Commando given orders to move, and it was due east from Troarn, not via St Pierre du Jonquet, as had been assumed. The axis of advance given to our Brigade, and to No. 3 Parachute Brigade, was Route Nationale 815, leading to Dozulé and Pont l'Évêque. 41 Commando's immediate orders were to advance as far as St Richer, about three miles away, and assemble there. The Patrol in the Janville area was to retrace its steps to Troarn and rejoin the Unit as soon as possible next morning. Commando headquarters was set up at St Richer by 0100 hours on the 19th without having made contact with the enemy.

I passed a second night in Janville and next morning was sent off alone to report to HQ. It was Saturday 19 August, dull after a night of rain, and on reaching Troarn I found that, in 48 hours, the town had been unbelievably transformed. The N.815 was now carrying an unending stream of nose-to-tail military traffic of every conceivable type and it was fortunate that a military policeman was on hand to slot me into the flow.

To the east of Troarn the N.815 has to cross the Rivers Muance and Dives – about five hundred yards apart at that point – and both bridges had been blown. These had been replaced by floating pontoon bridges and rough tracks bulldozed down the steep river banks linked them to the N.815. The bridges, however, could carry only one lane of traffic and, as many vehicles needed attempt after attempt to negotiate the wet and slippery tracks, there was one helluva double traffic bottle-neck. All the while the neighbourhood was being subjected to intermittent shellfire and the entire column could do nothing but wait in line and hope for early release.

To be stuck motionless between a pulsating truck belching exhaust fumes in your face and the hot radiator of another monster towering behind, with cold, uninviting water on both sides and shells bursting in your field of view, is not an enviable position. It was a huge relief, therefore, to be able to ride off the end of a bridge, sit back along the luggage carrier to increase traction on the rear wheel, open the throttle and bounce and slither up the opposite bank.

Once across the rivers the congestion quickly subsided as vehicles dispersed into the countryside; then the N.815 became largely the domain of the infantry. The Paras were 'at the sharp end' a mile or so ahead and much of 41 Commando was moving forward in the traditional manner of foot-slogging. After I had reported back, I found that my own role was, largely, just to be there. On occasions I was sent up or down the marching column with messages – giving the marchers a target for more ribald remarks – but often it was just a matter of waiting by the roadside until they had passed.

Then it filtered down that the CO had been called forward to an 'Order Group' at Brigade HQ in Goustranville, about two miles ahead. It was learned that the Paras had secured the crossing of the River Doigt some three miles further on and a mile short of Dozulé, but had been unable to achieve the hill feature in front of the town. 46 RM Commando were to make an attack on this high ground that night, while 41 and 48 would initiate an out-flanking movement to the south of Dozulé at dawn. I wasn't to be involved and passed the night by the roadside, where I was able to crawl under a truck to gain protection from the overnight rain, until dawn stand-to next morning.

That Sunday dawned bright and fair. By first light elements of 48 and 41 Commandos had crossed the river via a small pedestrian bridge south-east of Goustranville. 41 advanced to Putot-en-Auge and later in the morning the Commando was moved up to fill a gap between 48 and 46 Commandos. The Germans had become very active in the area and their mortar fire was inflicting casualties. A number of 'S' were wounded, including Captain Grant, the CO who had been hard to find in the brickworks near Troarn. Patrols pushed forward to Clermont-en-Auge, taking prisoners, and by afternoon were advancing northwards from Panniers. St Léger was occupied that evening; our forward Troops remained there overnight.

While this had been going on I was shuttling up and down with the Transport Column as it moved along Route N.815 towards

Dozulé. Some distance short of the town the vehicles were halted and the officers and men of Rear Headquarters continued on foot through dank and shady woodlands, along narrow tracks, made soft and slithery by the overnight rain. For Despatch Riders it was a major achievement just to stay in the saddle and, more than once, a file of foot-sloggers had to hop rapidly off a track which wasn't wide enough for them and a motorbike.

In the late afternoon we moved into bright sunshine to find ourselves on an extensive straw-covered farmyard area, bounded by rough wooden buildings. Almost immediately a score or more of French civilians were milling around with glasses and bottles to welcome their liberators. One perspiring Marine gratefully accepted what he assumed to be a tumbler of water and had taken a gargantuan swallow before discovering that it was Calvados, the local apple brandy! His reaction verged on the cataclysmic.

HQ was set up in one of the outbuildings and despatch riders were immediately called from the liberation celebrations to deliver messages. The portable radio sets then available could be unreliable at any time, but in the woods above Dozulé they were useless and Despatch Riders had to make up the deficiency.

As the shadows lengthened, riding along slippery woodland tracks without lights and with the trees cutting off what little daylight remained became more and more difficult. In the very late dusk I was given a signal for Brigade HQ, established in a large house more than a mile away through the woods. I managed to make the delivery just as the last vestiges of daylight were fading; there was no reply, so I started back immediately, but after perhaps five minutes of slipping and sliding through a black maze of trees I had to accept defeat. A DR who just couldn't find his own way home slithered back to Brigade to spend the night on the floor of their SDO.

It was raining heavily next morning, but in full daylight I was able to negotiate the treacherous tracks and return to HQ. I learned that, at 0430 that morning, aided by the light from some burning buildings, a combined force of 41 and 47 Commandos had entered Dozulé without opposition. During a sweep through nearby orchards at first light, however, 'X' Troop and Advanced HQ had suffered casualties, including two killed. Later in the day the unit was pulled back to St Léger, leaving only a Standing Patrol in the town. For the rest of the day British troops, including the 5th Parachute Brigade, streamed through burning Dozulé in pursuit of the retreating Germans.

For most of that day much of the Commando was occupied in little more than keeping dry as rain continued to deluge down. The DRs, however, were continually out and about, but by evening conditions had deteriorated to such an extent that this couldn't be accomplished on two wheels and, with visibility down to almost zero, it became a two-man job, a driver to handle the jeep and a DR to find the way.

In the almost total darkness of those woodland tracks it was still a very dicey business and at times progress depended largely upon the driver proceeding at a snail's pace, gauging the amount of resistance he was getting from the flanking bushes to keep him on the track. The DR, meanwhile, head bent low and well inboard, strained his eyes to see as much as possible and give such directions as he could from his knowledge of track junctions and gated entrances. Surprisingly, we all got home that night.

Next morning we wondered what the previous two days' problems had been about. Even at dawn stand-to the air was sweet and dry and, as the early morning mist lifted, the sky became bright and crystal clear. We moved down into the valley, passed through shattered Dozulé and resumed a rather slow progress along the N.815. It was uneventful until reaching the high ground above the town of Pont L'Évêque, when the column moved into a confused medley of incoming missiles and nearby explosions. Pont l'Évêque – Bishop's Bridge – is a crossing point of the River Tougues, which the Germans had clearly decided was a good line on which to fight another rearguard action.

HQ was set up in a farm a short distance from the main road leading down into town where a group of French civilians appeared to have sought refuge. That night we shared with them the straw-covered stone floors of a long row of single-storey outbuildings extending from the farmhouse towards the road. The stout stone walls were probably adequate to withstand the blast and shell splinters from near-misses but the lightly-tiled roofs would have been shattered by a brick.

At some time after midnight I was called from the fuggy warmth of our communal resting place to deliver a signal to one of the

Troops. The night was filled with the rumbles of explosions and, in the valley below, the glow of many fires and clouds of red-tinged smoke hung over Pont l'Évêque. The Germans had obviously started blowing up anything that might be of use to us. The flames, reflected from low clouds, helped me find my way; I completed the delivery and returned without incident.

Morning was sunny and comparatively quiet. After stand-down a cheerful *entente cordiale* atmosphere pervaded Commando head-quarters as we hunted for receptacles to hold water for a wash and shave. In this we were helped by cheerful civilians and it wasn't long before one old lady had been 'conned' into thinking that she had learned a little English.

A popular nonsense song of the day began with the 'words', 'Mairsy Dotes 'n dozy dotes 'n little lams-ee-tivy . . .' subsequently translated into 'Mares eat oats, and does eat oats, and little lambs eat ivy'. A signaller got the idea of responding to the lady's 'Bonjour' greeting with a polite 'Mairsy Dotes' and it wasn't long before she was proudly airing her 'English' by greeting others in the same way!

During the morning it became known that the Commando was to take over a sector previously held by some of the Airborne Division which, for reasons not divulged, had been withdrawn. I was sent with the leading elements to report where the positions actually were and, leaving my bike by the roadside, accompanied them on foot. We crossed a number of fields, passing scores of well-dug but empty slit trenches – many more than could have been filled by the entire Commando. The weather was now overcast and a feeling of foreboding seemed to hang over those abandoned positions, which was heightened for me during my solitary long walk back to the road. Enemy guns had opened fire again and shells were falling in the immediate neighbourhood. Back at HQ, I found that the civilians had been evacuated.

That shelling was the start of one of the most prolonged barrages we experienced there. For the remainder of the day I alternated between the comparative safety of HQ and solitary trips around the Commando area, all to the accompaniment of mortar and/or 88 fire. Despite the very good Airborne holes, the unit suffered a number of casualties in those positions, including the Medical Officer and some of his Sick Berth Attendants.

In the afternoon I was given a message for one of the Troops positioned on the high ground overlooking the River Tougues and was shown their approximate position on the map. It meant going about three-quarters of a mile or more down the main road towards Pont l'Évêque, then taking a farm track to the left, along the top edge of the river valley; the Troop would be in the third or fourth field on the left-hand side.

Three-quarters of a mile is a long way when you are completely on your own and there are no friendly troops between yourself and the enemy. I seemed to be getting uncomfortably close to Pont l'Évêque and had reached the stage of thinking 'Must have missed it – another fifty yards and I'm turning back' when I came upon a break in the hedgeline and turned on to a narrow track. A hedge ran along the left-hand side and to the right open fields fell away towards the river. At that point it was hidden by trees, but beyond a wide panorama of countryside on the enemy-held bank was clearly visible. I was counting the gateways on the left, paused at the third, but, seeing nothing, carried on and rode directly into the fourth field. It was small, largely bounded by trees, and it too appeared empty until, some 10 yards away, a head and shoulders appeared above ground level, arms waving wildly and a voice bawling, 'Drop that bloody thing QUICK! – AND GET OVER HERE!'

I didn't have to ask why. Even as I obeyed and started to run, the urgent screaming approach of shells announced that a salvo was going to land very, very close. As I fell on top of the Troop Sergeant the shells were bursting all about. 'You silly bastard!' he was spluttering angrily. 'They've got that bloody gateway taped to an inch. Any movement and we get twenty minutes of this fricking lot.' 'Sorry, sarge, but they didn't tell me.' We both used the word 'they', but I knew he meant the Germans and he knew I was talking about Commando HQ. When things had quietened down sufficiently for me to flit across to the Troop Commander's hole more heads poked above ground level and I was followed by a barrage of bad language and baleful glares. 'At least,' I reminded them, 'you lot always have holes to jump into.'

After receiving the officer's reply I was ready to go, but it was obvious that I would have to find some other way back. I righted the bike and rode into the trees at the rear of the field to find one.

103

It was only a small copse and soon gave way to a wide, rolling hill-side falling away from the Troop position. All was plain sailing until progress was halted by a stout wire fence, too high for me to 'topple' the bike over – a technique used in training – with the bottom strand almost at ground level. I rode back and forth, searching for a gap or a weak spot, but the posts were too stout to move and the wires were strong and unbroken, nor was there any way round, yet it was unthinkable to return the way I had come.

Trying not to panic, I reasoned that as the bike was too heavy to lift and couldn't be toppled over, it would have to go under. I laid the machine on the ground as close to the fence as possible and climbed over. Then, lying close to the fence, I began a combination of heaving up the bottom strand of wire, manoeuvring the handle-bars and other parts of the machine underneath one at a time and dragging hard. In short heaves, as handle bars, footrests, hub nuts, etc, gouged furrows in the earth, I managed to inch the bike forward. It required long pauses for deep breathing and resting muscles in between heaves, but the process was eventually successful. It probably took half an hour to complete the job, by which time I was weak and wringing with perspiration.

When my thumping heart had settled down I started off again and was soon riding down a hillside falling steeply into a grass-covered valley a few hundred feet deep. At the bottom, near the hedge boundary, a battery of field guns was set up, the gunners apparently getting ready for a shoot. Barely had I been heartened by the sight of British troops than a salvo of shells shrieked over-head to burst, in puffs of black smoke, about midway between me and the guns. Instinctively, I opened the throttle, zoomed down through the drifting smoke, flew past gaping artillerymen picking themselves up off the ground and slithered through a muddy gateway on to a farm track.

The track led me to a farmyard from which I regained the N.815 and returned to HQ. In the Signals Despatch Office a radio set had been tuned to receive the BBC Home Service News and I was just in time to hear cultured tones announce, 'This morning, our troops entered the town of Pont l'Évêque'!

The Germans knew that Allied troops would soon be moving into the town and were continuing their demolitions. They were still at it when, in the darkness of late evening, I was handed a signal for another of our Troops. Their HQ was in a house on the outskirts of the town, standing isolated at the top of a steep *pavé* street leading down towards the river. My trip was probably in connection with a crossing of the river at Pierrefitte-en-Auge, a few miles to the south of Pont l'Évêque, which had been planned for that night.

I was sitting in the kitchen, awaiting a signal to take back, when a batch of particularly large high explosives blasted off. They were so close that the building shook to its foundations, as we did to ours. We surmised that it had been a salvo from one of the German large-calibre multi-barrelled Nebelwerfer mortars, some of which fired rocket-propelled missiles up to 32 cm calibre – as big as 12" shells. As has been mentioned previously , the translation of 'Nebelwerfer' is 'Smoke thrower', something of a misnomer, but at least those ones hadn't had our names on them.

Back at HQ, my tour as Duty DR was finished for the day, another one would sleep in the SDO, so I was forced to spend the night in the open, in the transport lines. It was an extremely noisy night. The German rearguard must have had lots of ammunition left and, rather than carrying it away, were blasting it off in our direction.

There were no holes available so I crawled under a truck as protection against falling bomb and shell splinters, despite realizing that it could be a foolhardy thing to do. Suppose the truck was hit and the petrol tank blew up? I didn't go too far under. Then what if shell splinters slashed the tyres, dropping the thing on top of me? I kept away from the sump and differential housing. A combination of such thoughts, plus the whines and explosions of shells, kept me awake much of the night, but it all helped to pass the hours of darkness.

Chapter 8

ACROSS THE RIVERS TOUGUES AND SEINE

By dawn, however, all the threatening noises had gone and an un-accustomed blanket of silence lay over the countryside. Pont l'Évêque was still burning, but, as hour followed hour without any enemy activity, it was clear that the Germans had pulled out. It was learned that the crossing of the Tougues at Pierrefitte planned for the previous night had been called off at the very last moment when the Commando was actually moving up to the jumping-off point. News also filtered down that elements of Sixth Airborne were already across the river, pushing forward to regain contact.

Throughout the day the Commando remained in position, waiting and wondering. That night I was Duty DR again, so at the nub of things when, at half past four in the morning, the Commando received orders to make an immediate move forward. The Fighting Troops were roused, to climb into TCVs and be taken forward some eight miles beyond Pont l'Évêque. They debussed in the vicinity of Beuzeville and began an early morning pursuit on foot. The 8th Parachute Battalion, advancing on the same axis, was ahead of 41 and I was ordered forward to report to their HQ to act as liaison link for Brigadier Leicester.

The Paras had set up their Headquarters in a recently-vacated German bunker built in the corner of a wood where it had commanded the approaches to an adjacent crossroads. The location, shown on a map, posed no problem, but to reach it circumspectly from the rear entailed a final approach ride of about two miles over rough farm roads meandering between high hedges

1. Ply/x 111113 Marine H.T.W.B. 'Geordie' Swindale, killed on D-Day. Taken in Catania, Sicily, after the Salerno operation, September 1943. This book is dedicated to his memory.

Royal Marine Commandos embark on LCI(S) – Landing Craft Infantry (Small) – at the *ising Sun* jetty, Warsash on the River Hamble, 5 June 1944. *(Royal Marines Museum)*

3. LCI(S) carrying Royal Marine Commandos, nearing *Sword* Beach, Normandy, D-Day 6 June 1944. *(Royal Marines Museum)*

4. Royal Marines coming ashore from LCI(S). The man at the foot of second ramp is being helped carry a parascooter.

5. Sword beach on D-Day; men take brief shelter behind an AVRE.

6. Prisoners taken by Royal Marines at St Aubin being marched away.

7. The outskirts of Lion-sur-Mer. On D-Day the shop bearing the name 'Martin' was the Post Office. The Author's small group of stragglers took the road leading straight ahead. *(Photo taken by the Author in 1976)*

8. Ranville, where 6th Airborne Division had their Headquarters, commemorates the fact that it was the first village in France to be liberated. *(Photo by Author)*

PLACE
du 6 Juin 1944

RANVILLE
LE PREMIER VILLAGE DE FRANCE
LIBERÉ A ETÉ PRIS AUX ALLEMANDS
A 2H 30 LE 6 JUIN 1944
PAR
LE 13TH (LANCASHIRE) BATTALION
THE PARACHUTE REGIMENT

WIN OR DIE

THIS MEMORIAL IS RAISED BY ALL RANKS IN MEMORY
OF THEIR COMRADES WHO FELL IN THE CAMPAIGN

Pegasus Bridge in June 1944. (British vehicles are still driving on the left!). In the background are two gliders of the 6th Airlanding Brigade.

10. and 11. Pegasus Bridge in 1976. Open for road traffic (left) and canal traffic (right). *(Photos by Author)*

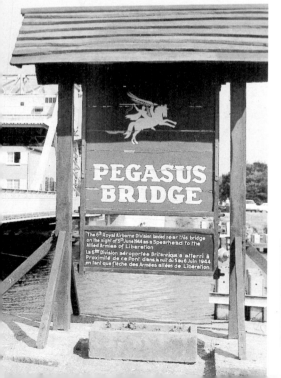

12. The station house at Cany-Barville, standing derelict in 1976. In August 1944
Signallers and DRs of 41 RM Commando were billeted on the ground floor, while
the stationmaster and his family lived in the upper storey. *(Photo by Author)*

13. A Welbike is taken from its container, having been dropped by parachute.
(Airborne Forces Museum)

14. Squatting on their loaded Buffaloes, men of the Commando wait as their LCT approaches Walcheren. *(IWM)*

15. An LCT of 41 RM Commando nearing Westkapelle.

16. An LCT touches down after passing through the breach in the sea dyke.

17. The Buffalo blown up by a German mine at Serooskerke on 8 November 1944, with the loss of 20 lives, including 14 men of No.48 Royal Marines Commando. *(Jacob van Winkelen)*

and tortuous muddy tracks snaking through intermittent stretches of woodland.

As at Troarn, I was instructed to leave the machine at the edge of the wood lest the noise of the engine should alert the enemy. Long before reaching there, however, the futility of such an instruction was obvious. Almost continuous explosions were splattering the area and the rattling of automatic small arms fire, uncomfortably close by, made any other noise irrelevant. Nevertheless, I dropped the machine and doubled the few score yards to a massive blockhouse, nodded to a paratrooper sheltering in the doorway and headed down a flight of concrete steps.

At the bottom I entered a completely different world, but my eyes needed time to adjust to the gloom. It was a confined, dim, shadowy place, illuminated only by a few hurricane lamps, around which indistinct figures were poring over maps or talking into microphones. The crashing noises above ground had been replaced by no more than the low mumbling of voices of officers discussing the situation and signallers reciting call signs and dictating messages.

I reported to the Signals Officer and was told to wait while a message for Brigade was finalized, so there was time for a smoke and to absorb the absolute safety engendered by a yard or two of reinforced concrete. In due course I was handed the message, but on starting back up the stairs the Para at the top called down, 'Hang on a bit, DR, its rather noisy up here.' After a while he came back with 'OK, it's quiet now,' and I was on my way.

On emerging into daylight it was clear that his 'quiet' was only relative as there were still many unfriendly noises in the real world. With them came the realization that my brief stay in complete safety had engendered a degree of reluctance to get back to the 'normality' of bombs and shells. The feeling returned each time I had to leave the Paras' bunker, but apparently, like stage fright, it evaporated once back into things. There was no major problem in being 'outside' when that was the only way of life you knew, but having it interspersed with periods of complete safety brought home a realization of how dicey the whole business was.

After that first trip to 8 Paras I spent the day shuttling back and forth between their bunker and Brigade along those rough, muddy tracks. In marked contrast with the Paras' bunker, Brigadier

Leicester's 'Headquarters' was no more than a small clearing in a wood. There, sitting on logs near a wood fire where a dixie of tea was constantly kept hot, he, with some of his officers, map cases on knees, conducted the Brigade's business.

After delivering one message from the bunker, the Brig asked if it would be possible to take his Intelligence Officer back with me for a discussion with the Paras. I replied that it could be done, but the ride was rough and often touch and go whether I could keep the bike on an even keel, so there was an even chance of him coming off. The Brigadier clearly thought the risk was worth taking, so the officer straddled the luggage rack and off we went.

Nearing 'bunker wood', I was engrossed in watching the track and keeping the pair of us on the bike, and it was only at the last moment that a glance forward revealed a figure in German field grey emerging from the trees. Then I saw a rifle and bayonet at his back, in the hands of a grinning parachutist.

After conducting the Officer to the bunker and waiting until he had completed his discussion, I delivered him unscathed back into the presence of the Brigadier. The two officers exchanged welcoming pleasantries, then the IO dipped a mug into the dixie of tea, but, before allowing him to make his report, 'Jumbo' dipped another mug into the dixie and handed it to me, saying, 'I think the DR deserves one too'.

After that tea break I returned with a signal to 8 Paras which could have been the order to put in an attack. In any event the Germans pulled back and when 8 Para HQ vacated the bunker and moved forward about two miles I accompanied them. When they were settled in their new positions I was given a signal for Jumbo to inform him where they were.

It was evening when I reported once more to Para HQ and artillery and mortar fire had subsided to a 'desultory' stage. The entire countryside was quietening down so that the noise of my engine had become an embarrassment. I was thanked kindly for my efforts during the day and politely told to return to my own Unit.

The rest of the Commando hadn't been idle either, In the morning our scouting patrols had bumped the Germans between Beuzeville and St Maclou, then maintained contact during the day. When I returned to HQ it was dusk, dull and overcast, and some

108

of our Troops were moving forward. 'A' was to be accompanied by tanks, therefore the noise of a motorbike engine wouldn't be any problem, and I was sent along with them.

Tanks and Marines moved together along a narrow country road with hedges set high on dikes along both sides. The column turned through a gateway on the right-hand side of the road up a steep track which turned almost immediately sharp left into a field of stubble. One tank slithered sideways, crushing TSM Hazelhurst against the stone gatepost; he was crippled for the rest of his life. A short while later the tanks laagered up for the night and I was sent back to Commando HQ.

It was then about nine o'clock and I was dismayed to learn that 41 and 48 Commandos had been alerted to set off at two o'clock in the morning on a cross-country march on St Maclou, some six miles away. However, Colonel Palmer must have been aware of my very full day as he motioned me across to him and said, 'You needn't come, Mitchell. Stay here for the night and catch up in the morning.' I snuggled down into the straw of a barn and knew no more until the cocks were crowing next morning.

The operation had been a complete success. After the approach march in almost complete darkness the two Commandos had descended upon St Maclou in the early hours, only to find that the Germans had decamped. 48 had been given the job of leading the way and their Commanding Officer, Lieutenant Colonel 'Mouldy' Moulton, came up with an effective way of keeping the long file of men on the right track. Individual Officers had been given stretches of the route to commit to memory and they moved forward in turn to act as 'point'. Even amidst the many major news items of the time, that night march of 48 and 41 warranted a few column inches in the National Press.

Immediately after breakfast I set off to catch up, riding alone along deserted country roads, the verges littered with the aftermath of infantry activity. Unlike the outskirts of Caen, there were no shattered wrecks of tanks or trucks. The debris of war this time was no more than scattered odds and ends of military equipment – water bottles, steel helmets, ammunition carriers, etc, with, here and there, bodies of the dead. I passed perhaps a dozen or so; two, I noted, were Canadians, lying side by side on the grass verge, but the rest were German. One still remains in memory as a short, podgy youngster, lying face down in a shallow ditch, steel-rimmed spectacles and coal-scuttle helmet still in place.

My introduction to St Maclou was having to find my way around a very large crater where there had recently been a major cross-roads. Then I became engulfed in the jubilation of people liberated after four years of enemy occupation – cheers and smiles, hugs and handshakes, tears of joy and kisses, with some glasses of wine, cider or calvados. The Commando would be staying in St Maclou for a few days; it was Saturday, so there were hopes of a weekend off the war. Quite a lot had happened in the week since leaving Troarn.

The Despatch Riders and some Signallers had been allocated a recently-vacated terrace house as their billet. All furnishings, fittings, crockery and cutlery, even to a well-stocked drinks cabinet on the living-room wall, were still in place. Presumably the absence of the previous occupants had been linked with the precipitate departure of the Germans. We quickly adapted to living in a house again, for the first time since leaving Hastings three months earlier.

It was said that, in consequence of all the to-ings and fro-ings of the previous day, Colonel Palmer had put my name forward for a commendation. Whatever the reason, in due course I did receive a certificate which reads:

'It has been brought to my notice that you have performed out-standing good service, and shown great devotion to duty, during the campaign in North West Europe. I award you this certificate as a token of my appreciation, and I have given instructions that this shall be noted in your Record of Service'. It bears the signature, 'B.L. Montgomery, Field Marshal, Commander-in-Chief, 21st Army Group', so that was one occasion when Monty's instructions weren't carried out. My Record of Service bears no mention of the certificate!

For men in the Fighting Troops it *was* a weekend off because, in the words of the Unit's War Diary, theirs was to 'rest, wash and recuperate'. That didn't apply to the DRs as there were still messages to deliver. To make matters worse, it started to rain next morning and it continued almost non-stop for two days; while the troops sheltered indoors, we travelled the wet roads of France. Nevertheless, it was enough to have a house in which to sleep and a drinks cabinet on the wall.

As usual, the easing of tension and our static situation opened

110

the flood gates of rumour; the buzz-mongers came into their own again. 'Home next week!' some said. 'SS Brigades are to be re-organized as ordinary Infantry Brigades.' 'Not so,' said others, 'We will become Mobile Reconnaissance Brigades.' The 'hottest' buzz of all was that the Airborne Division and No 1 SS Brigade were to be sent back to Blighty.

Wednesday came, with no positive news nor developments until, out of the blue after lunch, transport was laid on for 'shore leave' in Honfleur, the coastal resort some eight miles distant. The town had been liberated by the Canadians on the same day as the Marines reached St Maclou and was still in festive mood. Streets and buildings were decorated with flags and bunting, while every Allied vehicle received spontaneous waves and cheers. Café owners and restaurateurs, however, had returned to 'business as usual' and the prices being charged verged on highway robbery.

On our return to St Maclou that evening we found that the with-drawal of Sixth Airborne Division and No. 1 SS Brigade was a *fait accompli*; they were on their way home. No. 4 SS was to 'soldier on', apparently to demonstrate the unofficial motto of the Royal Marines – 'First in, last out'.

The DRs at least received 'sweeteners' by inheriting some of the Airborne Division's motorcycles. In place of the long-in-the-tooth Ariels we each became the proud possessor of a state-of-the-art 350cc Matchless, with teledraulic (telescopic hydraulic) front forks. As if to stress that it was 'all change', the operational element of the unit was moving forward next day, leaving me behind as the DR with Rear Echelon.

On the Thursday morning I was quite happy to wave 'Cheerio' to the other DRs as they rode away, shepherding the Unit convoy towards 'the front'. My stay in St Maclou was short-lived, however, as next morning I was handed a despatch for Advanced Head-quarters, which I would find in Yvetot, a small town on the far side of the River Seine, beyond Barentin. In 1944 the first bridge over the Seine was at Rouen, but I was to make for a point opposite Duclair to be ferried across.

I set off with a mixture of glee at being able to try out the Matchless on a trip of almost fifty miles and some trepidation as to what conditions might be like so far away. For the first twenty miles via Pont Audemer the road was awash with a continuous flow

111

of military vehicles all heading for the Rouen bridges. At Bourg-Achard, however, I had to turn off onto the minor road leading into the horseshoe loop of the river towards Berville-sur-Seine, my ferry point. Then, for ten long miles, I was completely alone on a deserted forest road, passing more and more wrecked German vehicles as I drew nearer to the river and with the stench of rotting flesh growing ever stronger in my nostrils.

During the previous two weeks German troops in headlong flight had been trapped in such loops of the Seine and, at the mercy of Allied aircraft, untold numbers had perished. In the adjacent larger loop of the Forêt de Brotonne, where even more German troops had been trying to escape, the carnage had been particularly horrendous. As I drew near the river I passed lines of those German vehicles which had managed to survive the air attacks. The lines continued down to the water's edge and some vehicles had even been driven deep into the water, as though the drivers hoped that their trucks would float and carry them to safety.

The 'ferry' turned out to be no more than one of the pontoons used for building floating bridges, fitted with an outboard motor and being operated by two REs. Despite having seen no sign of life during my ride, there were files of British infantrymen lined up waiting to board, but they were halted until my bike had been manhandled over the gunwale. An Army DR with bike was already on board, so there wasn't much room left for infantrymen. The crossing, of about five hundred yards, was rather hairy as the pontoon was buffetted by the adverse current of the river. We were hard put to keep our bikes on an even keel, but eventually grounded safely within a few hundred yards of Duclair. 'Vive les REs!'

Only then did it sink in that the Commando had not gone forward into shot and shell, but into vin blanc and kisses. I had to join a long string of military vehicles moving slowly through the streets lined with cheering people waving flags and bottles of wine. If any vehicle stopped, even momentarily, the occupants were deluged with hugs, kisses and glasses of wine; the air was filled with 'Vive les Tommies'.

Motorcyclists were particularly vulnerable as children lining the kerb poked Union Flags and Tricolours into their faces. The obvious defence was to stop and accept a drink, but more positive evasive action was needed if my message was to be delivered. Even

112

beyond the town there was little easing off in the rapturous welcome being accorded the stream of vehicles by groups of people gathered by the roadside. The six-mile journey to Barentin was a continuous triumphal procession, but then I had to turn out of line. The main flood of traffic was heading northeast towards Pavilly and Tôtes, following the German retreat, but my route to Yvetot was 'back' to the north-west. The road was only sparsely trafficked, but I still encountered group after group of French folks wanting to say 'Thank you' to any passing Allied serviceman. The sight of a waving wine bottle seemed to bring my machine to a rapid halt automatically, until I steeled myself to resist temptation.

Yvetot was in a state of euphoric turmoil, the streets were thronged with a noisy, boisterous *mélange* of Marines and civilians. I located the Signals Despatch Office with some difficulty and delivered my message. It evinced no great stir, so I regretted not having delayed longer. I was simply told to find the other DRs and stick around. By the simple process of grabbing every passing jolly Royal and bawling, 'Where are the DRs?' I eventually located them. The Commando had been the first Allied troops to enter Barentin and Yvetot, so had been welcomed as liberators. The square outside the Barentin Mairie has been renamed Place de la Libération and the building itself bears a plaque attesting to the fact that 41 RM Commando were the first to arrive.

In Yvetot hundreds of Royal Marines were almost inextricably mixed up with the local population. The top brass were undoubtedly aware of this and may have been a little concerned about the unit getting too attached to the place. During the evening orders were passed around by word of mouth that 41 would be moving out next morning and all ranks had better be there.

Chapter 9

CANY-BARVILLE, LE HAVRE AND DUNKIRK

On Saturday, 2 September, together with 46 and Brigade HQ, the Commando marched to Fauville-en-Caux, some ten miles away. Commando Headquarters had been allocated the Château de Bourville on the outskirts of town and arrived to find a main gate guard already in position, courtesy of the French Forces of the Interior (FFI), all armed with German light automatic weapons.

The FFI were much in evidence, as their major preoccupation was to organize public 'shearings' of French females who had consorted with Germans. 'Stages' had been set up in the market square of every town and village and, one after another, struggling women and young girls would be held down in a chair in full public view while a barber went about the job. As each handful of hair was snipped off he would twirl it around above his head to rounds of applause and cheers from the crowd, before casting it to one side and taking hold of another. After that he resorted to hand shears and finally removed the last vestiges with a razor leaving the victim's pate as bald as a billiard ball. Only then was she released to fight her hysterical way through the spitting, buffeting, jeers and catcalls of the crowd.

Even before one victim had managed to escape the concentrated hate of her townsfolk, those nearer the platform were starting up with new rounds of cheers as more handfuls of hair were being waved aloft. I witnessed only a small part of one of those ceremonies; they were too much like the citizenesses of the French Revolution knitting beside 'Madame Guillotine' as the heads dropped. For months afterwards a headsquare was the hallmark of a shorn collaboratress.

Although the Brigade was on 4 hours' notice to move, nothing had happened by Monday afternoon, so Jack Horsfield and I, being off-duty, sallied forth in search of eggs to supplement the compo rations. With Jack riding pillion, some tins of food for bartering purposes and a supply of 'invasion money', we set off. However, as Rouen was only about thirty-five miles away, we decided to make a detour there first.

As we drew near the city centre the bike was sucked into a main street awash with nose-to-tail traffic before there could be any thought of evasive action. Two Bailey bridges, built across the Seine to replace those demolished by the Germans, were carrying endless streams of vehicles into the city. Clouds of dust raised by the multitudinous wheels and tracks soon clogged our noses and throats, and Rouen's bombed buildings looked no different from any others. I took the first opportunity to turn into a side street and escape. Back in the quietness of Seine Maritime, we soon located a farmer's wife who was happy to exchange eggs for some of our tins of food and we returned to the thanks of our oppos for a successful egging expedition.

The following day began quietly, but around mid-morning the Commando received 'Immediate' orders to move out. The journey was again of the order of ten miles and Headquarters, with 'S' Troop, were located in Cany-Barville, five miles from the Channel coast and twelve miles due east of Fécamp, home of the Benedictine monastery and its liqueur. The rest of the Commando was spread out in nearby villages, with Brigade Headquarters in Ourville, some four miles away, all in an attractive rural area completely untouched by the war.

The Despatch Riders and some Signallers, about a dozen of us in all, were billeted in the empty ground floor of the house of the station-master who, with wife and two children, was still in occupation of the upper part. It stood on a triangular grass plot bounded by a low, wooden pale fence, one side of which abutted an irregularly shaped station yard, while it backed on to a narrow unmade road separating it from some disused railway tracks. An interesting feature of the station yard was a small café in the far corner.

Although the Unit was 'resting', the flow of messages continued and the DRs were kept busy, pleasantly riding around in the warm sunshine. I was soon doing much more riding than any of the others, especially on my off-duty days because my smattering of French had cast me in the role of unofficial egg procurer. I became known around the nearby farms and quickly established a 'round' of likely suppliers, where negotiations invariably started with a glass of wine or a nip of calvados.

Sardines and corned beef were most sought after by the French, but there was also an insatiable demand for petrol. With the area around the station house littered with motorbikes, jeeps and trucks, it was obvious that there was petrol somewhere around; no sooner had we moved in, than enquiries were being received for, 'D'essence?' I was invariably called to the fore and soon adopted the Gallic attitude of hunching the shoulders, head on one side, displaying empty hands saying, 'Je regret, M'sieur . . . !' The DRs received a jerricanful of petrol when necessary to top up their tanks, but there was none to spare for the black market business.

Two days after our arrival, however, I was turning away an enquirer when someone called out, 'Hey, Mitch, if it's petrol he's after, there's a jerricanful here you can flog'. I agreed a price for the twenty litres and told the Frenchman to bring his vehicle along the track behind the house. It was a gigantic 'camion', which pruned most of the trees en route, and it was crammed with dozens of passengers.

The driver jumped down, whipped off the vehicle's petrol filler cap, then took a quick sniff at the jerrican I handed him before pouring the contents into his tank. I had received the money and the big truck was trundling away when I saw that my comrades were 'rolling in the aisles'. They had conned me into selling four gallons of water with a few inches of petrol on top! That was my first and last petrol sale. For days thereafter I kept out of sight, with one eye always on the lookout for a big French truck.

Friday was a red letter day – our first pay parade on French soil! Each man received 100 francs – equivalent to ten shillings or six pints of beer in the UK – and we didn't have far to go to spend it. The café in the station yard was little more than two rows of five or six marble-topped tables along the sides of a strip of carpet leading to the bar. Both walls were lined with mirrors bearing adverts for such French beverages as Byrrh and Dubonnet, but we wanted to try Benedictine. Madame was apologetic, she would have to charge 20 francs a glass as she had to buy on the black market, but we accepted. After four, one more would make us penniless, so we changed to cider at one franc a tumblerful and still had a few francs left when wandering back to our billet.

At 0800 hrs next morning I began a twenty-four-hour tour as Duty DR. It was Saturday and business was slack and, around noon, I told the signallers where they could find me and wandered across to the café. Before I had time to order anything, a Frenchman asked me to join him in a particular apéritif. My French didn't extend to 'I have never tasted it', so M. André Lecop, I still have his visiting card, taught me the words '*Je ne l'ai jamais bu*'. He also invited me to his home for a meal the following Wednesday evening, with the suggestion that I might perhaps take a tin or two of British rations.

Next morning, minutes before relief, I was handed a signal for Brigade and, as there was no answer, decided to take an 'exploratory' route back. I didn't have my map and became doubtful of the way, so stopped in a village to ask. The man I approached had been on his way to a café for an 'eye opener' coffee and he invited me to join him, which I was pleased to accept. He insisted that it should be 'un café/cognac', then suggested that I joined him for breakfast – he lived with his sister. Afterwards he changed into his 'Sunday best' and we went to meet his girlfriend coming out of church. Thereafter I was happy to be drawn into a succession of visits to family and friends, but, after a late lunch, insisted that I really must report back to HQ. My new-found friend was reluctant to let me out of his sight – he had arranged more involvements for me – so rode pillion back to Cany. He waited while I washed, shaved and changed into best battledress, then we returned to the fray. The finale was a formal dinner, with more wine glasses on the table than I had seen in my life, at the home of one of his girl-friend's bosses. She worked in the Town Hall.

Whilst I had been enjoying those junketings, some thirty-five miles away at Le Havre, British and Canadian troops were finalizing the surrender of the Germans still holding out there. When Allied forces had swept forward from the beachhead substantial garrisons had remained in all the major Channel ports to deny their use by the Allies and Le Havre was the first to be liquidated. At

Cany we learned of the imminent fall of the port on Monday 11 September, when the unit was alerted to move into the city immediately after German capitulation. 48 Commando was to take care of prisoners, but 41's job would be to 'Act in Support of the Civil Power' or 'keeping the peace'. It seemed incredible that there were fears of disturbances by civilians, but it was even said that there could be French *francs-tireurs* firing upon us.

The garrison of Le Havre capitulated on Tuesday 12 September and early the following morning the long convoy carrying 41 Commando moved off. It was a slow and, especially for the DRs escorting it, a very dusty journey. When the string of vehicles started to negotiate the ruins of the city progress became desultory and spasmodic. The nearer the convoy came to the centre the damage encountered was progressively worse; in places it was impossible even to distinguish where streets had been. The very few civilians encountered gave us nothing but blank stares or glares of hatred.

The trucks finally came to a halt in the docks area, the very centre of the desolation, and just stayed there. By the time the brass hats were satisfied that there wasn't going to be any civilian uprising it was late afternoon; the convoy turned around and returned to Cany. Our arrival came as a surprise, but everyone seemed pleased to see us, especially Madame at the café.

At the time we simply assumed that hostile French reaction had been feared because their city had been destroyed to force the Germans out and thought no more about it. Not until many years later did I learn that, only a few days before our arrival, no less than three thousand French civilians had been killed in a single air raid, the culmination of a week of unnecessary bombing. Allied ground commanders had made it clear that they did not want air attacks, being confident of effecting the surrender of the city without any. In addition, offers by the German commander, Colonel Wildermuth, to allow civilians to leave and ensure that none of his troops would be in the city centre, where most of the civilians were gathered, were refused. For some reason the RAF not only went ahead with unwanted attacks, but concentrated upon the city centre, rather than the German defensive positions on the outskirts.

Nevertheless, that chance return to Cany enabled me to take up the invitation to supper given by M. Lecop the previous Saturday.

We had a pleasant meal in his home in the village of Theuville-aux-Maillots, four miles from Cany along the Fécamp road. He pressed me to call on him again and thrust a bottle of calvados into my hands as a parting gift.

Three days later came the final farewell to Cany-Barville, with the DRs conducting the road convoy to an unknown destination. The first town en route was Yvetot and 41 Commando rumbled through its narrow streets with no reaction whatsoever from the people who had been so ecstatic only two weeks earlier. Liberation was already a thing of the past.

As the journey continued it became clear to those of us with maps that the convoy was making a wide detour around Dieppe, still occupied by the Germans. An overnight stop, sleeping in barns, sheds and outhouses, was made in a small town with the even smaller French name of Eu, three miles inland from Tréport. By 0700 hours next morning, we were on our way again; it was a very chilly morning for the DRs, but M. Lecop's calvados helped. It was young, raw stuff, very different from the pleasant café/cognacs of the previous Sunday morning, but we endured the taste for the warming effect.

The convoy meandered on, crossing the Somme at St Valéry, then via St Omer and Cassel to come to a final halt, in the dank dark dusk of a September evening, outside another of those massive German reinforced concrete bunkers. 41 HQ had arrived in Loon Plage, a small town about two and a half miles from the coast, straddling the road to Dunkirk, another port still held by the Germans, which lay some six miles further east. Our Brigade, now under command of the Canadian First Army, was to take over the job of 'containing' the garrison. The Commando was relieving the Calgary Highlanders and the first order given in our new location was 'No green berets'. The Germans could find out for themselves who was their new opposition.

The Commando had inherited the blockhouse, dimly lit with hurricane lamps as the power was cut off, for their Headquarters building and the DRs were allocated one of the many small compartments as sleeping quarters. Hardly had we settled down on the concrete floor, however, than it was reported that the German garrison in Calais, eighteen miles to our rear, had broken out and we were in danger of being surrounded. The unit was put on 50%

119

stand-to throughout the night, increased to 100% for the hour before dawn, and everyone spent most of the night in extremely cold firing positions in the open. Then it transpired that it had been a false alarm; the Germans were still in Calais. There may have been no connection, but that Sunday had seen the start of Operation MARKET GARDEN, which secured the river crossings at Eindhoven and Nijmegen, but failed to capture Arnhem, 'a bridge too far'.

It was understood that the Dunkirk garrison numbered about ten thousand men, while No. 4 Brigade couldn't muster two thousand, and these were very thin on the ground. 41, with less than 450 men, had almost six miles of front to cover, a line running almost due south from the Channel coast east of Mardick to the left flank of 48 Commando at Brouckerke. It being impossible to form a continuous perimeter, the Rifle Troops held small, widely spaced positions based upon farmhouses and other buildings, with the gaps covered by mines and frequent patrolling.

As well as getting back into an active role, the Commando had moved into a completely different environment. Instead of the rolling, wooded countryside around Cany-Barville, our new location was an empty, flat terrain, criss-crossed by innumerable canals, dykes and watercourses. The featureless landscape was relieved only by almost leafless roadside trees and a few widely scattered farm buildings. The weather too had changed almost beyond belief. The warm bright sunshine of Seine Maritime had been replaced by leaden skies, dank mists and cold drizzle.

From a DRs point of view the situation was very similar to that which had prevailed at the radar stations. With the Commando strung out along the perimeter of a large German position, long detours were necessary to get to the various Troop headquarters. All trips to Troops positioned to the south of the road to Dunkirk had to start by heading inland for three miles to Bourbourgville, then working your way around to the east, before riding in towards the coast.

There were no such complications in getting to 'B' Troop, as their Headquarters was close to the road to Dunkirk. Shortly after our arrival the Troop had probed forward for almost two and a half miles without meeting any opposition, therefore Captain Sturgis had positioned his Troop in that area and established his

Headquarters in adjacent Ferme Hameral. As the road was almost perfectly straight and under German observation, a 'limit of visibility' had been created by stretching a wire hawser across the road and draping it with camouflage netting.

On the coastal flank were 'X' with Headquarters in the handful of houses known as Mardick (Fort Mardick, two miles further east, was in German hands) and 'S' was a little further on in Le Clipon. Unfortunately a short length of the road to Mardick was completely open and under German observation, which meant speedy runs to get out of harm's way before the inevitable began to arrive.

In Mardick, in addition to 'X' HQ, there were some of the local FFI. They were militarily dressed in knee breeches and jackboots, had Lüger pistols at their belts and carried Schmeissers over their shoulders – and they were female! I didn't learn if they had any military duties, but did wonder whether their get-up might be more of a deterrent to advances from Allied troops rather than German.

After one running of the gauntlet return from 'X', the SDO received an emergency call from them – a knocked-out German truck and a defunct British Bren Gun Carrier were blocking a strategically important road and a breakdown truck was required immediately to clear the way. I led a massive recovery vehicle to the spot, which, luckily, wasn't under direct observation, but it was clear that the Germans were aware that something was happening and were doing their best to make things uncomfortable. For a disconcerting half-hour I could only stand by as truck and carrier were slowly manoeuvred on to the narrow road for towing away, while the Germans sent over salvoes of 'Hope these catch you in the open' shells.

A few days after our arrival a battery of Bofors Light ack-ack guns came under unit command. The gunners had never previously fired their weapons at the enemy and were delighted to join us. Although their normal role was against low-flying aircraft, the 40 mm calibre guns, firing 2 lb shells at a rate of 120 a minute, were quickly brought into action against German ground targets. A farm occupied by the enemy was soon burned to the ground and we began to get deserters protesting about the 'new weapon', which was much feared by the Germans.

The Fighting Troops were sending probing patrols to seek out and harry German positions, and the Germans were doing very much the same thing. On the Wednesday 'Y' moved up, bumped a German patrol, suffering one casualty. That same day 'B' pushed a patrol almost two miles up the road towards Dunkirk and they managed to collect a German prisoner. Ironically, on their return journey he trod on one of his own people's mines; he was killed and his two NCO escorts were badly wounded.

More often than not these patrol clashes were nocturnal affairs and on most nights there would be noisy confrontations in the darkness. At times our men were involved in hand-to-hand clashes close to their sleeping quarters, when infiltrating Germans were detected and pounced upon. One such incident took place during the night of Wednesday/Thursday.

I was Duty DR and shortly before dawn was roused from sleep on the SDO floor. 'B' troop was requesting transport and an escort for three German prisoners taken in a night encounter. The Duty Officer arranged for a jeep and driver, and ordered me to be the escort. I left the drowsy warmth of the HQ bunker for a freezing cold ride to Ferme Hameral in an open jeep. On arrival we learned there were only two prisoners to take back as the other one had 'got himself shot'.

There was just sufficient light in the early morning sky to make out the young, rather bristly, expressionless faces of my two charges as I waved them into the back of the jeep with my Colt 45. When they were settled, I squeezed in too, facing them with gun at the ready. They looked so small and inoffensive that the whole affair seemed rather ludicrous, but I waited until we were all back inside the HQ bunker before handing each of them a cigarette and returning to my disturbed sleep.

At 0800 I was off-duty, so could undertake an egging expedition. Around Loon Plage my smattering of French was no longer so effective as most of the farmers spoke only Flemish, but I had managed to pick up enough words to stay in business. When I knocked on a farmhouse door, whether or not there were eggs available, I was invariably made welcome. Even without eggs, there would be a drink or two, now beer rather than wine, and I would reciprocate with cigarettes.

At one farm I found the lady owner still incensed by the fact that when the Germans had pulled back into Dunkirk they had taken three of her horses. She told me that the commander of the Dunkirk garrison had lost an arm on the Russian Front and she knew how she would deal with him: 'I'd cut off the other one,' she said, 'and let the . . . starve to death.'

Another advantage of the DR job was to be able to stop at cafés to get warm and practise the language. There weren't any in the immediate vicinity, but on Saturday evening I was given a trip to Brigade HQ and on the return journey decided to stop at a café in Wormhoudt. I got into conversation with two Frenchmen, one of whom said that he had spent four years as a prisoner in Germany. I couldn't work out just how he had managed to get home, but was pleased to drink to his achievement.

On Monday buzzes about a move started again. The hot one was that we were heading for Holland to support the First Airborne Division at Arnhem. We never did learn if there had been any truth in that one because that was the very day the airborne troops were pulled back across the Rhine. Nevertheless movement orders did come through and we were bound, not for Holland, but Ostend in Belgium. The Commando's positions around Dunkirk were to be handed over at midnight next day, Tuesday, 26 September, after which we would 'proceed' to Ostend during the night. By a remark-able coincidence, the relieving unit was to be none other than the Black Watch, from whom 41 Commando had taken over respon-sibility for the radar stations at Douvres/La Délivrande shortly after D-Day. Now, four months later, at Loon Plage they were to take over a similar pocket of enemy resistance from us and we repaid the compliment with interest. The radar stations had yielded little more than two hundred Germans, but at Dunkirk we gave them a quarter share of ten thousand!

Chapter 10

INTO BELGIUM, TRAINING FOR WALCHEREN

The handover took place at midnight 26 September as planned, but it wasn't until an hour later, after many tricky manoeuvres in fitful moonlight, that the long convoy of more than fifty vehicles was finally assembled. Twelve 3-ton trucks had been borrowed from nearby units to enable the Commando, with all weapons and stores, to be moved all at once. A Despatch Rider rode down the line giving the 'Start up!' signal and the long string of vehicles rumbled off into the night. The DRs rode behind the 'Pathfinder' jeep until a doubtful part of the route required one of them to remain behind to ensure that all vehicles kept to the planned route. Then came the hair-raising job of regaining position at the head of the convoy.

The truck drivers, travelling without lights along unfamiliar roads made slippery by drizzle, tended to hog the crown of the carriageway; therefore, for DRs needing to get past, with only a few feet between a swaying 3-tonner and a muddy ditch, it was a leap in the dark every time. A few trucks slithered off the carriageway, then one DR would stand-by while another went for assistance, but, surprisingly, no Despatch Riders came to grief that night. With only the drivers, DRs and a handful of officers awake, the convoy rumbled on throughout the hours of darkness, travelling via St Omer, Cassel and Poperinghe. It was still trundling forward when the wet night gave way to warm September sunshine.

Around mid-morning the convoy came to a halt in sight of

Ostend. Then, as hour succeeded hour, rumours passed up and down the line that Commandos weren't wanted there. It was late afternoon before the unit eventually moved into town – Other Ranks to an empty convent building, with parts of the outer walls missing and devoid of any glass in the windows, Officers to the Hotel Manchester. Next morning the Commandos moved on, 41 and 48 to the coastal town of De Haan, some six miles further east, while 47 travelled three miles further along the coast to Wenduyne, and Brigade Headquarters carried on ten miles inland to Bruges.

De Haan (Le Coq) had been used by the German Gestapo as a Headquarters and Recreational Area, and a number of hotels had remained fully operational. These, however, had long since been taken over by the Headquarters staffs of the Canadian Army and the RAF Tactical Air Force, so empty buildings, which had provided seasonal pre-war holiday accommodation, were opened up for the Commandos. One such building, the Pension du Nord, became 41's HQ offices, plus living quarters for the Signals Section and Intelligence personnel, the DRs' being allocated a room on the top floor. It contained a single item of furniture – an iron bedstead with wire base – which Frank Heggarty and I, who got there first, promptly appropriated. It seemed fitting that the Auberge des Rois – Inn of the Kings – became the Officers' Mess!

All ranks were warned that, before pulling out, the Germans had carried out extensive and indiscriminate booby-trapping and everything in and about the buildings should be carefully examined before touching. Despite this, only sloppy German workmanship saved one of the Sick Bay staff from injury when he opened an oven door and out came a length of fuse with pull-igniter attached, which hadn't been securely fastened to the explosive charge. Two men of 'X' Troop weren't so lucky and were injured by a booby-trap fitted to the roller shutter of an empty house they were investigating.

Once settled in, the CO's first Daily Orders stressed that the Commando was in De Haan for 'rigorous training and general toughening-up'; it was understood by all that a specific operation was already in mind. Details of German defence works were needed for training purposes, so the Intelligence Sections of both 41 and 48 Commandos collaborated in surveying those in the neighbourhood and preparing plans. Two Royal Engineers clearing a beach to be used in training were badly wounded when a mine they were working on exploded.

Morning parades were re-instigated; boots and uniforms had to be clean, webbing equipment scrubbed and there was a ceremonial sentry at the entrance to Commando Headquarters, to the great delight of children when he sprang to attention to salute officers. The DRs received a jolt when told that they too were expected to get fit and a few route marches and other strenuous pursuits were interspersed with delivering messages.

Twice a day there was a round of delivery runs beginning with the various Headquarters offices in De Haan, then continuing along the coast to Wenduyne, inland to Nieuwmunster, where other elements of the Brigade were stationed, and on to Brigade HQ in Bruges. The round trip back to base involved some 25 miles. Brigade had taken over a medieval convent near the town centre, standing close to a main road but completely screened from view by a frontage of tall buildings of a very much more recent vintage. Access was gained via an unremarkable archway in the street façade, but, only a few score yards further on you had travelled back in time some six hundred years to a secluded courtyard bounded by shady cloisters, with a statuary centre-piece.

Shortly after our arrival those of us who frequently travelled from De Haan to Wenduyne began to notice that unfamiliar tracked vehicles were being accumulated on the lower slopes of the dunes bounding the seaward side of the road. In shape they were similar to Churchill tanks, but had open 'holds' in place of gun turrets and were very lightly armoured. They were parked nose to tail in tight rows and completely covered with camouflage netting. In time we learned that they were amphibious landing craft, officially designated 'Landing Vehicles, Tracked' (LVTs) but generally known as Buffaloes. They stood eight feet high, were twenty-five feet long, and could carry twenty-four fully equipped men or three tons of supplies on land at twenty-five miles an hour and in water, floating with a freeboard of barely two feet, at about five knots.

The vehicles being assembled near Wenduyne belonged to the 11th Battalion Royal Tank Regiment and were arriving as and when released from active operations with the Canadian 3rd

126

Division, little more than twenty miles away. Buffaloes had proved invaluable in a slogging battle to clear the Germans from their last foothold south of the river, the flooded countryside at the mouth of the Scheldt estuary, around the port of Breskens, the so-called 'Breskens Pocket'. Their next job was already lined up – to carry commandos ashore, somewhere.

A smaller amphibious tracked vehicle, the 'Weasel', was also to be used in the coming operation. Although sometimes looked upon as an amphibious jeep, there was no development nor manufacturing link between the two vehicles, the only similarity being their size and carrying capability. The load limit of a Weasel was about half a ton, including crew, and, like the Buffalo, it could travel at 25 mph on land and 5 knots in water. Weasels were to be handled by our own drivers and those selected for the job began training immediately. Paradoxically, one of them was 'Pegler' Palmer, driver of Gunga Din, the unit's water truck, so he who had spent much of his time transporting water was now learning to drive a vehicle where water would be transporting him!

For the Fighting Troops a much more strenuous programme had been drawn up by Major Wood, the Second-in-Command. This covered every aspect of fitness and military training and laid down precisely what each Troop would do every morning and afternoon during the coming weeks. They were even required to indulge in sessions of battle drill or Troop attacks before attending noon church parade on Sundays.

A large proportion of the programme, naturally, involved weapon handling. First, 'zeroing', i.e. having the sights checked and adjusted, then the whole range of small arms weapons (automatic pistol, rifle, Bren gun, Tommy gun, Sten gun, Vickers medium machine-gun) had to be fired to set proficiency standards. For some there were sessions operating flamethrowers, hurling hand-grenades and firing 2" and 3" mortars, while others handled explosives – fixing beehives onto concrete fortifications, thrusting pole charges through gun slits and detonating Bangalore torpedoes to explode mines and blow gaps in barbed wire defences.

An important weapon in the Commando's armoury was its only anti-tank weapon, the PIAT mortar – an acronym for Projector, Infantry, Anti-Tank. This was a very effective close-range weapon capable of penetrating 4 inches of armour plate at 120 yards, although, despite its name, it wasn't strictly a mortar at all, being fired in the prone position by means of a trigger. Tragically, practice with this weapon at De Haan resulted in four of our men being killed – three when a bomb exploded prematurely and the fourth when another ricocheted off the German strongpoint being used as a target.

In addition to the training programme within the Commando there were exercises involving the rest of the Brigade and other units earmarked to take part in the operation. Tank support would be provided by Shermans and Flails of the 1st Lothian and Border Yeomanry, and there would also be armoured vehicles of 87 Assault Squadron RE, while the Canadian First Army Corps would be providing medical teams. As it was to be, largely, a mechanized landing, everyone had to become accustomed to working with both Buffaloes and Weasels – loading them, boarding them and getting in and out of them in a hurry!

As usual, no sooner had the Commando become settled than the 'buzzmongers' became active. As usual too, each of them knew just where the landing was going to take place and could forecast that it would be either 'a piece of cake' or 'a bloody suicide job'. One of the names frequently bandied about was Walcheren, the Dutch island at the mouth of the River Scheldt, but it was given no more credence than a number of others being put forward.

Walcheren had 'hit the headlines' in the English-speaking Press on 3 October, a week after our move from Dunkirk, as the 'Tea saucer island'. On that day, at the instigation of General Guy Symonds, Commander of the Canadian First Army, No. 84 Bomber Group RAF had blasted the first gap in the sea dyke at Westkapelle. As the greater part of Walcheren lies below sea level, once the protective dyke was breached the North Sea poured in and much of the interior of the island 'filled up like a saucer of tea'. The great military importance of the island of Walcheren lay in the fact that German gun batteries, particularly those at Westkapelle and Domburg, prevented vessels from entering the River Scheldt, thus preventing the use of the port of Antwerp, which had been in Allied hands since September.

As day succeeded day, with the fighting echelon of the Commando deeply involved in the training programme, the off-duty DRs were able to exploit their mobility to explore adjacent

128

towns and villages. With three months' back pay to draw on, they were also able to investigate what lay behind such signs as 'Café' and 'Bieren'. On one such occasion, in a café near Jabbeke, our group was surprised to be greeted by the girl behind the bar, not in French nor Flemish, but in English! She was an American, about nineteen years old, who had been staying with relatives in the area at the outbreak of war and had been unable to return home.

Such local runs were generally made in the company of two or three others, but I also indulged in more protracted solo trips – generally on the pretext of 'trying her out', after some minor repair or adjustment! The first of these was a probe of about 35 miles to Ghent, which was subsequently extended by another 20 miles to St Niklaas. The most protracted was a 150-mile round trip to Brussels, where peace had already broken out, but the most memorable was a tour of some of the places familiar to my father during the First World War.

This one took in 'Wipers' (Ypres), with its sadly impressive Menin Gate bearing the names of tens of thousands of men with no known graves, then on to 'Popperingee' (Poperinghe) and Armentières, passing many awesomely extensive military cemeteries en route. In stationers' shops, too, I found evidence of that earlier war. Picture postcards of Hellfire Corner, Plugstreet Wood, Hill 60 and The Menin Road were still on sale. As I rode back to De Haan in the dusk of an autumn evening I could almost imagine the shades of my father's generation of soldiers travelling at my shoulder.

At De Haan I renewed contact with Ben, our Moroccan volunteer. In the moves of the Commando immediately before, during and after the breakout from Normandy, our paths hadn't crossed, but, with the Unit settled down again, Ben's cheerful face was once more in evidence. We had only a few brief encounters and never got back to more language-swapping sessions, but there was always a spontaneous exchange of greetings on meeting. By this time Ben was unquestionably 'on the strength', attached to the Intelligence Section, presumably because some of them spoke a little French. Sadly, some weeks later, it was probably after my first leave, I returned to the unit to learn that Ben had been fooling around with a primed hand-grenade when the pin came out and he had been evacuated to hospital, badly wounded. I never saw him again.

During the last days of October the likelihood of the island of Walcheren being our objective seemed to have evaporated. Breskens had been captured by the Canadian 3rd Division on the 22nd and units of the 52nd (Lowland) Division had then crossed the East Scheldt to land on South Beveland. It is ironic that the 52nd, specifically trained for a possible invasion of Norway and bearing the word 'Mountaineer' on their shoulder flashes, should first go into action on the flattest terrain in Europe! By the 26th they had linked up with the Canadian 2nd Division, attacking along the peninsula, and these combined British and Canadian forces were nearing the causeway linking Walcheren with the mainland. It looked as though the island was already 'in the bag' and that No. 4 Special Service Brigade would be going elsewhere.

By then it was known that only four DRs would be going with the assault force – Tuckwell, Thompson, Barker and Mitchell. Also, that there would be no motorbikes; the Despatch Riders would be primarily employed as 'ammunition wallahs', getting ammunition up to the forward Troops. Colt automatics would be left behind and the four of us were to be issued with rifles and bayonets. Like all those taking part in the landing, we painted our names on big packs, filled with a change of clothing, greatcoat, etc, which would go ashore sometime after the initial landing.

Towards the end of October the 'FOO' and 'FOB' people joined us. These were the teams of the Forward Observation Officer (Royal Artillery) and the Forward Officer, Bombardment (Royal Navy) who would call up and direct artillery fire when and where required. Their arrival was invariably an indication that an operation was 'on' and that its start would not be long delayed.

On Friday 27 October Colonel Palmer breezed through the Orderly Room in the Pension du Nord with a bundle of maps under his arm. As he passed a group of us – DRs and Signallers – he teasingly remarked, 'I bet you'd like to have a look at these!' The 'top brass' already knew what our objective was to be, but the rest would have to wait until De Haan had been turned into a top security camp before being let into the secret. Royal Engineers were erecting a high wire-mesh fence to enclose the entire northern part of the town between the tramway and the sea. When complete, and with everyone to be involved brought inside, the gates would be closed and armed patrols would ensure that no one entered or left until the planned operation was under way.

On the morning of Sunday 29 October it was announced that De Haan would be sealed off that evening. Killer and I were off-duty and, after lunch, we decided to pay a farewell visit to a café in Breedene, about a mile from Ostend, which, due largely to the landlord's two pretty daughters, had become the favourite retreat of Despatch Riders. We left the café in good time to get back for the evening meal, but I collected a puncture. It was decided that Killer should carry on to ensure that some food was kept for us, while I set about the repair. Before the job was half-way through, however, he was back – our bikes were to be loaded after all and all HQ had been hunting high and low for us! I sweated to complete the repair and rushed back, but found that the loading had had to go ahead and another machine had been sent. Fortunately, in the overall 'flap' of preparations, there were no repercussions; the motorcycles were never landed, perhaps they never even left Ostend.

On Monday 30 October, with the 'concentration camp' of De Haan sealed, it was safe for us to be 'put in the picture'. We were marched across the road to the Auberge des Rois, where an Operations Rooms had been set up, and briefed for the coming landing. Only then was it learned that the objective was, after all, to be the capture of Walcheren.

In retrospect, it is difficult to comprehend why the operation which No. 4 Special Service Brigade and units of the 52nd Lowland Division were called upon to undertake on 1 November 1944 had ever been allowed to become necessary. Had the pressure on the Germany Army, fleeing in chaos through the coastal regions of Holland and Belgium in the early days of September, been kept up for only a few more days it wouldn't have been required.

On 4 September, after a swift advance from Brussels, tanks of the British Second Army had entered Antwerp. The Belgian Resistance Army, alerted in advance by a seemingly innocent message broadcast by the BBC – *Pour François: La lune est clair* – (For François: the moon is clear), had risen against the German garrison and, heroically, had managed to preserve the vast docks area of the city intact.

Next day, Tuesday 5 September, the Dutch of South Beveland, seeing their roads crammed with retreating Germans and knowing that advancing Allied armies were almost on their doorstep, believed that their day of liberation was at hand. They went crazy with joy and chased their oppressors from towns and villages.

But the rapid Allied advance came to an abrupt and unexpected halt. Had it progressed only a dozen miles beyond Antwerp the many thousands of Germans streaming across the Scheldt from Breskens to Flushing, and those who had already managed to get across, would have been trapped on the peninsula of South Beveland. The subsequent bloody battles of the next two months, on both sides of the estuary, would have been avoided.

In the event, the retreating Germans, realizing that the pursuit had stopped dead, returned to exact their revenge. The euphoria of that *Dolle Dinsdag* (Mad Tuesday), when the Dutch had belaboured retreating Germans, evaporated and they had to suffer German retribution, bemoaning the halted Allied advance.

Even now it wasn't entirely clear whether the failure to continue the advance beyond Antwerp wasn't due more to chance than having arisen from any need or design. A variety of suggestions have been put forward, such as: time was needed to build up supplies; the British Second Army had become too involved in celebrating the capture of the city; the Canadian First Army, responsible for the extreme left flank of the Allied advance, was more interested in organizing a memorial service for the five hundred of their countrymen who had lost their lives on the ill-fated Dieppe raid of 1942. What cannot be disputed, however, is that General Eisenhower, who had just assumed personal command of all the Allied land forces in place of General Montgomery, was more than 400 miles from the front, near Granville on the Cherbourg Peninsula, nursing a wrenched knee.

Whatever the truth of the matter, the net result was that, for two months, the only major port with the capability of supporting an Allied thrust into Germany had rested in Allied hands, completely intact, but unusable. The German guns on Walcheren guarding the Scheldt estuary made it impossible for ships to approach.

On 30 October 1944, in the 'Ops Room' in the Auberge des Rois, individual Troops of 41 Commando took it in turn to study maps and aerial photographs of Walcheren, were given 'the overall picture' and learned of their own parts in the coming operation.

Four gaps had been blown in the sea dyke protecting the island

132

from the North Sea. In addition to the first one at Westkapelle on the western tip of the island, there was another immediately to the west of Flushing, a third at Rammekens between Flushing and the causeway, and a fourth just west of Veere on the north-east coast. In consequence, most of the centre of the island was under water, which had inundated some minor German positions and also seriously hampered the manoeuvrability of the island's defenders by confining them to such parts as still remained above water, but heavy coastal batteries, sited on the massive sea dyke, were unaffected.

The seaborne assault was to be carried out by No. 4 Special Service Brigade (later re-styled 'Commando Brigade') under Brigadier 'Jumbo' Leicester. It comprised four Commandos, each of less than 450 men – No. 4 (Army) and Nos. 41, 47 and 48 (Royal Marines). The Belgian and Norwegian Troops of No. 10 Inter-Allied Commando (about 60 men in each) were to be attached to 41.

The attack was to be three-pronged. No. 4 Commando would make an early morning crossing of the Scheldt in LCAs (Landing Craft Assault) to land at Flushing, (this operation was code-named INFATUATE I) with the Royal Marines going ashore on both sides of the four hundred-yard wide gap in the dyke at Westkapelle (INFATUATE II).

No. 4 Commando would be spearheading a follow-up force of elements of 52 Division, whose task would be to strike towards the causeway and link up with the forces already attacking it from South Beveland. At Westkapelle 41 would land to the north of the gap, capture Westkapelle and the neighbouring heavy coast defence battery, then push on to Domburg and beyond. The task of 47 and 48, going ashore to the south of the gap, would be to deal with the German batteries between there and the Flushing gap, where they would link up with No. 4 Commando.

The attack of 41 Commando was to be 'double-barreled'. 'B' and 'P' Troops would land from LCI(S)s (Landing Craft Infantry, Small) on the face of the dyke immediately to the west of the gap, then move towards the gun battery W15. 'S' Troop would also land there and set up their mortars on the dyke top to give support where required. Five minutes later HQ, 'A', 'X' and 'Y' Troops would go ashore in Buffaloes and Weasels from Tank Landing Craft which would sail through the gap and beach themselves at the edge of the bomb-shattered town.

For INFATUATE II the Royal Navy would be laying down a massive softening-up barrage, to be initiated by the 15" guns of the battleship *Warspite* and the monitors *Erebus* and *Roberts*. As the range shortened, smaller naval vessels would join in, then close inshore support would be provided by a special squadron of small craft, 'firing down the gun slits'. All in all, the fleet carrying the assault force to Westkapelle would total over 180 vessels.

All of this was reassuring, but eyebrows were raised when it was revealed that the assault was to take place in full daylight. H-hour had been set at 0945 to ensure that the pilots of rocket-firing Typhoon aircraft would have a clear view of their targets. It was also disconcerting to learn of the 150-feet-high lantern tower at Westkapelle, which would ensure that the German defenders would have full knowledge of the size of the attacking force long before any vessel came within range.

While the Commando seaborne assaults on Walcheren were proceeding, the Canadian and 52 Division forces in South Beveland would be attacking the island via the causeway. This narrow strip of land, wide enough only to accommodate a two-lane carriageway, a railway line and a cycle track, some fifteen feet above sea level and twelve hundred yards long, provided the only link between island and mainland. Even as the Commando was being briefed a series of costly head-on attacks along the causeway had been under way, but without success.

INFATUATE had been set for Wednesday 1 November, two days hence, and we would leave De Haan next day, Tuesday 31 October, to join our Buffaloes, already loaded and waiting on LCTs in Ostend harbour. In the evening, when everyone had been briefed, the Officers of the Commando invited the Senior NCOs of the unit to the Auberge des Rois for 'Good Luck' drinks. I was Duty DR in the SDO just across the road, without the possibility of any such conviviality, so was feeling a little 'Bolshie' about it. Then a message came through for the Signals Officer. It was quite innocuous and totally irrelevant at that time, but I saw my chance. Donning riding gear and crash helmet, I walked across to the Officers' Mess. Then, as I eased my way into a maelstrom of boisterous, loud-talking, drinking humanity, I began calling out,

'Message for the Signals Officer! Message for the Signals Officer!' Before he had been located the anticipated had happened; one of the throng had started shouts of, 'How about a drink for the Dog Rodger?'

After lunch next day 'the Walcheren party' was fallen in outside HQ while those who had not been chosen to go looked on with a mixture of relief and chagrin which we could very well appreciate. It was something of a surprise to learn that there was to be no transport, so we marched off, to lots of unprintable advice and an exchange of vulgar 'V' signs, which we knew was the Rear Party's way of saying, 'Keep your heads down, lads, and come back safe'. Two hours later we were marching through the bustling, café-lined streets of Ostend, thronged with off-duty military personnel. The wags had their inevitable last quips, 'Hey, Sarge! How about a quick one?' 'Can I grab a couple of bottles for the boat?'

At the docks we were directed to our allocated LCTs, then assigned to the specific Buffaloes which would carry us ashore next morning. I was among those given the rearmost vehicle on the port side, an unenviable position, as it could very well be the last one to move ashore. In the well of the LCT we had to squeeze our way along narrow alleyways between the LVTs to reach our vehicles. Their gunwales were almost three feet above our heads and, at such close quarters, they looked huge monsters. Using the tracks, we clambered up the vertical side to find that the hold was already full, almost to the top, with boxes of ammunition, jerricans of petrol and other stores. We would be steaming towards the enemy guns perched on top of powder kegs.

After dumping weapons and equipment on the vehicles we were given 'the freedom of the ship', although there was very little of that – no more than a small upper deck, with a few capstans and winches, the open tank deck where the Buffaloes and Weasels were parked and the ablutions. In the early dusk of an end of October afternoon there was little time, and not much light, to study the nearby vessels which would accompany us, but they were reassuring. There were LCTs loaded with Sherman tanks and flail tanks to detonate mines on the beach, AVREs (Armoured Vehicles Royal Engineers) to attack concrete fortifications and armoured bulldozers to clear the way if Buffaloes couldn't negotiate a beach exit.

After an evening meal of the inevitable 'Compo' one blanket per man was issued, which was as much as our Royal Navy hosts could provide towards easing the overnight accommodation. Harry Tuckwell and I chose the upper deck and decided to squeeze into the confined space between a winch drum and its housing, which we felt would at least shield us from the cold breeze created by the craft's forward motion during the night. We were asleep before very long, but stirred into semi-consciousness in the early hours of the morning when the reverberating throb of engines signalled that we were on our way. The island of Walcheren lay only thirty-five miles distant and 'tomorrow is another day'.

Chapter 11

THE WALCHEREN LANDING

For Harry and me, squeezed together for warmth in the winch drum housing, the night passed quietly and not too uncomfortably. It was still dark when we were roused to stand in line for our turn to make use of the ablutions, then wait for a breakfast of tinned sausage and Compo biscuits, washed down with tea. Once those preliminaries were out of the way, it was 'All right, on your Buffaloes and get rigged!' – despite the fact that it would be more than two hours before we went ashore.

At first light that Wednesday morning, 1 November 1944, it was heartening to receive confirmation that our LCT had not been travelling alone in the darkness. Perched on top of the load of military supplies in our Buffalo we had an unrestricted view ahead and, as visibility gradually increased, more and more vessels came into view. With full daylight a vast armada of vessels could be seen, spaced out some hundreds of yards apart, covering many square miles of ocean, the more distant ones little more than dark smudges on the horizon; we appeared to be somewhere in the middle.

The impressive fleet moving towards the assault on Westkapelle, designated Naval Force 'T', under the command of Captain A.F. Pugsley RN, totalled 182 vessels. However, unlike the earlier landings of Sicily, Salerno and D-Day, when many tens of thousands of men had been put ashore, the total to be involved in Operation INFATUATE II would be only about two thousand. This made the overall ship-to-man ratio of 1:12 far greater than on any of those

WALCHEREN
November 1944

Battery W 19
Battery W 18
Battery W 17
Domburg
Vrouwenpolder
GAP
Veere
Battery W 15
Westkapelle
GAP
W 13
Zoutelande
Middelburg
Arnemuiden
Nieuwland
Flooded areas
W 4
Rammekens
GAP
Miles
0 1 2 3
Flushing
GAP
West Scheldt
Breskens

previous occasions, a consequence of the fact that the assault of Westkapelle was to be largely mechanized.

More than a hundred Buffaloes and some eighty Weasels would carry most of the men ashore, together with their food, stores and reserves of ammunition, and these were being transported in LCTs (Landing Craft, Tank) of only 600 tons displacement. Other LCTs carried tanks of the 1st Lothian and Border Yeomanry, of the 79th Armoured Division and the Armoured Vehicles Royal Engineers (AVREs), which, for this operation, were equipped with bridging equipment and fascines to cross streams and ditches, and also armoured bulldozers to create exits from the beach if need be.

Close inshore support would be provided by twenty-seven similarly sized vessels of the SSEF (Support Squadron, Eastern Flank), a naval unit which had been created specifically to protect the eastern flank of the vast amount of sea traffic needed to transport, reinforce and supply the Allied armies involved in the invasion of France. The craft were crewed by six hundred officers and men of the Royal Navy, with five hundred Royal Marines to handle the guns. The squadron, under the command of Commander K.A.

18/19. German battery (W 15) on the dyke at Westkapelle after naval bombardment *(H. Sakkers and J. Tuynman)*.

20. Lieutenant D.F. Murray (later Sir Donald Murray KCVO CMG DL) a Section Commander of 'A' Troop, outside a German bunker on Walcheren. *(Charles Leonard)*

21. Royal Marines returning from a patrol on the Maas Front. *(IWM)*

22. The author, second from right, outside his Dutch billet in Goes, Zeeland, in May 1945 with Marine Barker and the children of the Smallegange family.

23. Wesel, Germany, 19 May 1945. *(Photo by Author)*

24. Königs Allee, Düsseldorf, 19 May 1945: the only feature amid a wasteland of rubble.

25. Essen, 19 May 1945: the ruins of a Krupp factory. *(Photo by Author)*

26. The author in Cologne, 20 May 1945. The cathedral is in the background.

7. Cologne: the wrecked Hohenzollern Bridge. *(Photo by Author)*

28. Cologne: the skeleton of the railway station. *(Photo by Author)*

29. Cologne, the Cathedral Square: a German tank is just part of the litter. *(Photo by Author)*

. Parachuting course at Ringway, Manchester, August 1945. The Author with Marine Leggett.

31. Taking part in a Brigade motorcycle rally at Erkenschwick, September 1945.

. Major William Cunningham DSO RM, acting-CO of the unit, presenting a contingent of 41 Commando to Prince Bernhard of the Netherlands at a Royal Navy week in Rotterdam, August 1945. *(Charles Leonard)*

33/34. Dortmund, September 1945. *(Photos by Author)*

Sellar RN, hadn't long been released from duties in the Channel and men had to be recalled from leave to sail for Walcheren.

The bulk of the fire power of the squadron was housed in various adaptations of LCT hulls – LCG(L)s (Landing Craft, Gun (Large)) fitted with 4.7 inch guns, LCFs (Landing Craft, Flak) with 2-pounder pompoms and 20mm Oerlikon anti-aircraft guns, and the deadly LCT(R)s (Landing Craft Tank (Rocket)), of which there were five at Walcheren. The last-named launched 1080 (Mark 1), or 936 (Mark 2), 29lb rockets, with 7lb bursters, in a rapid succession of salvoes of twenty-four. The result was a carpet of missiles, one to every 100 square yards of ground, over an area of some 700 by 150 yards. There were also two smaller types of vessel, LCSs (Landing Craft, Support) with quick-firing 6-pounders, Oerlikons and machine guns and, in action for the first time, LCG(M)s (Medium) armed with quick-firing 17-pounders.

The invasion fleet was steaming unhurriedly towards the rising sun, which soon cleared away the early morning mists, giving almost unlimited visibility at sea level, although the sky overhead continued to be obscured by almost total cloud cover. We were still some fifteen miles away, with about one and a half hours before touchdown, when we gained our first sighting of the Westkapelle tower. It was no more than the top of the lantern, seeming to poke out of the sea on the horizon dead ahead, the rest of its 150-foot-tall bulk still hidden from our view by the curvature of the earth.

The craft moved inexorably forward in comparative silence, the only sounds being the low throb of the engines, the slap of the sea against blunt bows and our own small talk as we squatted on the military stores piled high in the Buffaloes. Minute by minute the lantern tower grew taller as it emerged above the sea and was soon standing like an admonitory finger, attracting us towards itself like a powerful magnet.

We had been briefed on the overall pattern of the assault. While the SSEF engaged the shore batteries, LCI(S)s (Landing Craft Infantry, (Small)) would put 'B', 'P' and 'S' Troops of 41 Commando ashore on the face of Westkapelle dyke, immediately to the north of the breach. 'B' and 'P' would clear the northern part of the town, then move towards battery W15, on the dyke top a few hundred yards away, leaving 'S' to set up their 3" mortars and machine guns to cover the landing of the rest of the

139

Commando. Meanwhile, the LCTs carrying the armoured vehicles and amphibians would be heading for the breach in the dyke and, five minutes after first wave, 'A', 'X' and HQ would go ashore to secure the southern part of Westkapelle, including the lantern tower. 'Y' and the attached Belgian and Norwegian Troops of 10 I-A Commando would land, in reserve, 25 minutes later.

The craft carrying 47 and 48 Commandos, together with Brigade Headquarters and Canadian medical units, were on the starboard flank of the task force, heading towards the southerly edge of the Westkapelle gap, their 'aiming point' being the ruins of a radar dish on the dyke top. The initial assault there would be by 48, followed by Brigade HQ and the medics, while 47 would land in support one hour later. Somewhere in the North Sea, far to port of the task force, the 'heavies', the battleship *Warspite* and the monitors *Erebus* and *Roberts*, would be heading towards their bombardment positions.

As the lantern tower continued to grow out of the sea ahead of us we could imagine German defenders having a leisurely breakfast before making final preparations for our reception. For us there was ample time to consider an unexpected snippet of 'information', that RAF airfields in Britain were fog-bound, making it impossible for aircraft to take off; therefore we couldn't expect any heavy bomber 'softening-up' prior to the landing.

At the time this announcement was accepted as 'Just the luck of the draw', but it transpired later that Air Marshals Tedder and Harris had flatly refused the Canadian Army's request for such assistance. Tedder is reported to have referred to the Walcheren defences as 'a part-worn battery' and added that the Canadians were 'drugged with bombs'. 'Bomber' Harris, for his part, is reported to have boasted that, after all the bombs dropped there, 'he could have taken the island with his batman'. It was a great pity that those two weren't with us. Nevertheless the fog in England had been real and it is possible that bombers couldn't have taken off in any case. More significant at the time was that the assistance of rocket-firing Tiffies, for whose benefit the attack had been scheduled for full daylight, also appeared to be in doubt.

With the mesmerizing Westkapelle tower pulling us forward, the overall quietude prevailed until about 0820 hrs when action was initiated by the *Warspite* and the two monitors opening fire. Far

140

away to the north we saw the muzzle flashes of their guns and fluffy white mushrooms began to spurt above the horizon to the left of the Westkapelle tower. There was no land visible, but the position of the shell bursts in relation to the tower indicated targets on the north-west coast of the island, which was defended by the string of German strongpoints and gun batteries, from W15 at Westkapelle to W19 at the northern tip of the island, all of which it was 41's job to liquidate. Ironically, in the W15 and W19 batteries there were a total of nine 3.7 inch guns, which had been captured from the British in 1940. This may have been the source of Tedder's reference to a 'part-worn battery'. Not until about half a minute after the muzzle flashes did the booms of the fifteen-inch guns reach us, followed quickly by the rumbling crumps of exploding one-ton shells.

For the next hour the fleet sailed irrevocably on, with the lantern tower growing taller by the minute. We could only sit and watch the spectacle, as more and more guns came into action, until the billowing puffs of exploding shells had built up into an ominous white curtain wall along the horizon. This began to grow darker in colour from the smoke of burning buildings, and then from ships, as the van of the task force sailed within range. The crashing explosions ashore and afloat grew in number and intensity. Waterspouts from bursting shells could be seen dotting the sea ahead.

At first all this was happening some distance from us, but, all too soon, our section of the convoy came within range. Shells began falling among the nearby ships and the sea ahead became a jumble of burning landing craft, shell splashes, smoke and noises. Walcheren, perhaps a mile away, was visible only as a low smudge on the surface of the sea, when the whole shoreline appeared to erupt into a continuous wall of waterspouts. My heart probably wasn't the only one to skip a few beats at the thought of having to pass through that sort of barrage until someone remarked 'Rockets!' It was a huge relief to realize that what we had seen had been the effect of our own rocket craft. It later transpired that a German shell had caused the premature release of an entire launch of rockets, which had fallen into the sea. There was another rocket mishap later, when a control fault caused salvoes to fall short, among our own craft, but enough rockets were on target to have a dramatic effect upon the enemy and many dazed and bemused Germans were taken prisoner as a result.

During our approach the SSEF had been moving ahead to engage the German shore batteries at close range, consciously attracting enemy fire upon themselves, and the squadron was badly mauled in the process. Of the original twenty-seven craft nine were sunk and only five escaped being completely disabled. The two craft fitted with 17-pounders, the first of their type to go into action during the war, had beached themselves close to German fortifications and both vessels, as well as most of their crews, were lost.

It must have been towards the end of the SSEF's sacrifice that our section of the assault force sailed within range of the smaller enemy guns. Shells began to shriek down, splashing into the sea around nearby vessels, sending up spouts of spray and solid water. Craft ahead could be seen to have been hit, were on fire, some belching smoke and drifting helplessly. Despite the shelling, there was no suggestion of taking evasive action. The landing craft held course, steaming steadily and exasperatingly slowly towards the shore.

Unknown to us, a stroke of good fortune had eased the final stages of our approach. Battery W13 to the south of the gap, comprising four 150mm guns and the one responsible for much of the havoc to the SSEF, had run out of ammunition, which couldn't be replenished because of the flooding. Fortunately, too, the Typhoons had after all been able to take off from fog-bound England. They came swooping low over the coast, the high-pitched scream of their engines and the deadly swishes of their rockets adding to the general turmoil of noise.

Throughout it all every ear had been attuned to detect that short, sharp, high-pitched swissshh which we knew meant that a shell was going to plummet down uncomfortably close. Each time that happened our bodies reacted automatically, but, sitting as we were, out in the open, perched on a load of military supplies, all that was possible by way of self-preservation was to hunch our shoulders and keep our heads down.

The approach of the Infantry Landing Craft carrying the dyke Assault Party had been more to the north than had been expected, putting them in clearer view of W15, and in consequence they had attracted more enemy fire than anticipated. Twice the craft were forced to turn away, first when some rockets fell among them and

142

then when two were hit and casualties were suffered. In consequence the initial landing didn't take place until 1012 hours, 27 minutes behind schedule.

The LCTs carrying the rest of the Commando also approached the gap in the dyke from the north, with smoke from burning shore installations drifting seawards towards them. The craft then made a sharp turn to port, to pass through the smoke and into the 400-yard-wide stretch of North Sea pouring through the breach. To the left came a brief glimpse of a wrecked windmill perched on the crest of the stone-faced dyke, while, to the right, the bombed radar station was clearly visible on the far side of the gap. All forward vision was cut off by the high landing ramp, where a matelot was positioned to ensure that it dropped rapidly on touchdown.

By this time most of the 'outside' noises were being drowned out by the impatient revving-up of Buffalo and Weasel engines. Drivers had been given the start-up signal and were eager to move off the instant the order was given. Like the rest of us, they were itching to get the hell out of there to the relative safety of dry land.

Then came another abrupt swing to port as the helmsman squared-up for landing and, almost immediately, the bows crunched ashore; the bow doors flopped open and the ramp splashed down into the shallows of a sandy beach which only a few weeks earlier had been rear gardens. Landing vehicles began to trundle ashore and we gained our first close-up view of Holland a few hundred yards away – the rear elevation of bomb-wrecked houses lining the main street of Westkapelle.

As the deckmaster regulated the rapid exit of Weasels and Buffaloes engine noises lessened and we again heard the swishes and bursts of shells. Our vehicle, being at the rear of the LCT, was last to clatter down the ramp, but we were finally ashore on Walcheren. Surprisingly, the drive up-beach was exceedingly brief; the LVT stopped more than a hundred yards short of the houses; we dropped the eight feet to the ground and raced across the sand to take shelter against the nearest ones.

Surprisingly too, there wasn't a great deal of activity going on. The LCT which we had just left was already pulling off and one other was still disgorging LVTs. Three or four Buffaloes had been hit and were abandoned in odd positions here and there. There was a dead

Weasel in the shallows at the water's edge and a knocked-out flail tank lay half-way between the sea and the town. The rest of the Buffaloes must have moved somewhere inland. We could see that a few craft had been sunk in shallow water and others were beached at awkward angles against the shore on the far side of the breach. No shells were coming very close to us, however, thanks to the fact, as we learned later, that the barrels of nearby German guns could not be depressed sufficiently to enable them to be brought to bear.

As we crouched against walls of houses, awaiting the next order, a Buffalo, moving rapidly up the beach towards us, suddenly stopped dead; all aboard her precipitately baled out and headed for cover. It wasn't apparent just what had caused the demise of that particular vehicle, but there was no time to ponder the question. Hardly had we caught our breath, still thanking our lucky stars for having seen us ashore unscathed, than we were summoned forward on to the road at the front of the houses.

We quickly formed up in single file, facing the familiar lantern tower, now visible for its full height at the end of the street perhaps half a mile away. Just as the Troop received the order to move off a British military policeman, webbing and gauntlets gleaming white, appeared on the far pavement, heading in the opposite direction. To the nimble brain of Frank Barker it was a heaven-sent opportunity. As we started marching, he sang out, in his perky Cockney accent, 'All coppers are BAH-stards!' and, raked with laughter, our column moved off, leaving a frustrated MP glaring impotently after us.

That main street of Westkapelle was little more than a succession of bomb and shell craters passing through a devastation of ruined houses. At one point, where probably a 4,000-pounder had landed, the carriageway, footways and flanking houses had been completely obliterated. In their place was an enormous crater, seven or eight feet deep and about thirty in diameter with a pool of water at the bottom, and edged with a jumble of brick rubble and splintered wood. Beyond the empty shells of buildings lining the left-hand side of the road there was nothing but an undulating wasteland of bricks and roof timbers, with only a handful of houses remaining recognizable as such. Close behind the houses to our right lapped the waters of an extension of the North Sea which now covered most of the low-lying island.

We moved forward slowly and spasmodically with intermittent minor explosions and bursts of small arms fire coming from ahead, as the Fighting Troops searched the ruins of the town, while the sounds of spasmodic heavier explosions reached us from the rear. On reaching the lantern tower we found that it stood at a staggered junction of four roads, although two of them led only into an inland sea, and our small party was on its own. At close quarters the massive brick-built structure looked higher than ever and much less slender than it had appeared from the sea. The entrance door, at the top of a short flight of external steps, stood half-open and I was one of a party of six detailed off to 'Search it!'

Thoughts of Schmeisser machine-pistols, booby traps and hand-grenades flashed through my mind as we started up the stairs, automatically doing it all 'according to the book', with covering parties and search parties leap-frogging from floor to floor, kicking doors open, weapons at the ready. The building was devoid of Germans, but the indescribable litter of clothing, equipment and general rubbish in every room told of a panic exodus. On reaching the top, puffing and panting after our rapid ascent, we found a single Spandau machine gun pointing seawards through the metal balustrading around the lantern. The view from the top was largely of sea, but there was only time to catch a glimpse; no sooner had we signalled the 'All clear!' than the bawling voice of authority came back up to us, 'All right then, don't loaf around up there! Come down out of it'. We trooped back down the stairs, glancing ruefully into the littered rooms where there would undoubtedly have been many interesting souvenirs.

Back at ground level again there was no immediate rush to go anywhere, so we wondered why we had been brought down so quickly. Later we learned that, after a few Piat bombs and an exchange of small arms fire, the garrison of the tower had surrendered to 'A' Troop some time before we had arrived. We were allowed to 'Carry on smoking' and gazed over an apparently limitless inland sea, dotted with the flooded farms and homes of the people who had lived there. In most cases no more than chimneys and ridge tiles were visible, but here and there the top storey of a 'Dutch bungalow' protruded above the water. Single lines of the skeletons of trees showed field boundaries and two rows close together marked the routes of submerged roads. Then came the order 'Out pipes!' and we began to retrace our steps through Westkapelle until reaching the vicinity of the huge bomb crater, where we were fallen out again to 'Wait here'. It was probably around noon by that time.

Another unexplained wait before we marched back through the ruins of the seaward side of the town, parts of which merged into the sea without any demarcation other than the line of seaweed and flotsam left by the receding tide. We crossed the 'foreshore' and climbed to the top of the dyke protecting the north-western coast of the island. A knocked-out armoured bulldozer stood half-way up the stone-clad face close to the slumped ruins of the windmill we had seen from the LCT.

It was in that area that Sergeant Musgrove, in command of his section of 'B' Troop after the officer, Lieutenant McKenzie, had been killed during the run-in, captured a German pillbox with a handful of men, for which he was awarded the Military Medal. 'Muscleman Musgrove' we used to call him when he was a lance-corporal PT instructor at Thurlestone in 1941 and I was Orderly Room Clerk. Then we were skirting the shattered masses of concrete which had once been German fortifications, and the more pathetic tangles of wrecked Dutch homes. Everywhere there was an air of deserted emptiness which, as the aftermath of a successful landing, was something completely new to us. On previous occasions the beach areas had been swarming with activity – ships being unloaded, supplies pouring ashore, Royal Engineers constructing steel roadways across the sand – but this time there was nothing. The task force had been put ashore and all craft still seaworthy had been withdrawn. There would be no streams of supplies, no back-up and no reinforcements; the Brigade was on its own.

After only a short march we were fallen out once again and 'put in the picture'. 'B' and 'P' Troops, after clearing the northern part of the town, had come under heavy fire from the W15 battery – a complex of artillery positions and strongpoints around the main coast defence guns. 'Y' Troop had been moved up from reserve to put in a flanking attack from the flooded side of the dyke, under covering fire from the others, and by 1230 the battery had been taken with a 'bag' of 120 prisoners. By the time we arrived on the dunes all German resistance in Westkapelle was at an end and

146

the Commando had been halted by the Brigade Commander to await his order to continue the advance.

The area in which we waited had obviously been an assembly point for Buffaloes. About a dozen of them, knocked out by mortars or shellfire, lay abandoned amongst the dunes and stunted trees. One was completely intact, but a neat hole had been drilled in the narrow bulkhead between driving compartment and hold by a shell which had failed to explode. There was no sign of any casualties, so they had obviously been evacuated to the south side of the gap where the Canadian medical teams and Brigade HQ were located.

The heavy guns of battery W17 at Domburg, less than four miles away, which had continued to fire upon the Westkapelle area, were silenced for a while by a Tiffie rocket strike early in the afternoon, but they came back into action shortly afterwards. That battery was the Commando's next main objective, but it wasn't until 1500 hours that Brigadier Leicester gave the order to move forward. The bulk of the Commando then began to move up the road which topped the broad dyke forming the rim of the flooded island, leaving 'A' and 'S' Troops, together with the two attached Troops of 10 I-A, in defensive positions around Westkapelle.

The Commando was soon passing some shattered casemates of W15. Massive concrete roofs had been sliced off their supporting walls by the devastating concussions of large-calibre shells. Guns, torn from their mountings, were slumped as long fingers of scrap steel in the ruins of their turrets. Gun crews must have been blasted into eternity or lay buried beneath the mangled wreckage, but we passed a remarkable exception. A German gunner sat in the devastation of his concrete emplacement, seemingly untouched by all that had happened around him, but obviously very much dead. Still cradled in his arms was the shell (it was about the size of those I had once handled for the 'twin four-incher' on HMS *Cleveland*, so it was probably a 3.7) he had been about to load into the breech at the very moment he had ceased to exist. 'Better you than me,' was my only thought.

For an infantry unit advancing against unknown enemy defences four miles can be a long way. The total width of the dyke base between the North Sea, hidden from us by sand dunes to our left and the water filling 'the tea saucer island' stretching away to our

147

right and some ten feet below the road, was only a few hundred yards, but that provided ample room for a variety of defensive positions, mines and booby traps, so progress was slow.

HQ Troop was generally positioned behind the leading Troop, which was alternated from time to time, and when the width of dry land widened into more open country 'X' Troop moved out into the dunes on the right flank. Darkness was falling when word came back that Domburg had been reached; the garrisons of both W17 and of a smaller battery immediately inland were surrendering and the advance was being slowed up by having to deal with the large numbers of potentially hostile enemy giving themselves up.

'B' Troop was left to deal with them, while 'P' and 'Y' moved into Domburg, reaching the centre at about 1830 hours. It was then completely dark, apart from the light given by buildings still burning as a result of the naval bombardment. A few German stragglers were dealt with en route, but many others had withdrawn into the wooded sand dune country beyond the town. Major Wood, the 2 i/c, decided that it would be inadvisable to pursue them in the darkness, so 'P' and 'Y' were formed into a defence line between the sea and the edge of the flooded interior, with 'B' to their rear in reserve.

The group of HQ I was with marched back to spend the night in Westkapelle where a two-storey shop premises at the seaward end of the main street had been taken over as a combined Quartermaster's store and HQ billet. Only the ground floor was reasonably intact, although, with neither doors nor any glass in the large windows, it was a cold, draughty place in which to spend a winter's night. Fortunately, we four DRs were able to appropriate the narrow space between a shop counter and an internal wall at the end of which was a fireplace, albeit completely sealed off with a thin steel sheet. We set to to remove it, but, despite strenuous efforts, could do no more than prise free one top corner. Nevertheless, that proved sufficient to enable us to kindle a fire in the hearth and, with an abundance of shattered timber close to hand, the steel was soon glowing warmly.

As we settled down for the night another difference between Walcheren and previous landings became apparent. With no fleet of supply ships lying off-shore, there was no air activity. Enemy action in our area was confined to sessions of shelling, which were

148

noisy, but the explosions remained sufficiently far away to assure us that the guns weren't being trained in our direction. Apart from a cold two-hour stint on watch outside, we passed a reasonably comfortable night, squashed together for warmth behind the shop counter.

It was a raw awakening next morning. The fire was out and the shop was filled with cold, damp air. The QMs managed to produce a mug of tea each and we finished off the remnants of the 24-hour ration pack each man had carried ashore the previous day. Then came a protracted delay, awaiting the anticipated order to move back up the dyke road to re-join the Troops in Domburg. German artillery continued to be very active and we had a clear view across the gap where most of the incoming shells were landing. There we saw that two Buffaloes had been hit and they began to burn; men baled out in a great hurry. Joined by a flurry of other figures, they raced for cover as ammunition in the vehicles began to explode and for half an hour or more we were treated to a spectacular fireworks display. Only later did we learn how deadly that 'entertainment' had been. The exploding mortar bombs and small-arms ammunition had been raking a crowded open beach area and a dozen or more British and Canadians, as well as ten German POWs who had been doing the unloading, had been killed.

We marched back along the dyke road and, just before entering Domburg, gained a glimpse of one of the guns of W17 to the left of the road. A large barrel, no doubt a '220mm-er', poked above a tall hedge, its ragged muzzle end indicating that it had been 'spiked' by its own gunners. Historically, muzzle-loading guns had been rendered useless to the enemy by driving a spike into the vent hole. Then, with the advent of breech-loaders, it became the practice to insert a shell nose first into the muzzle and, with a very long lanyard, fire another round from the breech. Something much less drastic must have been resorted to at W17!

By the time we arrived in Domburg the Fighting Troops were somewhere ahead, pursuing the enemy into a maze of gun emplacements and strongpoints in the wooded dune country to the north-east of the town. They had, however, left behind some two or three hundred prisoners and the DRs were among those assigned to guarding them. The Germans were being held in a large school, where the children's playground, secure behind high metal railings, provided an ideal exercise yard. We assiduously patrolled the perimeter of the building, but felt that our presence was largely symbolic, as none of the inmates appeared to show any interest in wanting to escape, being only too happy to buy, or barter for, cigarettes, knowing that for them the war was over.

We learned that 'X' Troop's advance the previous evening had been held up by determined Germans in a wired-in position on a high dune. As the Marines went forward the Troop Commander, Major Brind-Sheridan, and one Marine had been wounded, but their absence hadn't been immediately noticed when the Troop pulled back. Attempts to reach them during the night had been frustrated when the Germans lit fires near where they lay. Early next morning the garrison broke out to the north, coming under fire from 'B' who inflicted casualties. When the position was occupied the pair were found inside the enemy wire; the Marine was still alive but Major Brind-Sheridan had died of his wounds.

Information had also come through that 47 and 48 Commandos, on the other side of the gap, were having problems in their push towards Zoutelande. 47 Commando alone had lost more than twenty men killed in a series of abortive attacks on battery W4 and 41 was to go to their assistance. The two Troops of 10 I-A were to remain to continue engaging the Germans in the dunes, but the rest were to be pulled back, to march to Westkapelle and cross the gap by Buffalo. That night, while the German prisoners passed an undisturbed night in their intact prison building, we alternated between periods of guard duty in the open and trying to sleep in the empty shell of a house with no windows and no fire.

Next day, 3 November, was my 24th birthday and my fifth in uniform. I was growing old in the Service! On such a day, even in wartime, a Marine on one of HM ships would have had 'sippers' of rum from his messmates and there would have been the likelihood of 'big eats' at the messtable. For Marine Commandos serving ashore there was no rum ration and, for those on Walcheren, few rations of any description. A severe storm was making it impossible for landing craft to cross the ten miles of open water from Breskens to replenish food supplies and we were getting hungry.

During the morning the DRs were abruptly relieved of their POW guard duties, told to assemble equipment, clean weapons and stand by to join the last batch of 41, as riflemen, when it passed through Domburg en route to reinforce 47 and 48. An apparent increase in enemy activity north of Domburg had made the CO of 10 I-A reluctant to remain there with only his own two Troops and, in consequence, two Troops of 41 were to stay with them. Maybe we were 'make-weights'!

The afternoon was well advanced when we tagged on to the end of a column of marching men and it was dusk by the time we were fallen out at the edge of a torrent of black water scudding through the Westkapelle gap. It was high tide and the North Sea was pouring into the interior of the island like a mill race. There was a shortage of LVTs, so it was quite dark by the time our turn, as 'tail-end Charlies', came to be ferried across.

No sooner had we all climbed up the tall side and dropped into the hold than the Buffalo trundled back down the beach and into the swirling water. It was our first trip afloat in an LVT and we were surprised to see just how little freeboard there was between the gunwale and the sloshing sea. As we buffeted the current the windscreen of the driver's compartment was continually awash and every other second it disappeared completely beneath the water. With its 200hp engine racing at full throttle, our noisy splashing craft was tossed about alarmingly, but in only a minute or so we were nearing the indistinct blackness of the far side. Then, completely unexpectedly, the driver switched on powerful headlights and, at a stroke, the indistinct blackness ahead was transformed into ranges of brightly-lit fairytale sand mountains. From that moment the trip became a fantastic Jules Verne journey.

Our roaring amphibian grounded in the shallows, slewed sharply to the left and, engines still at full throttle, began to follow the water's edge along the dyke foot. One track remained splashing through shallow water while the other churned through soft sand a few feet up the slope. As we bucked and plunged forward the headlights would suddenly pick out a grass-tufted hummock, bright and clear against the dark sky. Then that would disappear as we climbed to the top of the rise, with headlights becoming searchlights sweeping the heavens until, flopping over the crest, the Buffalo would crash down into a shallow inlet to send a shower of illuminated spray over the Marines packed in its belly.

High tide had lengthened our watery trip to Zoutelande, as so much more of the island was submerged, but the intriguing journey

151

came to an end much too soon. The LVT crawled clear of the inland sea and came to a halt on a metalled roadway. The dream-like interlude was over and we jumped down. If ever a vehicle was in the right place at the right time it was surely the 'Landing Vehicle, Tracked' on the island of Walcheren in November, 1944.

We marched off and soon found ourselves moving from the raw darkness of a November evening into the cosy brightness of a spacious German bunker, made even more attractive by an issue of hot food. Briefing for the attack next morning began immediately after the meal, but, within minutes, it was terminated by the announcement that the Germans had already surrendered! Our presence in Zoutelande wasn't required after all, so my birthday ended on an unexpected high note, as well as a hot meal, a night of warm safe sleep and the knowledge that there would be no early reveille for a dawn attack next day.

The surrender of W4 and the subsequent link-up by 47 and 48 with No. 4 Commando, who were on the other side of the Flushing gap, had put all of south-western Walcheren in Allied hands. A substantial enemy force, however, still held the centre of the island, including Middelburg, which had remained above water. The north-western part of the island too remained in German hands, so next morning 41 headed back across the gap to resume its operations there.

On reaching Domburg it was learned that the CO of 10 I-A had planned an attack by his joint force for that afternoon, to be supported by two Sherman tanks and two AVREs. These were the only serviceable armoured vehicles to have made it ashore out of the original twenty (2 Shermans, 6 flails, 8 AVREs and 4 armoured bulldozers). Our CO and 2i/c immediately went forward to witness the attack, leaving the rest to be allocated billets for the night.

Commando HQ had taken over the Bad Hotel, a large country-mansion-type building set in its own grounds, which had recently been vacated by German HQ personnel. The DRs' bedroom was fully furnished, even down to an unbelievable collection of toiletries on the dressing table. The cellars had clearly been well stocked with liquor of many varieties and in vast quantities, much of it by the carboy rather than the bottle, but stocks had been greatly depleted. Nevertheless, the fortunes of war had given us a very cushy billet for a change, the only drawback being the scarcity of food, of which we had received very little that day.

Hardly had we moved in than I was handed a message for Brigade Headquarters; there being no transport available, I had to walk the four miles back to the Westkapelle gap. While waiting for an LVT to take me across, I spotted a cake of 'dehydrated porridge', still in its cellophane wrapping, lying on the sand. Manna from Heaven! I quickly scooped it up and, stifling pangs of conscience at keeping it all to myself, started to eat. A Buffalo was preparing to come across for me, so I did it quickly!

Brigade Headquarters had been set up in the reinforced concrete control centre built into the sea dyke which had formed the base of the radar dish, so delivery was quickly effected. As there was no answer, before starting back I had a look at Brigade HQ's two open air 'annexes', neither of which would have been there had not stormy seas isolated Westkapelle from mainland Europe. The first was the prisoner of war cage, no more than a depression in the sand, bounded by a few strands of barbed wire and covered by Bren guns. There hundreds of German troops, packed shoulder to shoulder squatting on the ground, had to spend their November days and nights with no more creature comforts than they had been able to provide for themselves. Only a few hundred yards away a much more saddening 'annexe' was the mortuary. There, arranged in neat military rows, lay some scores of Allied and German dead. Each man was shrouded in an army blanket, many still on the stretcher used to carry them there, all awaiting transport across the Scheldt.

It was evening by the time I arrived back in Domburg, to be greeted by the other side of war. The entire town was buzzing with noise and jollification and at the Bad Hotel it was 'Saturday night in the Enemy HQ' with a vengeance. There was very little food but plenty of liquor; such wines, spirits and liqueurs as the Germans had left behind were flowing freely. I luxuriated in the first wash and shave for four days before joining in.

German artillery continued to be active, demonstrating that Domburg was still within range of their guns, but we were too occupied with other things to worry much about such things. Before going to bed that night the DRs decided to 'clear the decks' and, opening the windows of their bedroom, spent an enjoyable few minutes hurling bottle after bottle of perfume, face cream and body lotion into the darkness.

Next morning, despite it being Sunday and 'the morning after the night before', we had to return to serious business. As DRs without motorbikes, we were put to our assigned task of 'ammunition wallahs', getting ammunition up to the forward Troops. Under the command of a sergeant, we loaded a Buffalo with a lethal assortment of mortar bombs, PIAT bombs, 303 cartridges, hand grenades and Bangalore torpedoes, then climbed on top of the load for the ride.

We had learned that the attack of the previous afternoon had been halted when 'B' Troop was enfiladed by heavy machine-gun fire from woods on their left flank. Further advance would have been impossible without incurring heavy casualties, so they had been ordered to pull back a few hundred yards to consolidate and await the return of the Troops sent to Zoutelande. While we were loading up the reserve ammunition these Troops had moved out of Domburg to participate in an attack on W18, the next major battery along the coast.

Our Buffalo headed out of town towards the coast, then turned off the road and began ploughing its way over undulating sand dunes. We caught glimpses of the North Sea over the dunes to our left, while, to the right, there was little more than extensive straggling woodland. After a bumpy journey of about a mile or so the LVT climbed to the top of a particularly long, steep, sandy incline and came to a halt near one of the many bunkers the Germans had constructed in the area.

We began to off-load our explosive cargo and carry it into the protection of the interior. This seemed to be the signal for German artillery to open fire and shells were soon falling in the vicinity. We were allowed to take shelter in the narrow entrance passageway, but no further, so remained near the doorway, with the LVT standing in the open, directly in front of us. That particular Sunday happened to be Guy Fawkes Day in the UK, but we were under no illusions about what sort of fireworks display would ensue if a shell were to fall on or near that load of ammunition.

The worst of the barrage was over when accustomed ears warned of the approach of another missile, which was undoubtedly coming to earth unpleasantly close. We were still looking out towards the LVT at the moment when there should have been a shattering explosion, but saw only a vicious spurt of sand kick up on the brow of the dune, only feet beyond the vehicle. Seconds later an explosion blasted off near the bottom of the hill. The bloody thing had bounced! Had it pitched only a little to the right there could very well have been a few more stretchers to line up outside Brigade HQ.

Things quietened down after that, the off-loading was completed and the Buffalo returned empty to Domburg. We were set marching forward with the rest of HQ Troop to maintain contact with the Fighting Troops advancing towards the battery. Breasting another dune, we suddenly gained a wide panoramic view ahead. The narrow sandy track along which we were trudging in single file led downhill until being lost in an extensive band of trees perhaps a mile ahead. Far beyond the dunes to our left were blue patches of the North Sea, while more dunes and trees stretched away to the right. Almost concurrently, the overall stillness was broken by the increasing roar of aircraft engines rapidly approaching from the rear. With rockets slung under their wings, they were instantly recognizable as Typhoons and they were clearly coming in for a strike.

As each plane in turn swooped low, directly above our heads, its engine noise rose to a high-pitched scream, quickly joined by flesh-tingling swwiiissshes as two deadly rockets left the aircraft's wings. Our eyes followed their converging trails until the white puffs of exploding warheads rose above the trees, followed a few seconds later by the crump of explosions. My reaction at the time was similar to that expressed by the Duke of Wellington on receiving a draft of recruits during the Peninsular War: 'I don't know what effect these (men) will have upon the enemy, but, by God, they terrify me'.

The effect of that Tiffie strike on battery W18 was to pave the way for a completely successful assault by 'A' and 'Y' Troops, but, sadly, there had been casualties. Two of the four killed were Captain Peter Haydon DSO, who had been my Section Officer in 'Q' Troop, and his MOA Byron Moses, who had gone forward to help him. Three more died of wounds two days later, including a signaller friend, Harry Page. By dusk all local opposition was at an end and HQ had moved into one of the evacuated bunkers of W18. Apart from a spell of guard duty, the DRs passed a warm, peaceful night, with some assistance from a part-bottle of cherry whisky found in there.

The influx of prisoners resulting from the capture of W18 had over-stretched the accommodation available in the Domburg school, so next morning, 6 November, the DRs and two Signallers were sent back to town by Buffalo to act as escorts in transferring some of them to the Brigade POW cage. We reported to the Sergeant-in-Charge, then waited outside the school while he completed arrangements. Soon our charges began shuffling out and, for interest's sake, we started to count – ten, twenty, thirty, forty – but gave up when it go to two hundred, and they were still coming.

Our charges were of all shapes and sizes, but, almost to a man, they carried what we called a 'surrender suitcase' containing their belongings. We had to search the prisoners for hidden weapons, but found no more than a few forbidden penknives; all wrist watches had disappeared. As the long, straggling column of threes moved off it was obvious that six men with rifles and bayonets, plus a Sergeant with a Colt 45 automatic, would be hard-pushed to control them should they decide to get awkward. In the event the only awkward person was the Sergeant. He started to make the POWs double march, but we made it clear that *we* weren't prisoners.

At the Westkapelle gap the prisoners were fallen out while the slow process of ferrying them across got under way. The Germans were well prepared and, from suitcases and haversacks, produced bread and sausage for lunch, more food than we had seen in days. I was standing alone, some twenty yards or so from a group of them, wondering whether it would be British to pinch some of their grub, when a party of seven or eight started moving towards me. I waited, bayonet loosely pointing in their general direction, wondering 'What the heck?', until I saw that one of them had a loaf of bread in one hand and was making cutting motions with the other, saying, *'Messer? Messer?'* They needed a knife to cut the bread and we had taken all theirs!

There had been no guidance as to what to do in such a situation, but as the Germans were obviously more amused than aggressive I fumbled for my jack-knife and handed it over. The bread-holder inclined his head as he said *'Danke'*, opened the knife and proceeded to hack off rough slices for his comrades. I watched closely lest he should try to cut anything else, but as soon as he had finished he snapped the knife shut, handed it back to me with a grin, a slight flourish and a '*Danke sehr*'. Throughout this pantomime my hungry stomach had been suggesting that I should 'liberate' at least one slice of bread, but I persuaded it that it would have been *infra dig* to show the defeated enemy that we were hungry.

Only two LVTs were available to shuttle the horde of prisoners across the gap, so it was late afternoon before the last ones were off our hands. By the time we had marched back to Domburg it was pitch dark and there was no LVT to take us up to HQ. So, instead of a comfortable bunk bed in a cosy German bunker as on the previous might, we had to make do with the bare floorboards of a cold, small room in the school/prisoner-of-war building. Once again parsimonious rations sent us to sleep with rumbling stomachs and this time there wasn't any cherry whisky to help things along.

It was a relief next morning to climb on board a Buffalo and be taken back into the bosom of the family. On the previous day, although we hadn't known it at the time, the 52nd (Lowland) Division, as the culmination of their joint attacks with the Canadian 2nd Division, had accepted the surrender of General Daser, the overall German Commander on the island, with his remaining force of 2000 men. This meant that only in 41's sector beyond Domburg were the Germans continuing to offer resistance.

During our absence the previous day REs had been striving to open up a supply route to the forward troops, to enable them to continue their advance towards the next enemy positions, 'The Black Hut' and W19. So many mines had been encountered, however, that an alternative route had had to be found and this had occupied the entire morning. In view of these supply difficulties and the few hours of daylight remaining, Brigadier Leicester had decided to postpone the attack until next day and use the afternoon to build up stores. As a preliminary move, the Belgians of 10 I-A had cleared the adjacent woods and taken up forward positions near the line of the proposed attack. It was rumoured that the Germans had evacuated W19 and pulled back into the wooded country beyond.

After an early morning recce on 7 November the Commando put in its attack at 1000 hours with armoured support and 25 pdrs and by noon the first stage, taking the Black Hut, had been achieved. Unfortunately, when moving forward towards W19, the leading

AVRE was destroyed by a placed charge, completely blocking the track. The attack was continued without fire support, but after 400 yards, when 'A' had taken over the lead from 'B', they encountered a minefield and, when seeking a way around it, came under heavy and accurate mortar fire. They suffered a dozen casualties, so the CO decided to call off the attack until armoured support became available. It took the Adjutant, Captain De Lash, three hours to evacuate the casualties under fire.

Before daylight next morning, Wednesday 8 November, while we were still in the comfort of the HQ bunker, the attack was resumed. By 0715 an enemy position between the inland scrub and W19 on the seaward dunes had been taken and movement within the battery indicated that, contrary to previous reports, the battery was still occupied. Just before eight o'clock, in full daylight, an assault was launched, which took the Germans completely by surprise and they quickly surrendered. The advance and mopping up continued with No. 4 Commando, coming from the other side of the island, linking up and moving forward on 41's right flank.

At about 1000 hrs the 2i/c of No. 4 came across to 41 with the Brigadier's orders to cease fire, as the surrender of the entire German garrison on Walcheren had been arranged. This information clearly hadn't reached the Germans in the next strongpoint, codenamed FUJIYAMA, as our leading Troop came under heavy fire when approaching it. They were halted while a German officer was brought from Vrouwenpolder to explain the situation to the Germans and by noon it was all over. The area around FUJIYAMA had been cleared and all prisoners, said to number over a thousand, were on their way to the No. 4 Commando POW cage. Our men began moving back to W18.

With the news that INFATUATE was over, we DRs and Signallers began poking around German bunkers and other buildings in search of food. We found some rock-hard Knackerbrot, which wasn't at all exciting, then came upon a food store which had received a direct hit. Most of its contents had been splattered around the ruins, but, after digging deep, we eventually located a few undamaged tins of the German equivalent of spam (the American name for their Lend-Lease wartime food delicacy of spiced ham!). Thick slices were soon sizzling in a German frying pan and the meat made even Knackerbrot seem palatable.

We returned to Domburg next morning, into the same room in the Bad Hotel and were allowed time for a wash and shave before resuming the job of guarding prisoners. Off duty that evening, there was still some liquor left in the cellar but before long the more palatable ones had run out, leaving only arrack – the liquid distilled from dates or coco-palm – and Dutch gin. Both of these 'fire-waters' appeal only to their devotees or to really dedicated drinkers, so most of us were quite happy to call it a day at that stage. One of our number, however, had apparently kept at it, as he came prancing around the cellar dangling a cat by its tail. We were obliged to ensure that he acted more humanely, after which he quickly passed out. Next day Harry had to be kept away from the eyes of authority until regaining normality.

On the afternoon of that next day the burial ceremony of those who had been killed during the final stages of the Walcheren operation took place. I was one of the detail sent, with an LVT as communal hearse, to pick up the bodies from the mortuary of the local hospital and transport them to Domburg churchyard. There were over twenty, sewn up in army blankets, and identified only by a plain white card pinned to their chests bearing 'Name, Rank and Unit'. An imperishable identity disc, around the neck, where it had dangled throughout their Service careers, would be buried with them.

Apart from an RAMC man all were from 41 and 48 Royal Marine Commandos and the Royal Engineers, in roughly equal numbers. We piled the blanket-shrouded corpses one on top of another in the hold of the LVT for the short journey to the grave-yard. One parcel was particularly pathetic, no more than two feet long yet containing all the earthly remains of a man whose vehicle had been blown up by a mine. The name, rank and regiment are indelibly imprinted upon my memory, yet, unlike the others recorded as having been buried at Domburg that day, no such person was later re-interred in the Bergen op Zoom War Cemetery. More than that, neither his Corps nor the Commonwealth War Graves Commission has any record of such a man. It remains, for me, one of the war's little mysteries.

At the churchyard a burial party took over to carry the bodies to their communal grave, a rectangular excavation barely two feet deep, alongside a boundary hedge overhung by the branches

159

of leafless trees. The bottom was awash with water, but, with most of the island flooded, the water table was everywhere very close to the surface, so that was unavoidable. Nevertheless, it didn't seem fitting that our dead comrades should be put to rest in such a wet place. The bitterest thought in most minds, however, was that if the Germans had surrendered only a few days earlier these men would have still been alive.

Volleys of rifle fire crackled out over the grave and a bugler sounded the Last Post. It took my mind back, five years almost to the day, when my eldest brother, Rex, had been buried with military honours in Heaton and Byker cemetery, Newcastle upon Tyne, on Armistice Day 1939. A Sergeant-Pilot in Coastal Command of the RAF, he had been killed when the Lockheed Hudson of which he was second pilot had crashed on returning to its base at Thornaby-on-Tees after a patrol over the North Sea.

The day after the Domburg mass burial was Armistice Day 1944. 41 RM Commando marched out of Domburg to the cheers, waves, thanks and good wishes of the Dutch inhabitants, free at last after four and a half years of German occupation. We were bound for Flushing, twelve miles away, from there to cross the River Scheldt to Breskens and return to De Haan.

The Unit marched along the dyke road for the last time, passing the defunct batteries of W17 and W15, and at Westkapelle Buffaloes again acted as ferries to take us across the gap. The march continued via Zoutelande. At the Flushing gap there were more Buffaloes to effect the crossing and they trundled through the flooded outskirts of the town to set us down on dry land again. Daylight was fading by the time the last mile or so had been covered and we were halted alongside an LCT tied up at the dockside.

As the Commando trooped on board all eyes opened wide with disbelief and the air turned blue with lurid Royal Marine epithets. Stacked seven or eight layers high, and about twenty rows wide down much of the centre of the tank deck, were hundreds and hundreds of boxes of Compo rations. Seeing all that food heading away from Walcheren, when we had just spent a week on short rations, was enough to cause a riot! Ropes were cast off, bells clanged, engine noises rose to a crescendo, racing propellers thrashed the water, but nothing happened. The flow of bad language quickly changed to ironic cheers and gales of laughter as it was realized that the heavily laden LCT had missed the tide and was firmly aground. Everyone about-turned and trooped ashore again. Then it was realized that there wasn't a lot to laugh about. There was some food, tins of cold Compo were handed out, but for overnight accommodation it was simply a matter of being marched to nearby streets of bombed and derelict houses and told to make ourselves comfortable.

All the houses were lacking doors, windows, parts of the walls and roofs, even the entire upper storey, but a group of us finally came upon a reasonably intact rear room. It was just large enough to accommodate about ten, stretched out on the floor, and was approached through the shattered front room by picking a way along such floorboards as still remained in place. Where there was no flooring, the cold, black waters of the Scheldt could be seen lapping less than two feet below.

In the corner behind the door of our bedroom there was a very small fireplace and it was soon roaring with a fire of bomb-shattered timber. We ate our cold rations in the resulting warmth and, with nothing else to do, were soon cocooned in sleep and wood smoke, but it wasn't to be an undisturbed night. In the early hours urgent yells of 'Fire! Fire!' had us rushing out into the very chill night air to find that the wall outside our room was a sheet of flames. With water close to hand under the floor, the rapid use of mugs and messtins quickly doused the flames and we returned to sleep. Perhaps the fire was no more than an accumulation of wallpaper, dried out by the heat of our fire and ignited by a tongue of flame licking through a crack in the brickwork, but it could have become serious.

Sunday morning was bright and sunny when the Commando marched back to the harbour. The LCT, with its countless boxes of Compo, was still there and floating this time. There were no hitches; it left Flushing to a round of spontaneous cheers and forty minutes later nosed up on to a beach near Breskens. The ramp flopped down and we trooped ashore to find a beach bustling with activity. LCTs were being unloaded by German prisoners in field grey, while numerous trucks shuffled back and forth. There was even a Church Army mobile canteen parked near the water's edge serving tea and buns, so it felt very much like the last day of a 'stunt' back in the UK.

TCVs to move the Commando the forty-odd miles back to De Haan hadn't arrived, so there was time to queue up for tea and buns. Then it was realized that we were still in Holland, would have to pay in Dutch guilders and we had sailed from Antwerp with only Belgian francs in our pockets. Fortunately, some of our number had persuaded Germans taken prisoner on Walcheren to surrender their guilders as well as themselves, so we were all able to pay.

Reasonably refreshed, we watched, with little interest, as German prisoners continued to unload the hoard of food with which we had travelled from Flushing. One after another they filed on board, humped a box onto a shoulder, carried it some two hundred yards from the sea and dumped it on another growing stack. Then a 15-cwt truck belonging to the Commando's Signals Section arrived, simply to make contact, and Operation COMPO was rapidly initiated, the objective being to acquire some of those boxes.

The truck was positioned close to the route taken by the POWs from LCT to stack, while two of our number wandered down to the water's edge and nonchalantly positioned themselves one on either side of the foot of the ramp. This was to be quite sure that, on whichever German shoulder a box might be carried, the reference letter could be read. We had decided to go only for 'A' boxes, containing steak and kidney pudding for main course, with mixed fruit pudding for 'afters'.

When a prisoner stepped off the ramp with an 'A' on his shoulder an almost imperceptible nod alerted those by truck. That particular POW was then followed by six pairs of eyes as he drew nearer and, after a quick check that no one in authority was looking in our direction, all that was needed was for one of us to step in front of him and point, commandingly, to the back of the truck. The German had no option but to drop his box inside, where it was immediately covered with camouflage netting, as he headed back to the LCT.

Not wanting to be too greedy, we called a halt at six, or it may have been seven or eight, boxes. It was only a 15-cwt, so there wasn't room to hide too many. However, with a full day's rations for fourteen men in each box, we reckoned that the Signallers and DRs had adequately, and justifiably, recouped themselves for those hungry days on the other side of the Scheldt!

The TCVs arrived during the afternoon and by 1630 hours we four DRs were back in the top floor room of the Pension du Nord, exchanging news with those who had been left behind. They listened attentively to a bare-bones account of what had transpired since leaving them – a lifetime of thirteen days previously – before jumping in with the latest buzz that De Haan was destined to be used as a military convalescent area and 41 was to be pushed out, probably up to the front.

Chapter 12

RETURN TO HOLLAND, AND V-WEAPONS

During our absence from De Haan the power supply had been restored to the Pension du Nord, so, with electric lighting and a radio set, one of 'the spoils of war' brought back from Holland, the DRs room was becoming less spartan. However, the weather had turned decidedly chilly and, with the imminent onset of winter, and that of 1944/45 was destined to be one of the coldest for many years, some form of heating had become top priority. Next day the off-duty DRs set out on a rummaging expedition.

After poking around the ruins of bombed buildings in the neighbourhood a small pot-bellied stove with some lengths of metal piping were unearthed and hauled gleefully up the four flights of stairs to our room. As there was neither fireplace nor chimney, an outlet for the flue pipe was provided by the simple expedient of knocking a hole in a window pane. Fuel, in the form of coal briquettes, was 'won' from a nearby Army cookhouse, but, despite repeated attempts to kindle a fire, it proved impossible to get the stove to draw properly, the only result being a roomful of smoke.

The following morning the stove was jettisoned out of the window and a second expedition returned with a replacement, but that too refused to function properly. Four days and a succession of stoves later, by which time the garden below our window was well covered with shattered cast iron, success was achieved. Then, with a working stove, electric light and the radio, although not quite in the lap of luxury, we felt that we were at least perched on its knee.

164

During our first few days back in Belgium the Unit was given a succession of, 'Jolly good show, chaps' talks, first by our Commanding Officer, Lieutenant Colonel E.C.E. 'Pegler' Palmer, then by Brigadier B.W. 'Jumbo' Leicester, and finally by Major-General Sturges, GOC of the Special Service Group. The General, on our return from the Mediterranean in January, had apologized for being late and he had another apology this time – for not being able to send us on leave. Instead he talked about 'polishing-off a few more islands' and 'going into the line in Holland', so we knew just where we stood.

In consequence of the casualties suffered on Walcheren, there were insufficient Officers and Other Ranks to form five effective Fighting Troops, so the number was reduced to four by amalgamating 'A' and 'X' as 'Q'. The original 'Q Troop' had ceased to exist at Salerno in September 1943 for the very same reason that this second one had had to be created, casualties. The newly-formed 'Q', together with Headquarters Troop, became the core of FORCE PALMER, which was immediately put on two hours' notice to react to any German incursion which might take place.

To mark the end of a successful operation, the Fighting Troops were granted a week to 'Rest and Re-equip', but for the 'Ammunition Wallahs-cum-DRs' return to De Haan simply meant a resumption of the rota of duty trips. Nevertheless, for all there was a new facet to life – currency exchange. Those who had arrived back with pockets bulging with Dutch guilders had to decide whether to cash in at once or keep them for a likely return to Holland. Then there was the problem of getting money back to the UK in sterling. At one time it had been possible to buy British postal orders at the Orderly Room using local currency, but the authorities had cottoned on to the possibility of 'fiddles', after which such transactions had to be entered in your Pay Book as debits against pay. The affluent set about devising ways of getting around this!

The few guilders I had managed to acquire – the circumstances are lost to memory – caused me no such heart-searching and they were largely consumed as fish suppers! In Ostend at that time even the most prestigious hotels were attempting to attract the 'Tommy Trade' by displaying prominent FISH AND CHIPS signs in their windows. With a white linen table cloth and waiter service, it was on a rather higher level than a normal British 'Chippy' and the cost of almost a week's pay would have been prohibitive had it not been for our temporary affluence.

On 23 November, ten days after our return, the Commando was put under two days' notice to move back to Walcheren. On that day, too, the Belgian Troop of 10 I-A Commando was again placed under command and seven officer replacements joined the Unit. One of them was Lieutenant R.S. Bate of the South African Union Defence Force, killed in a raid across the Maas less than three months later; another, Lieutenant J.B.R. Grindrod of the Manchester Regiment took up Holy Orders after the war and ended up as Archbishop and Primate of Australia, while a third, Lieutenant John Cameron Stewart, was to lose part of a leg by a German *Schuh* mine, also in a raid across the Maas, and he too emigrated to Australia.

The return to the 'Tea Saucer Island' was to be by land, via Antwerp, into Holland at Putte, then along the South Beveland peninsula to the Walcheren causeway. Although the total distance was only of the order of 150 miles, an overnight stop en route was planned, in view of the slow overall speed when shepherding a long convoy of vehicles. On Friday 24th, therefore, Lieutenant 'Bud' Abbott, the Intelligence Officer, with Corporal Latimer of 10 I-A Commando as interpreter, left De Haan by jeep to arrange accommodation for the following night; I was the DR chosen to accompany them.

Our little party reached Antwerp in less than two hours and were surprised to find that the vehicular tunnel under the river was still intact, although the entrance had been damaged by one near miss. The city centre was thronged with Allied military traffic and personnel; it was time for 'stand-easy' tea and buns and we had soon located a very up-market NAAFI/EFI canteen. These establishments were strictly 'off limits' for commissioned officers, but, muffled up in my riding coat Bud's pips were hidden, so he passed as one of a quartet of Other Ranks.

When we arrived, more than two weeks after the surrender of Walcheren, the Royal Navy still needed a few more days in which to complete the work of clearing mines from the approaches to the port. Nevertheless, even without there being supply ships unloading, Antwerp was already being targeted by German V-weapons, so it wasn't a place in which to linger unnecessarily.

The first two V2s had fallen on the city on 13 October, killing forty-two civilians, and on 16 November ten V-weapons had killed 263. Three weeks after our NAAFI stop, on 16 December, the Germans launched their Ardennes offensive, the so-called Battle of the Bulge, aimed at the city, and the main weight of V-bomb attacks was switched from London to Antwerp. In the afternoon of that same day a V2 rocket fell on the Rex Cinema in the Avenue de Keyser, killing 567 people, including 296 Allied Service personnel. When Antwerp became the major inflow point for Allied supplies, it remained a prime target for V1s and V2s. By March 1945 no less than 1200 V-weapons had fallen on the 65 square miles of Greater Antwerp, of which 150 V1s and 152 V2s actually hit the port area.

The first of those *Vergeltungswaffen*, Reprisal Weapons, had been used against London on 13 June, and the even larger and more expensive way of delivering a similar load of death, the V2, became operational in September 1944.

The V1 was simply a flying bomb, an unmanned aeroplane; some were launched from aircraft but the usual method was from concrete or steel ramps on the ground. After being aimed in the chosen direction by its launch ramp, the V1 was kept on course by a gyroscopic autopilot linked with a compass pre-set to the required bearing, the range being determined by a log actuated by a propeller in the bomb's nose. However, any manufacturing defect (such as slave-worker sabotage), deviation of the flying controls or unexpected wind change could put the bomb off course. In consequence, most of southern Holland and northern Belgium was at the mercy of 'strays' intended for more distant destinations, in addition to those actually targeted on the area.

V1s were variously sized between 20 and 30 feet in length, had a wing span of around 16 feet and a fuselage diameter of the order of 2.5 feet. The ram-jet engine, fitted on top of the fuselage, emitted an unmistakable 'tonk-tonk-tonk-tonk-tonk' noise as it ejected a pulsating comet's tail of fire from its single jet tube. Commonly known a 'buzz bombs' or 'doodle bugs', the V1s carried a warhead of one ton of high explosive, had a range of about 200 miles and flew at an altitude of some 2500 feet at a speed in excess of 400 mph. On one surprising occasion, through a momentary break in a blanket of cloud cover over 's Hertogenbosch, I saw a doodle bug easily overtake an unsuspecting Spitfire in full flight.

The fiery tails of flying bombs made them easy to spot in a clear sky by day or by night, but when it was cloudy or if confined indoors there was only the engine noise to reveal their presence. When the tonk-tonk-tonk-tonk of a V1's engine heralded its approach, time stood still for everyone within earshot, holding their breath and wondering where it was heading. If the engine noise began to die away, it had passed over and everyone breathed freely again, but if the tonk-tonk-tonk-tonk kept growing louder you were near its flight path. Your brain crossed its mental fingers, hoping that the devilish thing would keep on going. Should the engine noise stop abruptly, one ton of high explosive was plummeting earthwards and nothing could prevent it from impacting somewhere nearby. It was time to dive for whatever cover might be available, until the juddering blast of an explosion signalled another lucky escape.

In marked contrast, the V2 was a rocket bomb which impacted at a velocity of more than twice the speed of sound, so there was absolutely no warning of its approach. The first intimation of the arrival of a V2 was the explosion, which might be no more than a heavy 'Thump!' in the distance, but could be the building in which you happened to be being shaken to its foundations, or worse.

The V2 stood 46 feet high, had a mid-height diameter of some 5.5 feet, a take-off weight (made up largely of fuel) approaching 15 tons and had a range of 250 miles. The rocket's initial vertical take-off lifted it to about 12 miles above the earth's surface, when a radio signal turned it into its calculated trajectory. The rocket continued its arc of ascent to a height of about 70 miles, then tilted earthwards to impact within a mile or so of its pin-point target, so, on balance, it was probably the more accurate weapon. There was no preferred way of having one ton of death delivered and it was no consolation to know that, if one of them 'had your name on it', you would never be aware of the fact.

The place chosen for 'overnighting' the Unit was the small village of Hoogerheide, some twenty miles over the Belgian/Dutch border, where allocation of sleeping quarters was to be arranged with the local Burgomaster. For the night we three other ranks were given the rubble-strewn front room of a small, shell-blasted terrace house. The previous occupiers were safe, living with their next-door neighbours whose house was relatively undamaged. We were later invited in to share the warmth of the stove and pass a pleasant evening conversing in a mixture of English, Dutch, French and mime. One thing that seemed international was the instinctive hunching of shoulders and exchange of rueful glances at every nearby explosion.

When the main body of the Commando arrived next day we were able to direct them to the various empty buildings in which they would spend the night. Early on Sunday morning I re-joined the DRs and we began shepherding the convoy towards Middelburg, some forty miles away. It was a slow, cold business, most of our time being spent on the roadside directing the trucks along the right road. All went smoothly until, around noon, the convoy came to an unexpected halt outside Nieuwland, a small village some two miles short of our destination.

Hardly had the noise of our engines died away, however, than a dozen or more Dutch youngsters, brandishing wads of guilder notes, besieged the trucks, wanting to buy almost anything. With kit packed for the move, there was little immediately available for sale other than the cans of Compo carried for lunch and some bars of chocolate, but, at the prices being offered, many elected to go hungry for a while. Chocolate was *the* big sell. Two ounce (57 gramme) bars were snapped up at the going rate of 3 guilders, no less than thirty times their retail price in the UK. Over the next months civilians would be seen wearing a number of items of 'War Office issue' which had been put to new uses – blankets reappeared as overcoats, towels turned into blouses and innumerable sets of ladies' underwear were created from parachute silk.

The unexplained wait by the roadside became prolonged. Those who hadn't sold their lunch ate it, and still we waited. Then, from time to time, wavering trails of white smoke could be seen snaking high into the sky a few score miles to the north of us over occupied Holland and we realized that we were witnessing the initial ascent of V2 rockets. On a subsequent occasion, when V2s were being launched in the gathering dusk, bright flashes of light seen near the peak of their ascent were puzzling until it was realized that the rockets had been passing from the shadow of the earth to be momentarily illuminated by the sun, which had already set so far as our earthbound eyes were concerned.

On that Sunday afternoon outside Nieuwland the message

eventually trickled down to us that the unit we had come to relieve, the 4/5th Battalion Royal Scots Fusiliers, would not be moving out until next day and we would have to double up with them in their barns, garages and attics. Two Troops carried on to Middelburg and the Belgians moved into Arnemuiden, while HQ and the remaining three Troops stayed in the Nieuwland area. The Signals Despatch Office and Signal Section billets were located in a two-storey building at the corner of the main road to Middelburg, where the DRs were allocated a draughty attic as sleeping quarters, but at least it had a workable stove.

We were aware that the Commando's new job would be in general guard duties for the island and the provision of a mobile striking force. As all the islands in the Scheldt estuary, apart from Walcheren, were still in German hands, and North Beveland lay less than a mile distant, this was rather more than a perfunctory assignment. Brigade Headquarters had been set up in Goes, the main town of South Beveland, some twelve miles away.

When the RSFs had departed, a primitive form of electric lighting was installed by utilizing one of the Signal Section's petrol-driven battery-charging sets. However, it soon became possible to use the original lighting system when a nearby Searchlight Unit sent one of their men with a Lister diesel/electric generator to hook up to the mains electricity circuit.

During the following few days 'S' Troops moved to Middelburg and 'P' and 'Y' to Veere on the north-east coast of the island, vacating a nearby school, which became the HQ billet. The DRs were allocated one of the classrooms, which was quickly reorganized by extending the flue pipe of the stove and moving it into the centre of the room. We had inherited straw palliasses, then managed to ferret out some bedsteads and, with a table draped with a spare blanket, had a very passable barrack-room. Jackie Horsfield had come across a paint store and set to work emblazoning our names in red and gold on the wall above each of our beds.

In very marked contrast to these improved living quarters, our working life was becoming daily more unpleasant as the weather deteriorated. Unprotected faces were buffeted by snow or sleet and, with many of the roads under water, we were obliged to use unmade tracks and, within minutes of leaving the SDO, our lower legs would be soaked to the skin. In an effort to combat this I hunted around, found a sheet of aluminium, cut and bent it to shape, and fixed it between petrol tank and footrests as a mud splash. Preliminary trials indicated that it was a practical proposition, but before it could be given a 'field trial' we were moved to Middelburg, although the Signals Office remained in Nieuwland.

The new billet had a central location on the 'Canal through Walcheren', close to the Bailey bridge which replaced the one which had linked the town with the road to Flushing and Goes, demolished by the Germans. As at De Haan, the room had neither heating nor fireplace, so the rigmarole of finding a stove and poking a hole in the window for the flue pipe started again. We soon achieved warmth, but during my first short stay there the room was never completely free from smoke.

Next day I had the noon trip to 'P' Troop at Veere, barely five miles from the Signals Despatch Office, but at that time a completely isolated community. The flooding of the island had drowned the road to the town, which could only be reached by using an unpaved track. Arrival in Veere, after a solitary struggle against the elements through a bleak and empty landscape, seemed like reaching the end of the world. Troop Headquarters was in a stark, stone-faced building on a deserted quayside which seemed always to be lashed by stinging rain or sleet; Captain Sloley, the Troop Commander, was dubbed by his fellow officers 'The Hermit of Veere'.

On that December Friday in 1944 I didn't complete the journey. Nearing the end of the track, threading my way between water-filled potholes, I saw a jeep and trailer coming towards me at speed. It was travelling much too fast for the state of the road and the trailer was bouncing about like a mad thing, so I pulled off the track to let it pass. I obviously hadn't gone far enough, because the trailer dealt me and my bike a swingeing blow; I landed in the mud, moaning involuntarily from the pain in my left shoulder, while the trailer ended upside down with its wheels describing ineffectual circles in the air. It was a jeep of the Dutch Grenzwacht, frontier guards, who bundled me inside, righting the trailer, heaved my motorbike aboard, new mudsplash crumpled out of all recognition, and took me to Middelburg.

The Medical Officer didn't think that there was very much

171

wrong with me, but when I reported back next day, after a sleepless night with a shoulder that was still as painful as ever, he decided to send me to hospital for an X-ray. Transport was laid on to take me to No. 82 CRS (Casualty Receiving Station), set up in a school in Goes (without empty school buildings it is doubtful whether wars could be fought at all!) but it was too late to be examined that day. The shoulder was inspected next morning and arrangements were made to transfer me to No. 9 BGH (British General Hospital), in the centre of Antwerp, for X-ray.

Arrival there on Sunday evening was again too late to be seen by a doctor, but in good time for the nightly session of V-weapon attacks, which could be guaranteed to divert a mind from lesser personal problems. All too often the menacing tonk-tonk-tonk-tonk of a flying bomb could be heard, while spasmodic violent explosions and dull thumps told of either V1s or V2s impacting in the City area. On more than one occasion the entire hospital shuddered to its foundations. That was Sunday, 17 December 1944, the day following the launch of Von Rundstedt's 'last fling' Ardennes offensive, and only the previous day the Rex cinema had been hit, with the heavy loss of life mentioned earlier.

Next morning a lady doctor examined the shoulder; she seemed satisfied that there was no dislocation, although no X-ray was taken to verify this. I remained confined to bed, with nothing more than regular checks of pulse rate and temperature by two young Belgian nurses, until Wednesday afternoon. Then, after an abrupt transfer, I found myself in bed in the British General Hospital in Duffel (the town which gave its name to the Royal Navy's bridge coat) some ten miles away.

At that time I was totally unaware of the strategic implications of the German offensive, so didn't appreciate that I had been moved ten miles down the line of their planned attack. In any case, with a score or more V1s per day coming within earshot, Duffel was not an ideal place in which to be confined to a hospital bed. Like the clock inside the crocodile in *Peter Pan*, V1s gave warning of their approach, but nothing could be done about it, except to put your head under the pillow if the engine cut out.

On 21 December, six days after the event, an X-ray finally confirmed that all my pain had been arising from no more than 'a contusion'. By that time too, on a wider scale, it had become clear that the Germans had caught the Americans completely off-guard and advances of up to 50 miles had been made. General Montgomery had been given command of all British and American troops in the sector to stabilize the situation. The American 101st Airborne Division, cut off at Bastogne, was completely surrounded for a week and had to be supplied from the air. This occasion attracted public attention by US General McAuliffe's single-worded reply when called upon to surrender – 'Nuts!' For many years after the war the Military Museum at Bastogne went under the name of The 'Nuts' Museum.

With confirmation of the contusion, I became an 'up-patient' (which meant a hospital dogsbody, taking meals to bed patients, etc) but had to report to the gym twice a day to exercise the shoulder, which was still unpleasantly painful. By that time I felt sure that there was no chance of rejoining the Commando before Christmas, but consoled myself with the feeling that Christmas dinner in hospital could very well be better than anything to be found in a box of Compo rations.

On Christmas Eve, as the hospital was settling down for the night, from the corridor outside the ward came the sound of voices singing a Christmas Carol. It grew louder as the singers drew near; then, as they filed into the ward, we saw that they were carolers with a very sad difference. It was a mixed choir of all ages, but with one thing in common – they were all amputees. Some were on crutches, some had parts of two limbs missing; all were civilian war casualties. They stayed in the ward to sing another carol, then distributed hand-made Christmas cards, courtesy of the Belgian Red Cross; I still have mine.

The Christmas Dinner fully measured-up to expectations. A meal of chicken and pork was undoubtedly much better fare than most troops in NW Europe would have been getting that day and few civilians in meat-rationed Britain could have enjoyed a comparable meal. It is a long-standing tradition in the British Armed Forces that, on Christmas Day, commissioned officers serve the meal to the other ranks and this was faithfully observed on that occasion. What was far 'over and above' tradition was the barrage of popping corks as bottles of champagne were opened for the Loyal Toast! No doubt that luxury came under the heading of 'spoils of war' and, despite being drunk from enamel mugs rather than fine glassware, the toast of 'The King' was none the less sincere!

After the celebration of Christmas, hospital life seemed even more restrictive. The shoulder was by now almost pain-free; my only wish was to escape, but, despite being officially discharged on the Friday, it was early Monday Morning, New Year's Day 1945, before transport arrived from Brigade HQ to return Commando personnel to their Units.

It was a bright, frosty morning, with a slight overcast and, something which hadn't been seen since beachhead days, German aircraft scooting about the sky. The German Ardennes offensive had coincided with a period of cloud and low visibility, which had greatly assisted the Luftwaffe in avoiding the attention of Allied fighters. On top of this, early morning mists over the more southerly German airfields had cleared long before Allied planes in England were able to take off, giving the enemy pilots a head start before Allied fighters could be brought into action.

The air activity on 1 January 1945, however, wasn't in support of the ground troops, as the German thrust had been halted on Christmas Day. It had been a 'last fling' of air attacks on forward Allied airfields in France, Holland and Belgium, in which, the Germans claimed, 400 out of a total of 579 Allied aircraft destroyed that day were caught on the ground. At Brussels' Zaventem aerodrome alone losses on the ground amounted to 180 aircraft, including Monty's own Dakota. The Allies' counter-claim was that, of 500 German planes which had taken part in the attacks, 364 were destroyed.

Back in Middelburg, I found that the smoking stove problem had been solved, but the major 'welcome home' news was of the introduction of a Home Leave Ballot. Everyone with six months' service in the War Zone had become entitled to seven days' leave, albeit in dribs and drabs. The names of all those so entitled had been 'put in the hat' and the first to be drawn had already left; my name had been drawn for the beginning of February, four weeks ahead.

For those with surplus Dutch currency, acquired during the Walcheren operation or from selling NAAFI rations, etc, the link with the UK created by this leave system proved to be an added blessing. Their money was only of real value if it could be converted into sterling and it soon became common knowledge that the currency exchange offices at the Channel Transit Camps weren't concerned with the amount nor the source of the money they changed. With men going back to the UK on a regular basis, an efficient 'courier service' was now available.

The New Year of 1945 brought a snowy freeze-up which rapidly transformed flooded Walcheren, and the rest of Holland, into a white winter wonderland, but made living conditions for front-line troops so much the worse. Despatch Riding became a cold and hazardous occupation, so jeeps were made available for longer trips; four wheels and four-wheel drive kept us moving, but the vehicles did little so far as warmth was concerned. The wartime models were open to the elements, apart from the windscreen and a flimsy canvas rear cover and, notwithstanding an issue of sleeveless sheepskin jackets donated by individual benefactors in South Africa, conditions were quite bleak. In addition, with a manually-operated windscreen wiper, one hand had to relinquish the steering wheel every time the screen became obscured by rain or snow, which could be a tricky business on ice-bound roads.

Nevertheless, the four-wheel drive and slick manoeuvrability of the Willys World War Two Jeep were qualities much appreciated by friend and foe alike. In Normandy we came across some, abandoned at the time of Dunkirk, which had been 'upgraded' for use by German officers, with the sides fully boxed-in, fitted with doors and the canvas of the seats re-covered with luxurious padded upholstery.

During the second week of January rumours about 'moving up' began to circulate and, on the 18th, the Despatch Riders shepherded a long string of vehicles away from Walcheren. After negotiating the completely deserted thirty miles of road along the South Beveland peninsula, the convoy turned left and, a few miles later, halted in Bergen op Zoom. 41 was to take over a sector of the Maas River front from 47 Royal Marines Commando.

Chapter 13

THE MAAS RIVER FRONT

In Bergen op Zoom, as in Deal some twelve months previously, the bulk of the Commando was housed in a barracks. It was an extensive, single-storeyed timber structure, built in the form of a large open square, and housed a multiplicity of barrack rooms, ablutions, cook-houses, messrooms, recreation rooms, offices and stores. A particularly welcome feature, in view of the wintry weather, was that it was well-provided with efficient solid fuel stoves and the complex was comfortably warm throughout.

Although some of the Troop Offices were now under the same roof as the Signals Despatch Office and a number of the DRs' 'trips' were reduced to no more than indoor walks, the greater part of our time was still spent on ice-bound roads. Offices in the vicinity of Bergen had to be visited by motorcycle, but, with Brigade HQ still in Goes and a number of other formations located between Bergen and Tilburg some forty miles away, round trips of 50–80 miles by jeep were not uncommon. These longer journeys were, inevitably, cold and lonely affairs, relieved only by tea and buns at any NAAFI/EFI canteens found en route.

The Commando's Operational Instructions in Bergen op Zoom were to be ready to move in support of No. 4 Special Service Brigade in Beveland, or of No. 1 Polish Armoured Regiment in the Tholen/Sint Philipsland area, and also to plan and execute raids across to the north bank of the Maas. Each Troop, therefore, had to familiarize itself with an allotted section of the river, between the island of Schouwen in the Scheldt Estuary and Geertruidenberg, a stretch of no less than thirty miles.

In addition to giving the Commando a more active role in the war, the move to Bergen had put it squarely on the V1 routes to Antwerp and more distant targets. On the day of our arrival six of them fell into the Scheldt near the town and that set the pattern. By day and by night the sound of doodlebug engines became commonplace and on too many occasions an engine would cut out close enough to freeze all movement until the thing had exploded. By day they could be seen passing over or heading earthwards and by night their routes were marked by their fiery tails. On solo drives along the deserted road to Goes it wasn't uncommon to see a doodlebug heading in the same general direction and, more than once, the engine stopped and the bomb crashed to earth in a blast of smoke and debris in a field, or as a spout of sand and seawater in the shallows of the East Scheldt.

Four days after the Commando's arrival in Bergen Captain Stevens of 'A' Troop led a raiding party across the river with the object of bringing back a prisoner from a known German position. The party, comprising two officers, sixteen men and a Dutch guide, started off from Drimmeln harbour in two assault boats at 0245 hrs. Impeded by the adverse current, however, and by having to laboriously break a passage through ice in order to reach the north bank, it took them an hour and a half to cover a distance of no more than 1200 yards. Then, once ashore, it was found impossible to move quietly across the icy marshlands of frozen reeds and willows.

Nevertheless, the patrol pressed on, cutting trip wires encountered en route, and they also cut a way through the double apron fence found to be protecting the German position. The first four men had passed through the gap when flares illuminated the area, two machine guns opened fire and grenades began bursting amongst them. Captain Stevens who, along with the Dutch guide and one of the Marines, had been wounded by this fire, ordered a withdrawal to a position nearer the river.

The patrol pulled back under mortar and machine-gun fire, but when they had re-grouped it was found that the wounded Marine was no longer with them. It was then 0550 hrs and, with two men remaining behind to wait for the wounded man, the others returned to the 'firm base' by the boats at the river's edge. At 0630, the wounded man not having shown up, the patrol started back across the Maas and, helped by the current this time, were back in Drimmeln harbour by 0705 hrs. On learning of the impossibility of moving quietly over frozen ground, the Corps Commander immediately issued instructions that there should be no further raids until after the thaw.

On Sunday 28 January Lieutenant Colonel P.C.W. Hellings RM took over as Commanding Officer and Lieutenant Colonel Palmer returned to the UK. The very next morning the unit was placed under the command of 10 Canadian Infantry Brigade and given 'immediate' orders to join them somewhere beyond Geertruidenberg, about 35 miles further up the Maas. The entire barracks was immediately enveloped in a frenzy of packing kit and stores. As Corporal Angel, the NCO-in-Charge of Despatch Riders, was on UK leave, I was detailed off to take two other DRs and accompany the Unit road convoy when it left that afternoon. All jeeps would be needed to transport personnel and stores, so we would have to use our motorcycles.

After lunch, with all my kit packed and stowed in a Signals truck, I went off on a final duty trip around the Bergen area. Returning in late afternoon, I was concentrating on keeping control of the Matchless 350, slipping and slithering on the icy road; consequently it wasn't until turning to enter the main gate that I noticed smoke and flames arising from the barracks. Propping my bike against the outer railings, I ran forward to see what was happening. A corner of the wooden building was already well alight; men were hurling kit, boxes of ammunition and stores out of windows on to the snow and others were humping them away; more men were rigging up hoses to fight the flames.

As I drew near, there came an urgent shout from Jan Maley, 'Hey, Mitch! – over here quick – *the petrol!!*' Flames were licking perilously close to our stock of 40-gallon drums of fuel, standing on end close to the building, and I spent a frantic few minutes helping to topple them on their side and roll them out of harm's way. That accomplished, I joined a chain of men passing stores, hand-to-hand, away from the building, until called upon to get hold of a hosepipe.

By that time the fire was gaining strength and had reached some remnants of ammunition still inside the building. The crackling of the flames was now punctuated by staccato bursts of exploding small arms cartridges and the intermittent thumps of hand-grenades. As we played hoses on the flames, an icy wind blew back the lesser droplets of water which, despite the heat of the fire, froze into a film of ice on the revers of our sheepskin jackets. Before long it was decided that nothing we could do was going to save the barracks. The fire had eaten its way over the main gateway and was rapidly and relentlessly consuming the timber structure in two directions; the order was given to 'Let it burn!'. In the failing daylight we began to collect a miscellany of articles strewn far and wide over the snow.

Fortunately the loading had been going on since morning and all the Unit's weapons as well as the bulk of its ammunition and supplies were already packed on the vehicles lined up on the road outside. In the gathering darkness of a bitingly cold winter's evening, wet and dirty Marines boarded their vehicles. Rather later than expected, the convoy moved off towards the front, leaving the barracks, which had been our home for only ten days, no more than a glowing square of red-hot ashes.

The three DRs conducted the string of vehicles from the barracks, through the town and on to the Breda road at the start of their journey into the night. By that time, however, we were all riding behind 'Tail-end Charlie', the last truck in the convoy. Normally we would have been working our way up to the head of the column again, but, as things were, that was manifestly impossible. In the darkness, without any lights, and all drivers 'hogging' the crown of a narrow road, slithering on the hard-packed snow, any attempt to overtake would have been foolhardy in the extreme. Even continuing to tag along behind the trucks, on a barely visible icy road, was to risk broken legs or worse. I decided that it was impossible to carry on and, after telling the men on the last truck what I was doing, led the DRs back to Bergen.

I knew that the Rear Party had been accommodated in one of the town's hotels, so made my way there to report to the Officer-in-Charge. He was, with the handful of others, in a bright, warm, basement kitchen, the complete antithesis of the freezing darkness outside. My explanation of the reason for our return was accepted

179

without question and we were allocated an area of the kitchen floor on which to pass the night. Civilian cooks were busy preparing a meal, obviously for the Rear Party, but we weren't included.

Next morning a jeep was made available to enable us to re-join the Main Body and (as OC DRs!) I elected to drive. By daylight there was a vastly different world outside. It was still freezing cold, but, instead of the blackness of the previous night, there was bright sunlight with a light morning mist, and the white, slippery road to Breda was now carrying a continuous flood of military traffic. The mist soon produced a coating of ice on the windscreen and it had to be swung up out of the way to enable me to see where we were going. As to our intended destination, all the information available was that the Commando would be 'near the Maas, beyond Oosterhout and east of Geertruidenberg', and on reaching that area we would have to make enquiries.

At Breda, after a 'stand easy' interlude at a NAAFI canteen, we had to turn off the road to Tilburg where, presumably, all the other vehicles were heading, and head for Oosterhout and the River Maas. From that point we were completely alone, travelling along a deserted road through a bleak white wilderness, relieved only by fences, hedgerows and leafless tress. Before long the unmistakable 'whoomps' of artillery fire confirmed that we were indeed heading in the right direction.

A few miles beyond Breda we entered Oosterhout and for a short while made contact with the human race again. The drive along the main street of the small town, white under a blanket of snow, was rather like passing a series of Christmas card scenes. Cafés were brightly lit with their doors open and muffled-up figures moved about the streets or warmed themselves at bonfires crackling cheerfully on open spaces. The fact that virtually all the figures were British or Canadian military personnel, whose guns and vehicles littered the streets, didn't destroy the illusion.

We didn't stop and were soon back in the barren whiteness beyond. I drove slowly and cautiously for mile after mile, eyes searching for some sign of life, or where some might be found, with the sound of the guns growing louder. Eventually we spotted a small sign at the roadside, bearing the name of a Canadian Artillery Unit and an arrow pointing up a narrow track. In a few hundred yards it led us to a farmyard crammed with trucks and jeeps, while the abutting buildings bustled with Headquarters Staff. On reporting to the Orderly Room the Duty Officer had no hesitation in saying, '41 Commando HQ? They're in Waspik. I'll give you a guide'. He immediately summoned a stumpy, roly-poly sort of Canadian private to show us the way. The Canuck led us back to the farmyard, grinned a cheerful 'Just follow me, Bub!' as he hopped into a jeep and shot out of the farmyard as though it was a Le Mans start.

There had been no opportunity to explain that I was something of a novice driver, but to be left behind would have been a sad reflection upon the British, so I too had to put my foot down. The freezing cold soon became a thing of the past. I sweated profusely as we slid along narrow ribbons of ice between menacingly deep roadside ditches, slithered round ninety degree bends and jolted over rough, crunchy snow. Eventually we arrived in a small town, where my escort skidded to a brief halt. He indicated the adjacent building with his thumb, gave a typical North American 'See you!' salute, executed a rapid three-point turn and disappeared in the direction from whence we had come before there was time to say 'Thank you'.

Commando HQ in Waspik had been established in the Gemeentehuis, the local council offices. The standard architectural pattern for such buildings was for the main entrance to be about five feet above pavement level, approached from both sides by flights of balustraded stone steps. Probably this was to provide a podium from which the Burgomaster could make public announcements. At Waspik directly below the main entrance was the doorway to a cellar which, I found, was 'home' for the HQ Signallers.

The cellar had obviously been a storeroom for the Town Engineer, as signboards bearing the name WASPIK, red warning lamps, picks, shovels, coils of rope, etc, had been heaped to one side to clear part of the cobblestone floor. This had been covered with straw to provide a communal sleeping area for about fifteen men, and the 'kitchen', a roaring pressure stove sited near the doorway, made it a haven of warmth. I reported to the Signals Officer, who was quite happy with my explanation of our late arrival and about receiving one jeep instead of three motorcycles.

On the previous evening lack of visibility and road conditions had kept the speed of the convoy down to little more than walking pace and it had been almost 2300 hrs before they reached Waspik. After that it took a further two and a half hours for men of the Fighting Troops to take over the forward positions. It was probably as well that they had been unaware of the Despatch Riders sleeping in the hotel kitchen in Bergen!

The reason for the Commando's precipitate departure from Bergen op Zoom had now been made known. 41 was needed by 10 Canadian Brigade to secure their flank for an attack upon a stubborn German position on an island between two arms of the River Maas. The roughly diamond-shaped island, some five miles long and one and a half wide, lies between the main river, the Bergsche Maas, and the more southerly, and narrower, Oude Maasje (little old Maas), one and a half miles north of Waspik. The island was known to Allied troops as 'Capelsche Veer' but 'veer' is the Dutch word for 'ferry' and that name relates to the ferry which, in peacetime, crossed the Bergsche Maas just beyond the point where the Oude Maasje joins the main river, on the line of the road leading north from Capelle, two miles east of Waspik.

For some time the Canadians had been trying to eliminate the German garrison of the island in order to regularize the Allied front along the line of the main river. Only two weeks earlier 47 RM Commando had almost managed the job, but, badly outnumbered and suffering heavy casualties, just couldn't make it. They had, however, confined the Germans to the eastern end of the island and 10 Canadian Brigade were engaged in completing the job.

Preliminary infantry attacks had started on 26 January while Engineers went ahead with building a bridge across the Oude Maasje. During the night of the 29th, when 41 was moving in, the Canadians built up a tank force on the island and, next evening, the day the DRs reached Waspik, they attacked the German positions once more. Two battalions of Canadians, the Argyll and Sutherland Highlanders and the Lincoln and Welland Regiment, supported by tanks of the South Alberta Regiment, were involved. It took most of the night, but by dawn on the 31st the island had been cleared, leaving 145 Germans lying dead and sixty-nine taken prisoner, the rest having escaped across the main river. After the capture of the island, 41 Commando was given the job of holding on to it.

That action had coincided with the thaw, but this proved a mixed blessing for the troops in forward positions, adding the problems of mud to those of ice and snow. Those of us back in the Gemeentehuis cellar were thankful that we could pass our nights, apart from spells of guard duty and the inevitable dawn stand-to, in our cellar with nothing to disturb us apart from the sounds of distant gunfire. On that occasion I had only two such nights as, on 1 February, it was my turn for Home Leave!

Late in the afternoon a truck deposited the leave party, washed, shaved and wearing best battle dress, at the Antwerp railway station. It was some hours too early for the 2030 hrs 'Blighty Express' for Calais, so there was ample time for a meal in the station canteen, then to wander into town for a few beers. By the time we were settled down with our glass of rather fizzy Belgian brew the city's nightly session of V-weapon attacks had begun and our minds became a turmoil of unpleasant thoughts. What could be worse than 'catching a packet' with a leave chit in your pocket, just waiting for the train to take you home?

We sat with eyes continually drawn towards the clock behind the bar as random explosions shook the city. Each time a V1 engine cut out I was probably not alone in offering up the silent prayer of 'Please come down somewhere else, I'm going on leave'. With still an hour or more before train time a crashing explosion shook the whole building, all the windows rattled and the swing doors squeaked open. A phlegmatic Scot at a nearby table, who was obviously one of those unfortunate souls for whom Antwerp was 'home', looked towards us and explained, succinctly, 'Vee-ee Too-oo'. We decided to get back to the station, in the vain hope that the train might leave early.

We pulled out on time, but, on bare wooden seats, in an unheated compartment and with one window completely missing, it wasn't a pleasant journey. It was also inordinately slow; the journey of 120 miles took ten and a half hours. At 0700 next morning, cold, stiff and hungry, we stumbled across numerous rail tracks into the vast Calais Transit Camp to tag on to the end of a succession of seemingly endless queues for breakfast, document checking and changing guilders into sterling.

Hopes of a ship that day lingered on until late afternoon. Then we were given shore leave until 2200 hrs and told that our ship would sail at 0600 next morning, Saturday 3 February. A hurried black market currency deal was necessary to provide French francs to ensure an enjoyable run ashore. It was bleak and shivery next morning, but the trooper left on time and eight hours later docked at Harwich. By 1500 hrs a 'Leave Special' was steaming towards Newcastle 'and all points north'. We gazed rapturously out of the windows, drinking in every detail of the bare winter landscape – not much more than innumerable hedges, gaunt trees and ordinary houses, towns and villages, but it was 'Blighty'! Only when fading daylight made it fruitless to strain the eyes further did we settle down to sleep or to play cards, using English money for a change.

It was just half an hour short of midnight by the time the familiar arch of the Tyne Bridge, then a moon-glint on the river far below, confirmed that this was indeed 'home'. A few minutes later the fuggy carriages were disgorging streams of sleepy, shivering uniformed Geordies onto platform eight of Newcastle Central Station. We waved cheerio to our Scottish pals, who had still more hours of travel ahead of them, then rushed outside to see if the tramcars were still running.

That leave followed the normal pattern of wartime visits home – luxuriating in hot baths, stoking up on home cooking, undressing and changing into pyjamas then curling up between white sheets in a real bed. Predictably, almost without exception, immediately after a first greeting, people would ask, '. . . and when do you go back?' I'm sure that I wasn't the only one who felt like thumping some of them.

Home leave in wartime was subject to the vagaries of travel and, in particular, the state of the sea in the English Channel. Our leave entitlement was 'seven days at home' and, on arrival in the UK, everyone received a chit bearing a 'Leave Party Number' and the date, time and port to which he was required to report for the return crossing. As the day of return drew near, all service personnel on leave from the continent would pay particular attention to weather forecasts and news bulletins on the radio. Storms in the Channel would raise the hopes of tens of thousands of men and women, all waiting to hear, 'The following Leave Parties will report to their embarkation ports twenty-four (or maybe even more) hours later than shown on their leave chits . . .'

On that occasion I was fortunate in getting a forty-eight hour extension, so it wasn't until the early hours of Shrove Tuesday, 13 February, that I was back in the dark, cold, almost-deserted Newcastle Central station to catch the 0230 train to Harwich, where we arrived around noon. The next sailing wasn't until 0100 next morning and I passed the crossing with no more accommodation than a steel deck, made a little more bearable by occasional sips from a half bottle of whisky which my father had somehow managed to obtain as a 'going back present'. The crossing took ten hours, then came another wait in Calais for the 2230 train which deposited us at Antwerp railway station at 0930 the following morning.

Congregated outside the office of the RTO (Railway Transport Officer) were six or seven men of 41 Commando all needing to get back to Waspik, and we obtained permission to try hitch-hiking, rather than waiting around indefinitely for a truck from the Unit. We found an Army driver heading for Bergen op Zoom who took us to our Brigade Rear Echelon there and they arranged onward transport to Waspik. By 1800 hrs I was back in the cellar from which I had departed fourteen days earlier to go on seven days' leave. With the best part of half a bottle of Scotch to pass around for 'sippers', I was made very welcome.

During my absence the Waspik sector of the Maas River front had been generally quiet, with little more than the spasmodic exchange of shelling, mortaring and machine-gunning across the river. The Fighting Troops had continued to take turns in occupying the forward positions on the island of Capelsche Veer and there had been a few patrols across the main river, the Bergsche Maas, to check on enemy positions. A few days after I went on leave three men were crossing the Oude Maasje to the island when their boat capsized. Two were immediately swept away and drowned and, although the third was pulled from the water, he failed to revive after two hours' artificial respiration. In a very much lighter vein, one cross-river patrol, charged with finding out whether a particular German position was occupied, had reported in the affirmative, adding a rider to the effect that 'it was also established that at least one man of the Unit holding the north bank of the Maas is called Wilhelm.'

On the night of my return from leave 'B' Troop mounted Operation 'HUSSAR', a crossing to the north bank of the river, with a view to capturing a prisoner for interrogation. They landed without incident, but, when moving towards their objective, came under heavy enemy fire which inflicted a number of casualties and forced the Patrol Commander to order a withdrawal. One officer and one Other Rank, both badly wounded, had to be left behind. Two nights later Operation 'HUSSAR II', another 'prisoner snatch', was mounted by 'X' Troop, under Captain Cunningham.

The patrol crossed the river in two LCAs, touching down on the north bank just before midnight. After a five-minute softening-up barrage by medium artillery and mortars, followed by close-in fire from five Brens raking the top of the dyke, they stormed up. On reaching the top, the first party came upon seven or eight of the enemy running towards their stand-to trenches. They opened fire with TSMGs at 5 yards range and, as the Patrol Report records laconically, 'all went down'. The second party saw four Germans running towards their positions and opened fire with a Bren at 30 yards range; 'two went down'. Then a German was found crouching in a trench and, having 'bagged' their prisoner, the Patrol withdrew. It was all over in fifteen minutes, with eight or ten Germans having been killed or wounded and one taken prisoner, with no casualties to our men.

The prisoner was a Franz Neuhauser, an Austrian by birth, who had celebrated his eighteenth birthday only three weeks previously. Under interrogation he volunteered much more information than just his own 'name, rank and number', giving the names of his Section, Troop, Company, Battalion and Regimental Commanders. He also revealed that Lieutenant Bate, the Officer reported missing on the previous HUSSAR raid, had been found badly wounded and evacuated to hospital, but the man, Corporal Joe McKenna, had been dead when found, and was buried with Military Honours at Hank. It was learned later that the officer, Lieutenant Bate, a young volunteer from the South African Union Defence Force, died of his wounds; both he and Joe McKenna are now buried in Werkendam Protestant Cemetery.

That successful attack was a fitting finale to the Commando's tenure of the Waspik Sector of the Maas Front. Later that same day Commando Advance Parties reconnoitred fresh positions to be taken over some fifteen miles further up river. On 19 February the Unit pulled out of Waspik and moved to 's Hertogenbosch, there to take over a sector of river from the Canadian Lake Superior Regiment. Since going on UK leave, almost three weeks previously, the snow had practically disappeared and the Despatch Riders were back in the saddle again.

At that late stage of the war Allied Armies were moving forward on most fronts. The 'Ardennes Bulge' had been nipped out by the end of January and, during the first days of February US troops had cleared the last occupied areas of Belgium. In Holland things had begun moving again on 8 February, when the Canadian First Army launched an attack SE of Nijmegen, crossing the German frontier through the Reichswald and striking towards Kleve and Goch. This, the nearest offensive activity to 41 Commando's position, was some thirty miles to the east of us; on the Maas the front remained static.

At 's Hertogenbosch the Commando was given responsibility for about eight miles of the river between Bokhoven and Het Gewande so, with less than four hundred men to deploy, a continuous defensive line was out of the question. The tactics adopted, therefore, were to have three Troops 'up', manning secure front line positions and observation posts on the river bank, and covering the gaps with minefields, booby traps and patrols. The 'up' Troops were based in the almost deserted villages of Bokhoven, Crevecoeur and Empel, while the other two Troops were held 'back' in nearby Voordijk and Orten, ready to provide assistance, if required. 'S' Troop, was centrally located at Engelen where their mortars and machine guns could provide support in both directions, while further firing positions were prepared and ammunitioned, so that their weapons could be rapidly redeployed there, ready for immediate use.

Commando Headquarters was set up in 's Hertogenbosch ('Bois le Duc' or 'Duke's Wood'), a town of some 60,000 inhabitants lying less than three miles from the river. The various offices were located in vacant houses on the northern fringes of the town, while most HQ personnel were billeted with Dutch families. Unlike 'civvy billets' in the UK, however, this was on an accommodation only basis, all food being issued from Section cookhouses. Initially we took our food back to the billet to eat, but the ordeal of having every bite followed by the envious eyes of young Dutch children, who seemed to exist on sugared bread and vegetables, proved too

187

much. Thereafter we ate our meals standing around the hydro burners in the 'cookhouse', an empty private garage where the tins of compo were heated, until a messroom was organized. Any food that was surplus, or could be scrounged, was gratefully received in the billets.

Every day would see some kind of harassing activity somewhere along our river frontage. Most fixed German positions had been pinpointed and some of these would be engaged by the Commando's mortars or machine guns, or, on occasions, HQ would ask for supporting artillery to carry out shoots on specific targets. Then, from time to time, a squadron of tanks would roll within range to do a shoot of their own. The Germans had similar patterns of harassment, so Despatch Riders delivering messages around the Troop positions or to nearby units could suddenly find themselves involved in a 'hate session'.

The Commando's immediate artillery support was provided by a Polish Field Battery, to whom we delivered frequent messages. These, no doubt, gave map references, times, rates of fire, etc, for the employment of their guns, so presumably someone in their HQ was able to read them! Personally, I never came across anyone who spoke more than one or two words of English, although even that was much more than my command of Polish.

In addition to these long-range exchanges, both sides engaged in patrol activity into the other's territory to check whether known positions were still occupied, to determine if routes for future planned incursions had been mined, or just to see if the enemy was on his toes. The Commando had been in its new location for about a week when orders were received to plan two more 'Prisoner Snatching' Patrols to be code-named MOUSETRAP and FLYCATCHER.

Reconnaissance Patrols for both operations were successfully carried out during the night of 2 March and MOUSETRAP was put in motion two nights later. During the crossing one of the assault boats was found to have sprung a leak and it sank some ten yards from the enemy shore, but there was no loss of men or equipment and the Patrol carried on. Moving up the dyke face towards the German position, however, mines were encountered which had not been there at the time of the reconnaissance and the Patrol Commander was wounded. Surprise having been lost, he ordered a withdrawal and the one serviceable assault boat managed to make two crossings to bring all men back. Next evening a Patrol went across to bring back one of the mines, which confirmed that they were, indeed, 'Schuh' anti-personnel.

FLYCATCHER went ahead on 10 March. 'A' Troop crossed the Maas in two LCAs and, after some softening-up artillery fire on an area known to be held by German troops, moved along the dyke. They used the standard 'Trench clearing drill' of throwing a hand grenade into a bunker position, then following it up with bursts of TSMG fire. After seven or eight positions had drawn blank, they were rewarded with a cry of pain and dragged out a wounded German – mission accomplished. On their return one Marine was reported missing, but he later swam across; there were no British casualties.

The NOIC (Naval Officer-in-Charge) of landing craft on that stretch of the River Maas, Lieutenant R.O.S. Salmon RNVR, was something of an extrovert. In his opinion, taking his craft across the river constituted a formal occasion, so he opted to wear a top hat and white gloves. He also considered that it was correct to leave a 'visiting card', so he had prepared a notice board which was erected on the north bank, proclaiming, in German, that the 'Rosstiny Taxi Service' was offering trips to England for enemy personnel at – Wehrmacht (Army) 2 Marks and Volkssturm (Home Guard) 1 Mark. It ended with the words 'Look out for the top hat' and was 'signed' with a drawing of one.

The German prisoner was *Oberwachtmeister* Georg Fickenster, who had suffered wounds in the arm and the thigh. He was interrogated in hospital soon after capture and, not unnaturally, as the interrogation report put it, 'he found concentration extremely difficult'! Only after being assured several times that there were no other Germans present did he agree to talk, and then he said that he was 31 years old, came from Frankfurt am Main and that his Unit was 3 Coy of 1 SS Polizei, but he stressed that he was no Storm-trooper. He had been given only two months' infantry training and, like all the others of his unit, considered himself to be a policeman, not a soldier. He gave information about his Company's arms and equipment, communications system, ration deliveries, etc, and alleged that the Commanding Officer spent most of his time in a cellar under Company HQ.

It wasn't only the Germans who took shelter in cellars, of course; the civilians in 's Hertogenbosch made good use of all that were available. Lying, as it did, so close to the front line, the town suffered frequent shelling by German artillery, which caused numerous casualties. The Signals Despatch Office had been set up in the front room of an empty house on the main road leading out of town and in the direction of a nearby cemetery. Frequently, whilst awaiting the next despatch, a funeral cortège would pass the window, and most of them were much more macabre affairs than in the UK. The horse-drawn hearse was virtually a glass-walled tank, with the ornately carved wooden framing painted in sombre black, but with each corner post surmounted with a grinning white skull!

As well as the civilians, the Commando was also suffering casualties, but more often from mortar bombs machine-gun fire and snipers, rather than artillery, although we also had one man killed when he trod on one of our own mines. An open-sided outhouse at the rear of the HQ building was used as a mortuary. It was a sobering experience, going out on a trip, to pass another blanket-shrouded figure awaiting burial, and particularly poignant when you had known the dead man, as was the case when one of our Signallers had been killed on the Maas the previous evening.

Despatch Riders were part of the Signals Section of the Commando and one of our jobs was to undertake spells of duty at the 'Advance Signals Post'. This had been set up in a house, one of a long terrace at the extreme northern edge of the town, which had an unimpeded outlook over the flat countryside stretching towards the river and far beyond. That was the direction in which we would look expectantly for the first morning flight of V1 flying bombs, launched from ramps far to the north in German-occupied Holland.

The show would start just before the sun began to put any brightness into the sky, when a number of small orange-red lights appeared above the horizon. Then, as they gradually increased in size, it could be distinguished that the lights were propelling black blobs through the dawn sky. Soon the tonk-tonk-tonk-tonk-tonk noise of engines would reach us and it became possible to discern the double-barrelled shape of the missile – an aircraft fuselage forming the bomb body and the ram jet engine perched on top.

It was commonplace to see a dozen or more 'buzz bombs' in flight at the same time, ranging far and wide across the morning sky, but we could watch them in safety, knowing that they were heading further afield, for Antwerp or London. Only rarely did we see a 'maverick' bomb drop out of the sky and never very close.

Another 'once in a lifetime' spectacle, during our stay in 's Hertogenboscsh, was to see the roads of southern Holland carrying many more boats than the rivers and canals! The British and Canadian armies were building up for an assault across the Rhine and appeared to be transporting anything and everything that would float through Holland into Germany. Canvas boats, pontoon floats, motor boats and infantry landing craft of all descriptions were travelling piggy-back on every kind of military vehicle capable of bearing the load. Huge tank transporters, massive enough to carry the biggest and heaviest of tanks, were dwarfed by large steamers strapped to their backs. To manoeuvre such loads through the tortuous narrow streets of Dutch towns, especially around sharp corners, took much time, patience and effort, leaving more than one scraped building to mark their passage.

A week after the FLYCATCHER raid it looked as though 41 Commando was all set to be relieved by 48 Royal Marines Commando and moved back to South Beveland. Advance Parties left to reconnoitre billets in Goes, the capital of the province; then, abruptly, the move was cancelled. That same day we suffered three casualties during a German mortar attack on Crevecoeur, which sparked off a prolonged 'hate sessions' by both sides. Typhoon aircraft attacked the Germans in Ammersooien, a town a mile or so from the river, and in turn the enemy moved a battery of guns into Hedel and proceeded to shell Crevecoeur. Cross-river activity remained at a high level during the next day when one Troop of 48 Commando joined 41 to take over 'A' Troop's positions, seeming to confirm that they would soon be inheriting our 's Hertogenbosch sector.

The increased belligerent activity could possibly have had some bearing upon the decision, which had already been made, to send one of our Troops across the Maas to destroy a known enemy post. The operation had been code-named HELEN; a preliminary reconnaissance of the area to be attacked was carried out and other

191

preparations put in hand. Immediately before the assault went in there would be the usual artillery softening-up and, in addition, two more Fighting Troops and the Support Troop would provide a strong 'firm base' on our side of the river, ready to assist in the attack, or to facilitate a withdrawal if either course of action might prove necessary.

A further Patrol reconnoitred the chosen route to the enemy position, to verify that it was mine-free and, at 0345 on 22 March, 'Y' Troop landed on the north bank from two LCAs. The position scheduled for the attack was found to have been evacuated, so the Troop Commander immediately ordered an assault on another one, a short distance further along the dyke, achieving complete success, with all the occupants being killed. The Patrol then searched nearby houses and, finding that the enemy had decamped, were returning along the dyke when fired upon by a machine gun which inflicted a casualty. The position was immediately attacked and the gun silenced; then the patrol went on to assault another gun position where, once again, the occupants were killed. At that point the Troop was heavily engaged by a number of machine guns, suffering more casualties, and the Patrol Commander ordered a withdrawal.

On that occasion, too, Lieutenant Salmon had been in charge of the landing craft, wearing his top hat and white gloves, and once again he left a notice board on the north bank of the river. This time he advertised an 'amazing special offer, for one week only' of a free passage to England for all Germans! It continued with the admonition that 'This offer cannot be repeated – the bombardment is coming'. Again it ended with 'look out for the top hat'. On 19 June 1945 Lieutenant Salmon was awarded the DSC for 'services to the 509th LCA Flotilla'.

Later in the morning German medical orderlies and stretcher bearers could be seen collecting casualties and our men were ordered not to open fire. In the afternoon, under cover of a white flag, the Germans sent a party across to the front of the dyke where the action had taken place and were seen to carry away a British casualty who was still alive. The Germans searched the area but found no more. 41 had suffered two killed, four wounded and two missing; nine Germans were confirmed killed.

Two days after HELEN, on 24 March, the Germans sent over an

early morning patrol of five or six men which was soon spotted and fired on; the enemy quickly withdrew under smoke. As usual, the Germans retaliated with a mortar attack on the Commando positions, killing one man and badly wounding three more, two of whom died soon afterwards.

That turned out to be the day on which the boats we had seen being moved through Holland by road returned to their own element – General Montgomery had launched the 2nd Army's assault across the Rhine. Airborne Troops and No. 1 Special Service Brigade spearheaded four landings in the vicinity of Wesel, the town being captured by No. 1 Special Service Brigade.

On that day, too, the Advance Party of 48 Commando arrived in 's Hertogenbosch and ours left for Goes. The main body of 48 arrived next day and the two units double-banked in Troop locations until midnight, when 41 relinquished responsibility for that sector of the river. On 26 March the DRs shepherded the Unit convoy out of 's Hertogenbosch, away from the war zone, and back to Zeeland.

Chapter 14

THE END OF THE WAR AND
OCCUPATION DUTIES IN GERMANY

In South Beveland the unit was to take over the civilian billets previously occupied by 48 Royal Marines Commando and, as suitable accommodation was at a premium in the area, the number one priority of the Advance Party had been to ensure that none of those billets was lost to another unit! Headquarters and two Fighting Troops were stationed in Goes (pronounced 'hoose'), the capital, and the other Troops were housed in the nearby small towns of 's Heer Hendrikskinderen, 's Heer Arendskerke, Heinkenzand and Wemeldinge. Wemeldinge stands at the northern end of the South Beveland Canal, the only shipping link between the east and west arms of the river Scheldt, so it was vital that the lock gates there should be guarded night and day.

Initially, Frank Barker and I were allocated to the home of Mevrouw van Opstal, a neat, modern house in Violenstraat on the outskirts of town. It was comfortable and we felt very fortunate with our situation, but it lasted only a few days, because the husband came home! Mijnheer van Opstal, a merchant seaman, had been at sea at the outbreak of war and ever since then had been serving with the British Merchant Navy. It was understandable that he didn't want a couple of foreign servicemen sleeping in his second-best bedroom, so we had to move.

Our next billet, in the home of Mijnheer Smallegange, a baker with house and shop premises at Oud Vismarkt 4 (No. 4 Old Fishmarket), proved to be even better. It was very conveniently located in town, barely fifty yards from the market square, and we were given a commodious room at the front of the building, over the shop. We soon discovered that we had become part of a large Dutch household, as, in addition to five children aged six to twenty, a local girl lived in to help in the house and shop, and there was also a young girl evacuee. The elder children spoke good English and, apart from taking our meals at Headquarters, we became part of the family, even to obeying Heer Smallegange's command, '*Boven!*' (Upstairs!) each evening when he felt that it was time to go to bed. He had to get up early to start his baking.

The Commando hadn't been moved back to Zeeland for a rest cure but to train as a mobile striking force for employment in the 'war of movement' which was expected to develop on the plains of northern Germany once the Allies had established themselves across the Rhine. In addition, with the Germans still occupying the islands in the estuary of the East Scheldt, strategic installations in the area were at risk and the Commando was required to provide a defence force for South Beveland.

The new mobile role envisaged for the Commando would require rapid and efficient radio communication between Headquarters and the Troops whilst on the move, so all command jeeps were fitted with brackets to take the more powerful '68' sets. Then Officers and Signals Personnel began perfecting signals procedures to maintain overall control of the Commando and to operate in conjunction with other units, including tank and artillery support.

For the men in the Fighting Troops, being part of a mobile force wouldn't make a great deal of difference to the basic infantry tactics to be employed once they had de-bussed in close proximity to the enemy. However, within a few days of arrival, they started on another serious 'refresher course', as laid down in a detailed day-by-day programme drawn up by Major Young. Once again, too, great emphasis was laid on the zeroing and firing of all infantry weapons to set proficiency standards. In addition, another weapon had been added to the armament of the Commando and two men per Troop were sent for training in the use of flame-throwers.

The Troops also brushed up on their infantry tactics, practising the various 'drills' for assaulting enemy positions, clearing bunkers, etc, but not at the expense of the parade ground aspect of Royal Marine life and 'saluting was to be punctiliously carried out'. There were also the usual 'Keep Fit' occupations such as P.E. and route marches, some of which, on occasions, included the Despatch Riders.

Commando Headquarters had taken over the vacant Oude Mensenhuis (Old Men's Home) and the main entrance was flanked with a pair of highly polished shell cases. It was also graced by a ceremonial sentry with rifle and fixed bayonet; during the hours of daylight the Union Flag flew above the doorway. The local children never tired of watching the sentry spring to attention, bring his rifle up to the slope and give a smart butt salute to every officer who entered the building.

Directly across the narrow street fronting the Mensenhuis stood a row of small workshops where our motor cycles were garaged, while the Signals Despatch Office was located in a room at the rear of the main building, looking out on to a secluded courtyard garden. The SDO was distinguishable by the score or so of telephone wires issuing from the top of the window, linking the hand-cranked exchange inside to the outlying Troops and other units on the Commando's network. DRs would also visit these local HQs daily, but in addition there was an appreciable number of much longer journeys to Army and Royal Marines Headquarters in Middelburg, Bergen op Zoom, Tilburg, Breda and Antwerp.

The run to Antwerp involved a hundred-mile round trip and, if the weather was particularly bad, the DRs might be allowed to use a jeep; if the bar of the Officers' Mess needed replenishment, a jeep was mandatory. On one such DR-cum-drinks journey, I managed to squeeze in a meeting with my brother-in-law Horace, who was stationed in Antwerp docks with an RAF Embarkation Unit. There wasn't much time to spare, so it was probably as well that he was teetotal and our meeting amounted to no more than a 'hello and goodbye' over a cup of tea in the rather basic dockyard NAAFI.

In the market square of Goes there was a much more attractive tea-and-biscuits canteen where, on some evenings, Mies, the eldest daughter of the Smallegange family, would help out as a volunteer waitress. There was little control over the number of packets of biscuits we could buy so on those nights I would head back to Oud Vismarkt 4 with my battledress blouse bulging more like an ATS girl than a Royal Marine. Arrival at the billet would be to the great delight of the younger Smalleganges.

In Goes the unit had become eligible to participate in a Second Army scheme of 48-hour leaves in Brussels and, only a week after arriving there, Frank and I were lucky. A three-tonner truck took the leave party of some twenty men the eighty miles to the Belgian capital, to be accommodated with full board, as non-paying guests, at the fully-staffed Hotel Metropole in Place Rogier.

We were given a list of Do's and Don't's for the leave period and a major one of the latter was 'Not to eat in any civilian establishment other than your leave hotel' because this would upset the city's food distribution arrangements. There were no restrictions on drinking in civilian cafés and bars, however, but this proved to be an overrated and expensive pastime. The simple matter of buying a beer was bedevilled by the compressed air delivery system which produced very much more 'head' than beer. Behind every bar counter there would be rows of partially-filled glasses waiting for the froth to settle before being topped up again, then after another squirt from the pump a wooden spatula would be used to scrape off the surplus head before the glass went back for a further period of settling down.

Spirits could be obtained much more quickly, but a combination of basically high prices, the inevitable 'hostess' system and a ten percent service charge made them exorbitant to us. That first evening Frank suggested cognacs as a finale, so we entered a café and he ordered two. A 'floozie' hostess sidled up to him saying, 'One for me too, soldier?' Frank reluctantly agreed and three very small glasses were lined up on the bar counter, hers no doubt containing only coloured water. When asked the price, the barman said 'Two hundred francs', about a week's pay to us, which Frank promptly queried. The barman pointed to each drink in turn saying, 'Sixty, sixty, sixty, plus service – two hundred francs'. Frank repeated the barman's words in amazement, put his money back in his pocket and said, 'C'mon, Mitch, let's get out of here!' We did.

Back in Goes the training programme went on apace, but, as the Allied armies continued to advance into Germany from east and west, it was becoming clear the Commando wouldn't see any action in Germany. On 5 April, the very day on which we went to Brussels, 45 Royal Marines Commando of No. 1 Special Service Brigade had taken Osnabruck and troops of the 6th Airborne Division had entered Minden. Further south, American troops were daily

197

moving further east, while the Russians pushed inexorably west-wards.

By 21 April the Russians had reached the suburbs of Berlin and it was clear that the end was near. On 4 May, on Lüneberg Heath, General Montgomery accepted the surrender of all German forces in North Germany, Holland and Denmark.

In Goes we had been able to follow the progress of the Allied Armies on a map displayed in the window of a small newsagent's shop close to Commando HQ, which the proprietor had updated daily by moving lines of coloured pins. On the day the war in Europe came to an end, this service was terminated with the single word 'KAPUT!' – 'Finished!' – written in large letters over the map of Germany.

The surrender of the German Armies in North-West Europe came into effect at 0800 hrs on 5 May 1945; Holland was completely free again, after five years of occupation. That evening the market square of Goes, illuminated by a blazing 'Victory Bonfire', became thronged with a jubilant, dancing, singing mass of civilians and servicemen. Long fingers of searchlight beams circled the sky to demonstrate the end of the long wartime blackout and the celebrations continued into the early hours of the morning.

Three days later the war with Germany came to an 'official' end, when the British Government declared 8 May a national holiday – 'Victory in Europe Day'. To mark the occasion the Commando organized a Victory Dance in a church hall near the market square, with a local band to provide the music and bar supplies trucked in from Antwerp, the liquor capital of the area.

The dance was in full swing and all was going as planned when the bartenders surprisingly announced that stocks of beer had run out. There was, however, still a goodly supply of spirits and liqueurs, and these the amateur barmen, having only one size of glass to hand, continued to dispense in liberal quantities. At some point during the evening we realized that Bill Smith was no longer with us and simply assumed that he had wandered off on his own. On making our way billet-wards very much later we discovered that this had indeed been the case, but he hadn't wandered very far. We almost tripped over him, stretched out flat on the pavement outside the hall, dead to the world. He was hauled to his feet and manoeuvred into headquarters to sleep it off. He should have been

Duty DR next day, but was in no fit state to ride, so we covered for him.

That there was no longer a war in Europe had no marked effect upon the Despatch Riders' work load. Bill and I, however, were soon to receive an unexpected bonus when, less than two weeks after VE-Day, we were abruptly detailed off to join a 'leave party' going to Germany next day on a purely sightseeing trip!

Those who were able borrowed cameras from their Dutch hosts and, on the morning of Whit Saturday 19 May, two 3-tonner trucks, packed with twenty or more boisterous Marines, together with a pile of blankets and some boxes of Compo rations, rolled out of Goes. The weather was warm and sunny, and the canvas sides of the trucks were rolled up to give an all-round view. The journey started off along the Despatch Riders' 'canteen trail' of Breda, Tilburg and Nijmegen, then, a few miles further on, we entered Germany and jolted in turn through the ruins of Kleve, Kalkar and Xanten, heading for the Rhine. We crossed via a floating pontoon bridge, leading directly to Wesel, but, before entering the town, experienced our first encounter with 'D.P.s'. Displaced Persons, people who had been separated from their homes by the war, whether confined in concentration camps, used as forced labourers in Germany or simply having been in the wrong country when war broke out, were to prove a major problem for Allied governments for many years thereafter.

In 1945, to ensure that none of those travelling from Eastern Europe were carrying any unwanted bugs on their persons, the River Rhine had been constituted as a *cordon sanitaire* and, before being allowed to cross over, all civilians were made to suffer the indignity of de-lousing. Long lines of men and women waited their turn to have a rubber hose attached to a hand pump inserted between underclothing and skin to be given generous squirts of anti-louse powder, downwards and upwards, back and front.

As we passed through Wesel the borrowed cameras clicked, even though there was little to see other than mounds of rubble, obliterated streets and shrivelled, leafless trees; there was no sign of life of any kind. Beyond the city the countryside, although unmarked by the ravages of war, was equally deserted; the entire land seemed empty and dead.

We were heading for Essen and for a while our route lay along one of Hitler's much-vaunted autobahns. It was devoid of any other traffic, so the drivers were able to indulge in an unaccustomed spree of speeding. To arrive in 'Kruppsville' was to enter another graveyard of a city, but one with a difference. The vast expanse of masonry rubble and the empty shells of buildings were interspersed with acres of twisted steelwork which had once been armaments factories.

The trucks made a 'photo stop' outside the ruins of one of these Krupp works, as two German girls were approaching it from the opposite direction, walking down an otherwise completely deserted street. In any other country of the world, notwithstanding any language problem, they would have been greeted with a barrage of wolf-whistles and facetious remarks, but not in Germany at that time. Immediately after the German surrender a strict Non-Fraternization ('Non-frat') Order had been imposed, making it a serious offence for Allied Service personnel to have any form of social contact with enemy nationals, of either sex, except as required in connection with their duties. The girls walked past, we looked at them and they looked back at us, but, apart from the clicking of cameras, all in complete silence. By dusk we were happy to have moved away from a succession of such scenes of devastation into unscarred countryside and spent the night in a vacant school put at our disposal by the local American Military Authorities.

Next day, Whit Sunday, was another gloriously sunny day as we moved on to Düsseldorf, there to find yet another empty, desolate wasteland of rubble and the sickly stench of rotting flesh. Where the original street pattern had been obliterated, Army engineers had bulldozed access roads through the ruins. During one brief halt in our bouncing progress through the city I looked around for something distinctive to photograph. The best I could find was a column of masonry some fifteen feet high, which had obviously been the corner of a substantial building at a road junction, the street name-plates were still in place. The names meant nothing to me, but, many years after the war, visiting a re-built Düsseldorf, I recognized one of those names, Königs Allee, the most prestigious shopping street of the city.

From Düsseldorf the trucks travelled back towards the Rhine, heading for Neuss and Cologne. We re-crossed the river by way of another pontoon bridge, but American-built this time, named the

Ernie Pyle Bridge after one of their most popular writers. Here we met up with more DPs when our 3-tonners had to join a long string of trucks heading for the bridge, taking hundreds of them to the West; no doubt they had all been properly de-loused.

Cologne was also a dead and virtually deserted city, although, like Essen, many substantial buildings were still standing as empty, roofless shells. The trucks trundled through the ruined streets to the Cathedral. The massive edifice, although scarred and slashed by bomb and shell splinters in a number of places, towered high above us, still amazingly intact. The cathedral square was a litter of broken masonry, felled lamp posts and a solitary German tank. On the far side stood the ruins of the Hauptbahnhof, the main railway station, no more than an arched steelwork skeleton rising from a carpet of shattered bricks and glass fragments.

Bill and I walked around the Dom, inspecting the external damage, then, finding the main door standing open, went inside. There were a few civilians moving around, some in clerical garb, but others seemed to be, like ourselves, merely sightseeing. Outside again, we walked to the rear of the building and found ourselves directly in line with the Hohenzollern Bridge. Like every other Rhine bridge, it had been blown and the roadway led down into the river instead of across it. We took photographs of each other with the huge twin spires of the Cathedral as a backdrop, marvelling at its survival in the midst of the destruction all around.

From Cologne it is about one hundred and fifty miles to Goes, so the trucks started back early in the afternoon. En route to Aachen, we passed close to another heap of rubble that had once been Düren, probably the ultimate example of 'saturation bombing'; the original street pattern appeared to have been completely obliterated.

Moving from Germany into Belgium at Aachen was to pass from an empty, dead country into one bustling with life. Although the frontier towns had been bombed and shelled, and were badly damaged, they were nevertheless crowded with people. It was Whit Sunday, everyone was dressed in their 'Sunday best' and religious processions were encountered in every town. In Hasselt it took half an hour for a procession to pass and the streets to clear sufficiently to enable our trucks to proceed. A brief halt was made in Antwerp for tea and buns, then it was over the border into Holland at

Putte and the drive through South Beveland back to Goes.

The very next day our Brigade received a Move Order with the unambiguous codename of Operation DEUTSCHLAND. We were to take up occupation duties in Germany. By the following Saturday morning all was ready and the DRs began their task of shepherding the long road convoy away from Zeeland. The 'specifics' were – Speed 15 MIH (Miles in Hour): Road Spacing 40 VPM (Vehicles per mile) and, as a rider: *The attention of all troops is drawn to the Non-Fraternization Order, and the severity of the punishment following a breach of the Order cannot be over-emphasized.*

Once again the route lay through Nijmegen and into Germany via Kleve and Kalkar, but on this occasion the Rhine was crossed at Rees. Once across, the snake of trucks was guided north east to Bocholt, where it split up, distributing the various elements of the Commando to a number of different locations around Borken, a small town which lies only six miles from the Dutch border near the town of Winterswijk.

The basic duties of the Commando in that area of North Rhine-Westphalia were to guard vital services, in particular the trains operating on the main railway line between Borken and Rheine some fifty miles away, and the local distillery! In immediate post-war Germany these weren't the perfunctory tasks that might be imagined, because the country was in a turmoil. Gangs of Russian DPs, many of whom had armed themselves, were roaming far and wide, engaged in murder, rape and pillage, hell-bent on exacting revenge upon the enemy which had incarcerated and maltreated them.

To go some way towards providing protection for the civilian population, the operational Troops of the Commando and 'B' Echelon were stationed in eight small towns scattered over more than a hundred square miles of Germany – Borken, Gemen, Heiden, Holthausen, Lembeck, Oding, Rhade and Weseke. By a strange twist of fate, Borken had been the home town of one of the German-born 10-IA Commando men who had been attached to 41 since just before D-Day, and it was soon common knowledge that the welcome home from his ex-girl friend had been anything but friendly.

In addition to providing a deterrent to roving bands of DPs, the widespread distribution of the Commando was also designed to 'Show the Flag'. During the hours of daylight the Union Flag was flown outside every Troop Headquarters and beneath it a large notice-board instructed all German males over the age of fourteen to doff their caps as they passed. Anyone caught trying to sneak past without complying could be dragged back and made to stand bareheaded, facing the flag, for as long as the Officer-of-the-Day deemed appropriate. Teenage cyclists, naturally, pedalled furiously past, shouting incomprehensible remarks and any driver or DR in the vicinity would be ordered off in pursuit of them. Such an order couldn't be disobeyed, but most of us 'came the old soldier' by simply keeping out of sight for a while then reporting back, 'Sorry, sir, but they got away.'

For those men detailed off for train guards sixty were needed every day to start a tour of duty lasting two and a half days; living and messing conditions en route, mainly on the train, were primitive. We weren't involved in these guards, but had our own problems, one of which was the potential danger from Werewolves. These were said to be Hitler Youth fanatics who had banded together to prey upon Allied occupation troops. A solitary Despatch Rider on a deserted road was particularly vulnerable as a baulk of timber flung on the road would catapult him out of the saddle, while a length of invisible piano wire, stretched taut between two trees, could probably take off a head as neatly as Madame Guillotine.

This latter possibility was taken seriously by the High Command and for a while DRs were permitted to use jeeps. This didn't last for very long, however – possibly Despatch Riders could be replaced more easily than jeeps – and we went back to our bikes. For some time thereafter we tended to ride more slowly than usual, bent low over the petrol tank.

A further problem was that the roads were in an appalling state of disrepair, necessitating a continual look-out for potholes. Nevertheless it was easy to forget about piano wire and potholes if you had passed safely down a particular stretch of road only an hour or so previously, as was brought home to me when returning from a trip to Wesel, some twenty-five miles from Borken.

The road was, as usual, completely empty and the throttle was quite wide open as I swept around a bend to be suddenly confronted by a deep pothole. I managed to steer the front wheel clear, but the rear wheel struck with a jarring blow. The impact was so great that the pillion stays crumpled, squashing the mudguard hard down on the tyre and, with a dead rear wheel, and a strong smell of scorched rubber, the bike slithered to a halt. In the gathering gloom of dusk, on a completely deserted woodland road, I could almost hear the howls of Werewolves scenting a kill! Extreme loneliness, and a dash of panic, must have supplied the brute strength needed to enable me to reduce the bending of the mudguard stays sufficiently to free the wheel and allow me to ride back to Borken.

The quirk of national pride, requiring the doffing of caps to the British flag, didn't last for long, but the 'Non-frat' Order remained in force for a full three months. For some time before it was rescinded, however, it had been, as Horatio remarked to Hamlet, 'more honoured in the breach than in the observance'. While it lasted, however, it had been pleasant to be able to cross into Holland and talk freely with the locals – within the limits of one's vocabulary.

One drawback, however, was that the invariable topic of conversation of every Dutchman was bicycle tyres. With so much of their individual transport based upon push-bikes, replacing tyres worn out during the years of war was top priority for them. Presumably, being a motorcyclist, they thought that I might supply their needs, but I was asked so many times that, whenever I saw a purposeful Dutchman approaching me, I would get in first with *Het spijt me, geen fietsbanden!*' – 'I'm sorry, no bicycle tyres'; they invariably shrugged and turned away.

The Germans too had bicycles, but most of theirs were seen, hooked by the handlebars, dangling over the backs of the massive leviathans of the road then being used to move people about the country. Those huge vehicles with slatted timber sides, rising to perhaps eight feet above the road, were often towing one, or even two, similarly-sized monster trailers, all jam-packed with humanity. On the narrow roads of the area they were things to be given a very wide berth, but it was an Allied, not German, truck which almost put me back in hospital one day as I crossed from Germany into Holland at Gronau.

I had zipped over the border – there were no customs or any other formalities for DRs – and was approaching a long line of military vehicles parked facing in my direction on my side of the road. I was almost abreast of the first in line when it started to move off, turning directly into my path. Instinctively, I yanked the handlebars away from it and effectively executed the self-preservation manoeuvre of 'riding to ground'. The bike and I covered the next few dozen yards of carriageway in a horizontal position, with me still in the saddle and holding on to the handlebars, as showers of sparks streamed from all parts of the machine in contact with the concrete. Surprisingly, neither bike nor I suffered any real damage and, when getting to my feet, it was to see the truck responsible had completed its U-turn without pause and was speeding off into Germany.

Our billet in Borken was a large empty house fronting onto the main street, where we slept on bare boards and ate compo rations out of mess tins. Despite the minimal labour content of cooking compo, those who had the job were given the benefit of some elderly German prisoners-of-war as a fatigue party. One luxury we were all able to enjoy, however, was being able to take baths in the local hospital, where a uniformed attendant was on hand to run the water and clean the bath afterwards!

In mid-June, some two weeks after our move, a scheme for releasing people from the Armed Forces back into civilian life came into operation. Initially it was restricted to skilled craftsmen needed in UK industry to continue the war with Japan and to produce exports to get the country earning foreign exchange again, and building workers to make a start on the reconstruction of bomb-damaged cities; after that it was to be on a 'first in – first out' basis. There was also talk about 'training for civilian life', so we began to think that there might really be an 'after the war' for us. Throughout our Service life we had been singing, 'When this blinking war is over, oh, how happy I will be . . .', but, as year followed year, many had come to wonder if their luck would hold out until then.

The war against Japan was, of course, still very much in progress and, concurrently with releasing men from the Forces, there were 'Far East Drafts' to transfer Servicemen from Europe to the Pacific. Lists of names were posted on notice-boards and it was generally reassuring to see that these appeared to be based upon length of service in the Corps. Those who had survived four or five years of war began to feel reasonably confident of being passed over for drafting, but one couldn't breathe easily until??! On 26 June the first Far East draft from the Commando, of three Troop Commanders, the Padre, six Subalterns, seven SNCOs and eighty-four Other Ranks left, and no one knew when the next one would be.

For Despatch Riders life had settled down to a routine signals delivery service, interesting enough in its way as we were operating in enemy territory, but, basically, still just shuffling paper. The possibility of leaving all that behind for a few weeks appeared attractive, so, on 3 July, I volunteered for a parachuting course in the UK, which had the bonus of a leave at home afterwards. Two days later, however, all such extraneous thoughts were pushed from the mind when an Advance Party left Borken to reconnoitre a new location – Recklinghausen, in the Ruhr.

This move was code-named Operation BELSEN, obviously chosen because the Commando's next task, together with No. 4 Army Commando, would be to guard almost four thousand German prisoners being held in No. 4 Internment Camp. It wasn't learned whether any of the inmates had in fact had any connection with Belsen, but undoubtedly many of them had been guards at equally infamous extermination camps. One of the inmates was Alfried Krupp the 'armaments king', who remained in captivity until 1951.

In Recklinghausen most of the Commando was billeted in blocks of flats near the camp, but HQ troop was given an estate of detached houses, surrounded by a high chain-link fence topped with barbed wire. This was probably not so much as a deterrent to Germans, although talk of Werewolves were still prevalent, but as protection against marauding DPs. It would appear that the Occupation Forces had created some 'Displaced Persons' on their own account, as the previous occupants of the houses were still in the vicinity and, on occasion, were allowed to enter the compound to harvest their garden produce. Some, however, seemed to find more to interest them in the swill bins outside the cookhouse. The houses were unfurnished, but had been provided with beds and the mains electricity was functioning, so it was an up-market move. The houses had cellars, accessed by a very steep ramp from the back garden, and ours proved ideal as a workshop and garage for the bikes.

In marked contrast with practically deserted rural Borken, industrialized Recklinghausen was bustling with civilian activity. Despite having been extensively bombed, the town was still relatively intact and the coal mine was in full production. There was work for the civilian population, and shops and cafés were open for business, although not available to us because of the Non-frat Order. There was, however, one civilian establishment available to us which didn't involve fraternization, the pithead baths. Bathing parades, when we were marched there in parties, became part of our weekly routine.

The 'changing room' was no more than a large expanse of tiled floor, above which dangled hundreds of metal baskets attached to ropes passing over pulley blocks fixed high on the ceiling. After being allocated a basket, each man would lower his to the floor, strip to the buff and, with clothing and towel inside, it would be hauled up out of harm's way, before heading for the showers. More often than not a few dozen yards away there would be another group of naked men, looking very little different from ourselves, who had been our enemies only a few weeks earlier.

As a motorcyclist, one of the things I had been looking forward to doing in Germany was to ride my Matchless 350cc machine 'flat-out' on an autobahn. We had been given no more than an 'outline' map of the area, with little detail, but it did indicate that the Rhineland-Magdeburg motorway crossed the road to Bochum, very close to Recklinghausen and, at the first opportunity, I set off to find it. I rode slowly for mile after mile without any sign of a bridge over the road and had covered the entire nine miles to Bochum before accepting the fact that there just wasn't one. On the return journey I continued to look out for the elusive bridge and was almost back at HQ before noticing massive masonry walls at either side of the road, clearly the abutments of a bridge which no longer existed. I later found the access to the autobahn, a slip road nearer town, but, after a brief inspection, immediately abandoned any idea of speeding along it. Without exception the bridges over all minor roads had been blown and very few of the gaps had been fenced off. Only some time later did it dawn on me that the grassy mound topped with a line of trees which skirted our HQ Troop compound, only a few hundred yards away, was the autobahn!

Ten days after moving to Recklinghausen my name had reached the top of the leave roster again and, early on Sunday 15 July, a truckload of boisterous bootnecks set off, 'bound for Old Blighty's shore', and seven days' at home. The first leg of the journey was an 80-mile run to the 'railhead' at the Dutch border town of Gennep, where we endured a disspiriting six-hour wait before boarding the 'Leave Special'. Its standard of comfort – wooden slatted seating, a few broken windows and no heating – was typical, as was its speed. The journey to Calais, barely one hundred and eighty miles away as the crow flies, took a full twelve hours.

At 0400 on the Monday morning we once again stumbled over the multiplicity of rail tracks to the adjacent transit camp. As early bird arrivals, we felt confident that our trainload of troops would be on the next ferry to leave, and so it was, but that wasn't until 0900 the following morning. On that occasion it was the short sea crossing to Folkestone, and by late Tuesday evening I was back in Newcastle to hear my first, 'Hallo Ray! Home again? When do you go back?'

Conditions in the English Channel gave me a 'windfall' extension of 72 hours, so I was in Newcastle until mid-afternoon on Monday 30 July; it was Wednesday evening when I arrived back to Recklinghausen, seventeen days after leaving.

After reporting in at the Orderly Room, my 'Welcome Home' was a bit of a shocker, 'Just in time, Mitch! You're off to Manchester in the morning, for that parachute course,' and someone added comfortingly, 'I hear they're crying out for paras in the Far East!' It was no consolation to me to know that I was probably the only man in the entire Commando Brigade who possessed a slim volume entitled *Colloquial Japanese*, bought for interest's sake some years earlier! Another piece of news was that the Non-frat Order had been rescinded during my absence, but that was of no consequence at the time, as I didn't even have time to say 'Hello' to my motorbike.

The start back next morning gave every indication of the journey to England being very much smoother than my previous one. There were only eight of us bound for Ringway Airport, Manchester, and a 15-cwt truck with driver had been laid on to take us straight to our port of departure, Ostend, some two hundred miles away. At a NAAFI stop en route, purely by chance, we met up with a Belgian youth who was also on his way to England, but his trip wasn't in any way connected with the war, or Service life – he was off to enrol at one of our universities! It gave us some food for thought, as we couldn't even guess when we might get back to civilian life.

In the event, the truck managed to cover barely half of the journey that day. We ended up almost a hundred miles short and passed the night in a monastery-cum-transit camp at Bourg Léopold. Next morning our driver had to return to Reckling-hausen, so we were left to hitch lifts on passing vehicles, and it was evening before we reached the Ostend transit camp. There were no more ferries that day so we had to acquire some Belgian francs for a night ashore. We found Ostend to be a much more lively place than it had been some ten months previously after our return from Walcheren when we had to pay so much for fish and chip suppers.

Next day was a hot Saturday in August, but there was no ship for us. Instead we were able to visit those beaches previously fenced off with German barbed wire, carrying skull and crossbones *Achtung minen!* warning signs. Wearing thick battledress, we mingled with crowds of barefoot Belgians in bathing costumes and mused about men of military age drinking beer beneath striped umbrellas, sunning themselves on the beach or bathing in the sea, while we still soldiered on.

Sunday was another gloriously sunny day and, as our troop ship sailed out of Ostend harbour, it was given a stirring farewell from crowds of holidaymakers lining the piers. It was the long sea crossing to Tilbury this time and our 2100 hours arrival was too late for trains, so we were bedded down in the docks area. Next morning we left on an early morning train, but it was late evening before our party eventually arrived at No. 1 Parachute Training School at Ringway Airport.

Only then, when trying to find someone to whom we could report, did it impinge upon us that it was August Bank Holiday Monday and virtually everyone was away on leave. Eventually we were marched to a satellite camp some distance from the airport, allocated to a Nissen hut, told where to find the mess-hall, then advised that it wouldn't be open until after 0545 reveille next morning!

Immediately after breakfast we met the RAF Corporal who was

to be our instructor, presumably awaiting his third stripe, as all the others were Sergeants. Our squad of about two dozen was a mixed bag of all ranks, including commissioned officers, but there was no distinction in the training and when Corporal McLean gave the order 'Jump!', whether Major or Marine, you jumped or risked being RTU'd. The rule book didn't seem to be entirely specific on the subject, but it was generally accepted that, if a man refused his first jump, he was simply classed as 'unsuitable for parachuting' and left the course. After the first jump, however, refusal was a serious matter, warranting the ultimate disgrace of being 'Returned to Unit'. The vast majority would rather have broken their necks than refuse and be sent back to their unit with 'RTU' on their chit.

Parachute Training courses normally began with a week of 'toughening up', including lots of P.T. and other strenuous pursuits, but, being from a Commando unit, we were excused this. No one raised the point that for the previous eighteen months I had been a Despatch Rider, not a foot-slogger in a Fighting Troop. The course would consist of eight jumps in all, starting with two from a tethered balloon, followed by five from an aircraft and ending with a 'night balloon'. Before any parachuting began, however, there had to be lots of lesser jumping, to perfect the correct 'roll over' method of hitting the ground without injury. The first jumps were therefore from a height of no more than nine inches above ground; then we progressed to more realistic landings in a parachute harness hauled by pulley block a few feet above the floor of the aircraft hangar which served as gymnasium and training shed. Once the victim had fastened his harness he was hoisted up, his mates giving him a few hefty swings, and the instructor, choosing the right moment, pulled a quick released cord, then there was no option but to make a landing.

Next came 'the fan', designed to give a realistic simulation of an actual parachute landing, which was a bit more scary. No larger than the cooling fan of a car but with its blades fitted square-on to the axis of rotation, it was attached to the end of a steel cylinder around which was wound a steel cable with a parachute harness at the end. The fan was bolted on to the steel framework of the hangar at eaves level, some thirty feet above the floor, and in operation it was simply a matter of fitting the harness and jumping off. As the cable unwound, the cylinder spun the fan which generated sufficient air resistance to slow a man's descent to the landing speed of a real jump. The coming down was great; it was the climbing up that was a bit scary.

All 'real' jumps would be by a 'static line' hooked onto a rail inside the balloon basket or aircraft fuselage, which automatically pulled the parachute out of its pack. We had sessions of practising hooking up to the static line, the correct way to 'stand to the door', moving quickly along the aircraft and, most importantly, making a good exit. Aircraft jumps were made in 'sticks' of from two to ten men, and the longer the stick the greater the need for rapid movement along the aircraft and quick exits to ensure that, in action, the men landed in a cohesive group or, in our case, didn't end up in the trees at the edge of the DZ (Dropping Zone).

The order 'stand to the door' applied only to the first man in a stick, the rest simply lined up closely behind and followed him through the doorway as quickly as possible. When the command was given, No. 1 would move to the doorway, stand with his left hand on the edge of the opening, left foot on the edge of nothing and right hand grasping his right trouser leg about half-way down the thigh. When the red light alongside the door changed to green the Despatcher would slap him on the shoulder and bawl 'GO!!' in his ear; he went. Once outside the aircraft, the drill was to get your feet together as quickly as possible and bring the left hand over to clasp the right wrist. If you weren't slick enough, the slipstream would catch any outflung limb and spin you round like a top, 'corkscrewing' the rigging lines, which could result in an uncontrolled landing. The parachutes of the time didn't have the 'steerability' possessed by modern ones; all that could be done was to pull down on the front or rear pair of lift webs, spilling some air out of the canopy and so urging your descent in the chosen direction. If the rigging was twisted up, you were likely to come down 'all of a heap'!

One of the aircraft jumps was with a kit bag containing 50lbs of sand to simulate ammunition or other supplies, strapped to the right leg, so it was necessary to practise moving with this encumbrance. The bag had to be heaved forward with the right arm in harmony with a kick forward with the right leg, and a line of men practising the 'left foot forward, right kick and heave', routine was always good for a laugh by those involved. Invariably someone would start singing the dwarfs' song from *Snow White* and all would soon be chanting, 'Heigh-ho, heigh-ho, it's off to work we go!' as they thumped along. Jumping with it attached to the leg was practised from an aircraft fuselage about two feet above the ground.

Time and again, for a week, we repeated the various 'drills', for moving along an aircraft, standing to the door, exiting and landing. Interspersed with practical training sessions were instructional lectures, attending film shows to give us some insight into parachute manufacture and operation, including shots of German parachutists (who seemed to have a completely uncontrollable 'chute), what to do if you landed in water and watching WAAFS packing them at long tables in an aircraft hangar.

Our first two real parachute jumps were from 'balloons'. These were standard wartime barrage balloons, in essence a form of the helium-filled airship which in earlier days had been known as 'Blimps'. This name had arisen during the 1920s, when the British government was experimenting with two types of airship – those with an aluminium framework encasing the gas bags, classed as Type 'A' (Rigid) – hence the reference letters of the only two built – the R100 and the ill-fated R101 – while those without any metal framework were Type 'B' (Limp), so 'Blimps' they were!

During the war balloons, or more correctly their steel anchor cables, were a useful deterrent against low-level air attack. Single balloons would be tethered to merchant ships, while the forest of cables created by scores of them, strategically sited, could protect a large area. For parachute training a metal cage capable of holding eight men, with a 'door' – simply an opening in the side – was attached below the gas bag. A steel cable tethered the balloon to a winch on the back of a standard 'anchor vehicle', which could let the balloon float up, haul it down and transport it where required.

We had been warned that the programme of live jumps was at the mercy of the weather, as there had to be little wind so that we wouldn't be blown away, and good visibility to enable instructors to see men coming down and so be able to give any necessary instructions by loud-hailer. On the Monday, therefore, after a truck had taken us to the DZ for the first balloon jump, it wasn't a great surprise to be told that the wind was too strong, so we were taken back to Ringway. We were returned to the DZ in the afternoon and conditions were suitable, although, with a backlog of jumps to work off, there was a long wait before a balloon became available.

Eventually our turn came for the first jump and we filed into the cage; the RAF crew of the anchor vehicle released the winch; the cable started to unwind, allowing the balloon to rise, slowly but irrevocably. During the silent ascent Corporal McLean did his best to keep minds occupied with innocuous chit-chat and reiterating points made in the training. At the same time there were the inevitable 'wise-guy' comments, such as 'Third floor – ladies underwear, bed pans and potties' or 'Stop the balloon, Corp! I've changed my mind, I wanna be in submarines'. The balloon just kept going up and up until halted at about seven hundred feet, tethered to mother earth by no more than a long length of very slim cable.

Balloon jumps, we later appreciated, are quite different from those made from aircraft. The static line was attached by a short length of thin nylon string to a small pilot 'chute, designed to open the canopy, affixed to the top of the main parachute, and everything was pulled out of the parachute pack until the nylon snapped under the man's weight. After exiting the basket, therefore, a man had to fall the combined length of the static line, pilot chute, main canopy, parachute rigging and parachute harness, a vertical drop of about 150 feet, before a reassuring tug under the armpits signalled that all was well. From an aircraft, on the other hand, the slipstream opens the canopy almost immediately and, in a good 'tight' stick, there is time to nod 'Hiya' to your nearest neighbour as you float in the air, before being wafted away from each other. There were no reserve chutes, so it had to be right first time, but, once reassured on that point, you could enjoy floating down to earth – until the time came to prepare for landing! The cup of tea after that first jump, bought at a mobile Salvation Army Canteen at the edge of the DZ, was one of the best ever! Late that same afternoon we were also able to accomplish the second jump and could progress to our first aircraft jump.

This was scheduled for the next day, but first we were given a dummy run over the DZ to show us how it looked from the air, before having to get down there on our own. For most of us that was our first ever flight so we weren't surprised to learn that there was also a 'take-off drill'. The aircraft used for parachute training were 'Good old Daks', Dakota DC3s, the ubiquitous aerial work-horse of WW2. The interior was just as it had left the factory, with all the construction ribs exposed, the only fitments being the slatted timber seating running along both sides of the fuselage and a steel rail for the static lines along the 'ceiling'. With a full load of parachutists these aircraft had a problem in getting their tails off the ground in order to take off. So, when it was time to go, the command 'Prepare for take-off' would be given. Then we all shuffled forward along the seating, squeezing together as tightly as possible towards the nose of the plane to take the weight off the tail. The plane could then proceed to take-off and, once airborne, the 'passengers' could spread themselves out, in comfort, along the seating.

When it came to that first aircraft jump I was somewhere in the middle of the stick and, following closely behind the man in front, was out of the door and floating on air with my parachute opening in the slipstream before really knowing what had happened. The descent was uneventful and, luckily, a front-facing approach to the ground made it just right for a copy-book roll-over landing. After the usual cup of tea, our truckload of budding parachutists returned to camp glowing with a sense of achievement, to be greeted with news that capped even that momentous day – Japan had accepted unconditional surrender and the war was over!

The government had designated the following day, Wednesday 15 August, as Victory over Japan (VJ) Day and declared it a public holiday, but this had no immediate effect upon our set routine. We kitted up as usual and drew parachutes, but it was declared too misty for jumping, so we spent the entire morning just waiting to be taken to the aircraft. Lunchtime came and went with no improvement, then, abruptly, we were given three days' leave! There followed a flurry of collecting leave chits, ration cards and rail warrants, being transported to the railway station and we were off.

It was mid-evening when I arrived in Newcastle Central Station and took a tramcar to High Heaton. From all sides came the crackling of fireworks and the swoosh of rockets criss-crossing a sky made bright with the glow of many bonfires; the air was filled with the smell of wood smoke. As I neared the family home I could see the silhouettes of my parents, elbows resting on their garden gate, absorbed in the spectacle. I was able to get right up to them before saying, 'Hello, Mum; Hello, Dad!' and see the amazement on their faces at my sudden appearance. Until that moment they believed that I was hundreds of miles away 'Somewhere in Germany', as I had left home to return there only two weeks previously. I explained that I had been sent back to England on a course at Manchester and they were quite content to accept that without pressing for details.

Like all periods of leave, that one passed all too quickly; on the Sunday I returned to Ringway for 0545 reveille next morning to carry on with the parachuting course. The first jump that day was a stick of four when it was my turn to be No. 1 and I had to stand to the door. Looking down from the open doorway of the aircraft, with a bird's eye view of the English countryside some 500 feet below, was a very different experience from simply tagging along in a string of men moving down the aircraft and suddenly finding yourself outside. It looked an awful long way down to mother earth and I wondered what I was doing up there. Then the dispatcher slapped me on the shoulder, bawled '**GO!!**' in my left ear and I went.

That afternoon it was much more comfortable to be near the middle of a stick of ten and simply go with the rest, but my exit must have been sloppy. I was spun around by the slipstream until the rigging lines became corkscrewed almost up to the canopy. As I began the drill of kicking in the opposite direction, starting to unscrew, a loud-hailer voice came up to me saying, 'That's right, No. 6 – kick them out'. The job wasn't more than half-finished, however, when the voice came again, 'Stop kicking, No. 6 – you're almost down – take up landing position'. The twisted lines brought me to earth backwards and, unable to perform a roll-over landing, all the air was knocked out of my lungs and I probably collected another bruise or two.

The most potentially dangerous landings, however, arose from the kitbag jumps. The bag, strapped to the leg with a quick-release toggle, was fitted with a twenty-foot line, but some men hadn't attached these to their belts, so, immediately after landing, heads would swivel skyward, ears cocked for yells of 'Kitbag!' which meant that another fifty pounds of sand was hurtling down to the DZ with potentially lethal results.

By this time, with a few jumps to our credit, we could consider all those who hadn't progressed as far as we had to be 'rookies'. Some even went to the extent of collecting pieces of the nylon string used to attach the pilot 'chute to the static line – which would be scattered over the DZ – and fixing a strip for each jump to their smocks, like long-service medals! However, we did feel justified in singing the 'para' songs and, surprisingly, one still in vogue was 'Jumping through the Hole', despite the fact that all jumps were then being made from a doorway in the side of an aircraft, not through a hole in the floor. The most popular one was undoubtedly 'I ain't gonna jump any more', the words which ended every 'verse'. These verses were no more than the repetition, three times, of such gems as 'I'm looking for the WAAF who put a blanket in my chute', 'I'm looking for the Sergeant who forgot to hook me up' and 'They scraped him off the tarmac like a lump of raspberry jam', so, naturally, 'I ain't gonna jump any more'. But, of course, we did.

The eighth and final jump was the 'Night Balloon', which proved to be a rather eerie business. Standing on the edge of the DZ, awaiting your turn to use it, the balloon, floating at 700 feet, was visible only as a dark smudge against a slightly lighter sky. Every few seconds the single bawled out word **'GO!!'** came down from the dark smudge, but there was nothing to be seen until, with a sharp crack, which hadn't been noticed in the daylight jumps, another parachute opened and could be seen oscillating earthwards.

The ascent in the balloon and exiting from the basket were much less traumatic than the daylight jumps because you couldn't see anything! However, coming down and not being able to distinguish the ground was disconcerting as you didn't know when to prepare for landing. More than once it was a case of thinking 'Here it comes!', pulling down on the lift webs ready for a roll-over landing, but nothing happened. Then, suddenly, when you weren't expecting it, you hit the ground with a sprawling thump. We returned to camp in high glee, with a group of Belgians who had also just completed their course, and joined in with them singing *Je te plumerais*.

Next morning, without any ceremony, we were handed our parachutist's wings and, after a speedy session with needle and thread, hied to the nearby airport hotel to 'wet' them. A camera was produced for photographs with the newly-adorned right shoulders of battle dress blouses prominently displayed, then it was off on another seven days' leave which, of course, had been one of the incentives for volunteering for parachute training in the first place.

The return journey to Recklinghausen was fraught with transport delays and took almost as long as the leave. In consequence, we didn't get back to base until Saturday 8 September; I had been 'otherwise engaged' for precisely eight weeks since first setting off for 'seven days' leave at home'. During that time my haircuts hadn't been strictly 'Royal Marine', so it seemed advisable to put matters to rights by visiting a nearby civilian barber shop. The shop was empty apart from two men standing talking near the chair, the barber and an exceedingly tall German. I was motioned to sit down and, nearing the chair, saw that the latter had the unmistakable scar of a sabre cut on his cheek. In turn he had obviously spotted the bright new parachutist wings on my sleeve and uttered a single word to the barber, '*Fallschirmist*!!' I knew enough German to know that he had said 'Parachutist' and I wasn't too happy about the tone in which he said it, which seemed to imply, 'I know what I'd like to do with *that* lot!', so my sojourn in the barber's chair was slightly uncomfortable.

During my absence a scheme of 'Civilian Work Experience' had been instigated whereby men could start getting used to their peacetime jobs again, e.g. ex-butchers would spend one day a week in the local abattoir and miners went to work in the local pit. There were also 'organized entertainments' designed to keep the troops interested and, a week after returning, I was selected for the Commando's team in a 4 SS Brigade Motorcycle Rally. It had been organized by 47 RM Commando near their home base of Erkenschwick, and each Commando (41, 47 and 48 Royal Marines and No. 4 Army) plus Brigade Headquarters, fielded a team of six riders. The particularly muddy course began with a steep hill climb, followed by a tortuous cross-country circuit through a wood, which brought us back to descend the same hill. 41 finished second to 47, but we consoled ourselves with the thought that 'If only we'd had as much time to get used to the course as they had'!

A few days later a middle-of-the-night spot check of an outlying district of the town had the entire Commando out on the streets at 0100 hrs, fully rigged and armed. In small groups, each with a German speaker of 10-IA Commando, we roused all the occupants and searched every house. The net result of four hours' lost sleep was one antiquated shotgun, a barrel of illegally acquired pickled pork and the discovery that a few people had been spending the night in beds that weren't their own.

Towards the end of the month the Corporal-in-charge of DRs was returned to the UK for release and I was promoted in his place. This didn't relieve me of the job of taking my turn as Duty DR, but it did enable me to take the off-duty DRs on what I classed, officially, as 'Training Runs', but a more correct description would have been 'Fun Runs'. With two or three of the others following, I would set off along the autobahn, looking for an inviting exit point where I could take off, up or down a grassy embankment, and head for the open country. Surprisingly there were few fences to impede our progress and the runs could go on for miles and miles, across fields and through woods, until I found my way on to another road and we could map-read our way back or to any likely place for tea and buns.

There were, however, some nasty moments. More than once I roared up a steep embankment only to find that it carried a railway line and the sleepers were almost at the edge of the slope. Then it might prove possible to make a sharp turn, bounce over a few sleepers and head back down again, but not for everyone. Those who didn't make it either did a rapid 'back-pedal' to keep their machines upright while they went down the slope backwards or fell off and bike and rider rolled to the bottom.

One incident did make me more circumspect for subsequent occasions. We had had a good run from the autobahn, through woods and open country, then came upon a narrow beaten earth track leading up a low grassy hill. With three others following, I speeded over the top and had no option but to carry on down a track on the other side which led only to a floating walkway of timber battens, about three feet wide, chained end to end, across a wide expanse of water. If I had tried to stop most of us would probably have ended up in the water anyhow, so the only thing to do was to trust that the battens would have buoyancy enough to support the weight of a man and a motorbike.

They had, but only just. The first length tipped slightly as I moved on to it, then sank until it was awash, leaving a four-inch step at the far end where it was linked to the next in line. Scarcely breathing, I rode on, with each section in turn settling down in the water as it took the weight. At the far side there was another steep narrow track up an embankment and I zoomed thankfully to the top before daring to look back to see how the others were faring. By great good fortune, or good training!, they all got across safely and were soon up alongside me, giving my ears a pounding. Consulting our maps to determine the route back, we found that we had just crossed the Dortmund-Ems canal.

On other off-duty trips we roamed far and wide, and on one occasion I was persuaded by less mobile comrades, to ride to Mönchen Gladbach some fifty miles away. There was an immense prisoner-of-war camp there and I was commissioned to barter cigarettes for wrist watches with the inmates. It was too depressing an experience to repeat.

On another of our exploratory journeys around Recklinghausen we would come upon deserted ash-surfaced horse-trotting tracks. Then we would race around them, picturing ourselves as speedway riders, and there could be one German lady, who was nine or ten years old at the time, who retains a vivid memory of one of those occasions. As our quartette of motorcyclists came roaring round a blind bend we saw her walking across the track only a short distance ahead. Fortunately for all of our sakes, she didn't attempt to run, but simply froze in her tracks. We flashed past, two on either side of her, and next time round she was gone.

At the beginning of November the Commando was uprooted from industrial Recklinghausen and transplanted a hundred miles deeper into Germany, in the afforested countryside between Paderborn and Kassel. Headquarters and most of the Troops were stationed in the small town of Warburg, with two 'outlying Troops' in Lichtenau and Hardehausen, small villages on the edge of the extensive Hardehausen Forest. Brigade Headquarters was in Paderborn, some twenty-five miles away through the forest, and every ride there filled the mind of a solitary motorcyclist with thoughts of Werewolves and piano wires.

Warburg, because of its rail links, was a major transfer point for DPs being moved around the country and the Commando's job was the overall control of the town. This involved patrols by day and night, enforcing the curfew, carrying out traffic checks and house searches, providing round-the-clock guards for food dumps,

219

including the Warburg sugar factory and, primarily, controlling the railway station and the DPs passing through. Headquarters Troop was billeted immediately adjacent to the station in a large two-storey building which had probably been a school before being taken over as a barracks. A few days after our arrival in Warburg the Commando was given another job, codenamed Operation BUTCHER – the killing of deer in the nearby forests to provide food for the Ruhr.

The boundary between the British and American zones of occupation crossed the road to Kassel a dozen or so miles to the south of Warburg, so a few of us decided that it would be a good idea to make contact with our Allies. We sought out a Yankee unit, found their cookhouse and made the point that it was extremely cold outside. Mugs of coffee were eventually produced, but so grudgingly that it was abundantly clear that they just didn't want to know us. We got the message and thereafter stayed near the comfort of the barrack-room stove instead of riding around a freezing countryside on any 'Hands across the Ocean' expeditions.

I was Duty DR on Sunday 11 November and so had the morning trip to Brigade Headquarters in Paderborn. It was the usual cold, lonely ride through the forest and, on Sunday morning, there was no sign of movement in the town either. I was nearing the city centre, riding along a deserted street, when a German policeman, resplendent in ornate Prussian helmet, stepped off the footpath and waved me down. 'Who the bloody hell does *he* think he is?' I thought, 'stopping a British Despatch Rider', but I pulled up beside him. He didn't speak, simply pointed to a nearby church clock, which was beginning to strike eleven o'clock – the eleventh hour of the eleventh day of the eleventh month – reminding me that it was Armistice Day. For two minutes we stood together in silence, at that time the customary commemoration of the end of the First World War, until a siren signalled 'back to normal'. The policeman saluted; I gave one in return and we carried on with our respective duties without having spoken a word.

As had been happening for many weeks, long-familiar faces were disappearing as more and more release groups of H.Os, Hostilities Only men, left for the UK and 'Civvy Street'. The C.Ss, Continuous Service Marines, would have to soldier on until the end of their individual twelve-year engagements, but there was no doubt that the Commando was running down. The year was also running down and, as the end of November drew near, it looked as if the Unit would have another Christmas away from home. Then, out of the blue, came the order to pack all kit for return to the UK, leaving all vehicles behind. Within 48 hours the unit marched to the station and entrained for the start of the journey home.

Chapter 15

FROM SERVICEMAN TO CIVILIAN

On 29 November we arrived at Borde Hill Camp, Haywards Heath, Sussex, and the DRs were allocated some ropey old motorbikes to go through the motions of carrying on a normal routine, but the Commando was dying on its feet. On 2 December we were paraded to hear Colonel Sanders give his farewell speech on leaving the unit to take over No. 46 Royal Marines Commando. Then, on 7 December, the entire Commando, less a small rear party, left camp on 21 days' disembarkation leave. For the first time since 1941 I had the pleasure of spending Christmas at home.

Two days after our return, on 30 December, Major General Wildman-Lushington, GOC Commando Group, and all officers and men of No. 4 Commando Brigade, from Brigadier 'Mouldy' Moulton (who had taken over from 'Jumbo' Leicester) to the lowliest Marine, attended a church service to mark the completion of the Brigade's wartime service. Next day, New Year's Eve, we were surprised to find that the regulation issue of turkey had been kept for us, so we had our second Christmas Dinner that year, although it wasn't served by the officers.

A few days later the Commando moved from Borde Hill to the Royal Marines' Training Camp at Wrexham, where the disintegration of the unit continued. My turn to say farewell to 41 Royal Marines Commando came on 11 January 1946 when I bade adieu to those friends still around who had a few more weeks or months yet to serve. It was time for those in my 'Release Group No. 32' (we weren't demobilized, just 'released to civilian life', which meant we could be recalled) to begin the discharge formalities and I was returned to my 'Home Division' of Chatham for the process.

The Royal Marines Barracks itself hadn't changed at all since I had worked in the Records Office there for a few weeks in October 1940. However, the complete absence of air raid warnings, which had then occurred a dozen or more times a day, made Chatham itself a very different place. Another major change was being able to sleep in a barrack room and not have to 'Proceed to the Tunnel', which had been mandatory in 1940, there to sleep on the concrete floor, if all the wooden forms set against the walls had been taken.

Then followed a week of standing in line with other Chatham Marines who had been brought back from whatever part of the globe they happened to have been serving in when their 'number came up'. Each separate step of our transition from servicemen to civilians required a different queue. The first was for the Quartermaster's Store, to return service clothing and equipment (apart from one set of clothing and a uniform to wear on the journey home); the Records Office, to make sure that you really were the person entitled to be released; medical and dental inspections, the issue of civilian clothes, release document, civilian identity card, ration book, leave chit, rail warrant, back-pay and authorization documents to draw war gratuity and post-war credit entitlements in your home town. They seemed endless.

In one of those queues occurred a coincidence which few people would accept in a work of fiction, but which obviously do happen in real life. It was a bright, not too cold, January day and a string of men were waiting in line for the next stage in their move into civilian life. All had the appropriate document in their hands, ready to be checked and stamped after completing whatever process it happened to be. Purely by chance I happened to notice the regimental number of the sheet of paper being held by the man immediately in front of me and my eyes popped when I saw 'Ch/X 100976'. Almost five and a half years previously, on 8 August 1940, I had been standing behind that very same man, in a very similar queue, when we were both waiting to be processed **into** the Royal Marines. I had been given the next number – Ch/X 100977.

It was Ron Walker. We had done our six weeks' initial training together in No. 48 squad at the Royal Marines Reserve Depot, Exton, Devon (which has since been completely redeveloped as the

Commando Training Centre Royal Marines, Lympstone), but we had never met again during our service lives. After our squad passing-out, I was posted to Chatham Barracks as a Records Clerk, while he had gone off with the bulk of the others for field-firing in Wales. By the time I had managed to get back to Exton, some three weeks later, in a vain attempt to catch up with them, they had moved on. Many of my squadmates, including Ron, had been posted to MNBDO1 (Mobile Naval Base Defence Organization, but often ragged as 'Men Not to Be Drafted Overseas'!) and were in Crete when German parachutists swamped the Allied defenders. A number of the squad were taken prisoner, but Ron had evaded capture and was later with Tito's guerrillas in Yugoslavia. Others of my squad would have been in the same release group, but I saw no other familiar face.

Moving about the barracks, going through the long release processes, we naturally came upon many youngsters who were in their early days of being processed in the opposite direction. I passed the King's Squad, doing their impeccable close order drill, and remember thinking to myself, 'What's the point of all that now? The war's over!' Later I realized that I had already been thinking like a civilian, as Rudyard Kipling shrewdly wrote: 'Oh, it's Tommy this, an' Tommy that, an' "Tommy go away" But it's "Thank you, Mr Atkins", when the band begins to play.'

The most difficult episode of the release procedure for me was selecting a 'civvy suit'. Every man heading back to civilian life was provided with a complete rigout of civilian clothes – shoes, socks, underwear, shirt, tie, hat – and a suit. I wandered along racks and racks of jackets, waistcoats and trousers of innumerable colours and patterns, and all with the same invisible price-tag of 'free', but hadn't the vaguest notion of what might be appropriate. In desperation, I picked a double-breasted navy-blue herringbone, as it was described to me later, which proved to be very suitable and gave good service during the next few years.

The complete rigout was packed in what was probably listed in military terms as 'Box, cardboard, brown, civilian clothes for the carrying of'. Those boxes were unmistakable and were the target of civilian touts and wide boys, looking for a quick profit. 'Ere, myte! I'll give yer ten quid fer yer civvies!' – and quite a lot of men succumbed and went home without a suit.

By 18 January all military procedures had been completed. I was transported to Chatham railway station, where I too received an offer to sell my civvies, but, realizing that there had to be some kind of life after the war, wasn't tempted.

Only when I had boarded the train for London, with the cardboard box of clothing stashed on the luggage rack above my head and was settling down for the long journey home, did the finality of the situation impinge upon me. The ticket in my pocket was for one way only; never again would I have to 'Report back at 2359 hrs'; my five-and-a-half year stint of service in the Royal Marines was over.

INDEX

228